Immigration and Children's Literature

Immigration and Childhood Education

This series addresses the realities, challenges and developmental experiences of immigration from the perspective of young children and their families. Using a forward-thinking approach, the series examines current and existing realities about immigration and reflects on its impact on childhood. Titles provide viewpoints and research-based implications of experiences and circumstances surrounding immigrant and refugee child and families leading readers to consider and ponder their implications for socially just practice. Each title is also intended to stimulate discussion and further awareness about immigration issues facing the young child in contemporary society.

Series Editor:
Wilma Robles-Melendez (Nova Southeastern University, USA)

Editorial Board:
Mari Cortez (California State University, Channel Islands, USA)
Ramon Ferreiro (Nova Southeastern University, USA)
Clodie Tal (Lewinsky College of Teachers' Education, Israel)
Kenya Wolff (Mississippi State University, USA)

Also available in the series:
Issues and Challenges of Immigration in Early Childhood in the USA,
Wilma Robles-Melendez and Wayne Driscoll

Immigration and Children's Literature

Stories, Social Justice, and Critical Consciousness

Wilma Robles-Melendez and Audrey Henry

BLOOMSBURY ACADEMIC
LONDON · NEW YORK · OXFORD · NEW DELHI · SYDNEY

BLOOMSBURY ACADEMIC
Bloomsbury Publishing Plc
50 Bedford Square, London, WC1B 3DP, UK
1385 Broadway, New York, NY 10018, USA
29 Earlsfort Terrace, Dublin 2, Ireland

BLOOMSBURY, BLOOMSBURY ACADEMIC and the Diana logo
are trademarks of Bloomsbury Publishing Plc

First published in Great Britain 2023
This paperback edition published 2025

Copyright © Wilma Robles-Melendez and Audrey Henry, 2023

Wilma Robles-Melendez and Audrey Henry have asserted their right under the Copyright, Designs and Patents Act, 1988, to be identified as Author of this work.

For legal purposes the Acknowledgments on p. xv constitute
an extension of this copyright page.

Series design by Adriana Brioso
Cover image: © FatCamera/ Getty Images

All rights reserved. No part of this publication may be reproduced or transmitted in any form or by any means, electronic or mechanical, including photocopying, recording, or any information storage or retrieval system, without prior permission in writing from the publishers.

Bloomsbury Publishing Plc does not have any control over, or responsibility for, any third-party websites referred to or in this book. All internet addresses given in this book were correct at the time of going to press. The author and publisher regret any inconvenience caused if addresses have changed or sites have ceased to exist, but can accept no responsibility for any such changes.

A catalogue record for this book is available from the British Library.

Library of Congress Control Number: 2023937755.

ISBN: HB: 978-1-3502-5591-3
PB: 978-1-3502-5595-1
ePDF: 978-1-3502-5592-0
eBook: 978-1-3502-5593-7

Series: Immigration and Childhood Education

Typeset by Integra Software Services Pvt. Ltd.

To find out more about our authors and books visit www.bloomsbury.com
and sign up for our newsletters.

To my mother, my best teacher, whose lessons of humanity and compassion continue to guide my life. To all the children of immigrants who continue to dream for a future and to the teachers that everyday make those dreams come true, and to all those who make borders disappear with their efforts, empathy, and commitment to children.

W.R.M.

This book is dedicated to my sons Hopeton and Ian and to my daughter-in-law Kimberly. And to the memory of my husband Arthur, who I am sure is smiling down at me for following in his footsteps and wondering what took me so long.

A.H.

Contents

List of Figures	viii
List of Tables	x
Preface	xi
About this Book	xiii
Acknowledgments	xv
1 A World of Children on the Move	1
2 Children's Literature, a Voice for Social Justice and Critical Consciousness	29
3 We are Immigrants: Children Crossing Borders	61
4 Growing Up as the Youngest Immigrants: Through the Eyes of Children	101
5 An Unending Saga: Forced to Leave Home: Children and Families as Refugees	159
6 At School! Immigrant Children Coming to School	191
7 Bringing Immigration Realities to the Classroom through Children's Literature	223
Appendix: Topical List of Children's Books on Immigration Experiences	249
Index	253

Figures

1.1	Some Factors Leading to Immigration	5
1.2	*Migrant*, an umbrella term covering multiple realities (United Nations 2018; IOM 2019)	9
1.3	Reasons pushing and pulling people to migrate (United Nations 2018)	11
1.4	Social justice perspectives to bring change	16
1.5	Selected stories of children and immigration	20
2.1	Multiple roles of children's literature	33
2.2	Multiple roles of stories	42
2.3	Key components of social justice for immigrant children	51
2.4	Exploring experiences of immigration for children: Three focal lenses	55
3.1	Moving is a multidimensional experience	64
3.2	Borders are of many kinds	72
3.3	Reasons to migrate	82
3.4	Transitions—children's emotions and feelings	84
3.5	Selected stories of immigration: Key reasons driving immigration for families and children	87
3.6	Emotional impact of moving: What we learn from some story characters	91
4.1	Challenges facing children of immigrants	104
4.2	Topical areas explored through children's books about immigration	107
4.3	Children's Well-Being: A conglomerate of experiences to support their needs	116
4.4	Some feelings and sentiments experienced by immigrant children: Selected Stories	126
4.5	Names are more than just a name	129
4.6	Key issues about immigration status: Selected children's books	146
4.7	Circumstances leading to family separation	147
5.1	Children's literature as windows into the experience of forced migration	161
5.2	A sample of active zones of war and conflicts in 2022	165

5.3	Some of the thematic strands in children's literature about refugees from the perspective of children	172
5.4	Selected titles serving as windows into stories about refugees and asylum seekers	173
5.5	Typology of people impacted by forced migration	177
5.6	Emotional bonds of children and pets	182
5.7	An agenda for children's protection: Six-point process to protect refugee and migrant children	186
6.1	Classrooms, another border that children cross	193
6.2	A focus on some of the immigrant children's experiences at school	197
6.3	Meeting immigrant diversity through story characters: Selected story characters	198
6.4	Stories about classroom responsiveness to immigrant children's needs	203
6.5	Selected stories addressing the topic about names	206
6.6	Teachers are Key in Supporting Language Acquisition of Young Immigrant Children	212
6.7	Ten Books Providing Windows into Responsive Experiences	213
7.1	Connecting children to stories of immigration: Some points to consider	229
7.2	Applying a Freirean approach to engage children in critically reading stories of immigration	234
7.3	Mapping possible themes and topics from a storybook	236
7.4	Roles of pictures and illustrations in stories of immigration	237
7.5	Suggested resources to help connect children with stories	240
7.6	Sample template for a story map	242

Tables

1.1	Global Immigration	8
4.1	Selected Children's Books about Immigration by Authors Who Arrived as Child Immigrants	115
5.1	Selected Examples of Empathy and Compassionate Responses through Children's Books about Refugees and Asylum Seekers	184

Preface

Everyday a new story is begun, taking shape through its power to share experiences, dreams, and the feats of people from times we know and those still to come. Every day, children and adults alike gather to hear or read a story that will make them dream and feel that it is their own story. We have always cherished stories because of the powerful way they convey the messages that touch our hearts, fill our lives with hope, and that move us into action. We both come from different cultures but share a tradition of sharing stories that anchor our heritage and our love for teaching. It is those stories we hear from children and families and our passion for teaching that have brought us to share the power stories have to reveal the struggles and dreams of people continuing to migrate.

Whether we read them or they are read to us, stories reveal the drama of people and of realities and places that make your imagination soar with hope, with intrigue, and that so many times motivate you to make changes. They also have a unique way to uncover and reveal realities of today, even those that many consider difficult but that must be addressed. That special power of stories coming to us from children's literature inspired our work, as we find in them a way to explore and delve into the saga of children and people who are immigrants. This work started out of our own experiences, working with our college students, and inviting them to learn more about children through the lens of children's literature that so vividly bring alive those milestone moments of childhood and especially of a childhood being an immigrant. It also emerged from our research, exploring and learning more about the potential embedded in stories.

Writing in the middle of the COVID-19 pandemic taught us and our world a painful lesson. It also revealed the need for documenting those important moments in the lives of young children. Our writing started to take shape during a time of challenges when the news continued to be flooded with the faces of immigrant children and families trying to escape their own homelands and in search of safe havens. The more we heard about children, the more we wanted to reflect their experiences that children's books so effectively present. Today as we conclude this work, we are still challenged by many difficult experiences facing children of immigrants and their families. We witnessed the specter of an unprovoked war in Ukraine that shook our spirit and that of society, seeing millions of children and families forced to leave in search of a place to feel safe again. This is an ongoing story, just as immigration is, but one reminding us, in particular, about those forced to leave their homelands, escaping the cruel attacks on the life and future of an entire generation of children. With every story, hope also is also planted in our minds and hearts. Hope of what we can each do as realities are learned and as we are invited to take action and bring hope to their lives and that of their society. There is always hope for a future where each child will welcome the illusion filled stories shared at home, at school or wherever they hear that inviting phrase "Once upon a time …"

About this Book

Every book is a personal experience. And this certainly is an example of that, guided by our commitment and professional experiences and interest in expanding knowledge on the impact of the immigration journey on immigrant children. It is, too, an opportunity to clarify and help understand that immigration is inherent to our world, that it has always been a part of who we are as a global community. A dream and a joint effort, it gathers our experiences and our efforts to support the needs of immigrant children seen from two professional perspectives that describe our experiences, one of an early childhood educator and another of a reading and literacy specialist. Working together for many years, this work also comes from what we have gathered from research projects where we learned and continue to learn about the voices of immigrant children through the special voice found in children's books and storytelling.

This book is an invitation to read, to reflect, to share, and to appreciate the power of words turned into stories. Through its pages, we explore the many factors defining immigration and the realities of a process that in the first decades of this century has multiplied. We take a stance placing the focus on children as participants in the experience of immigration, one with so many dimensions. The book takes a different approach to explore and learn about children and immigration. It is, as Sim Bishop (1990) told us, a window and a door, this time opening to learn about immigration through the lens of children's literature. As you read its pages, they will invite you to view the challenges and realities of young children becoming and growing up as immigrants. It also invites you to consider the needs of immigrant children through the lens of social justice and of the rights universally ascribed to every child. Through its chapters, the realities of life as child immigrants, gathered through the unique voice of children's literature, are unmasked, leading us to consider the needs and rights of children. This book presents another way for learning and expanding the repertoire of ideas about living and growing up as an immigrant child. It is our hope that it will also offer another approach in the exploration of the factors influencing the lives of young children who are immigrants. As immigrants, we recognize the power of narratives and stories to share the realities and experiences posed by immigration. With our knowledge of what children need, it is our aspiration to promote a deeper awareness about the challenges that young children face every day, and to bring attention to the urgent need to respond equitably to what they need.

Wilma Robles-Melendez and Audrey Henry

Acknowledgments

To say thank you is to say how much we value and appreciate what others have done to help us. Words will never be sufficient to express our deepest appreciation to those who believe that this book would become a reality. We long waited to turn into a book our experiences and practices, using children's books to open up conversations, and to engage in knowing more about realities many avoided talking about.

Our thanks to our reviewers for their comments and helpful suggestions. We want to express our most sincere thanks to our editor, Mark Richardson and to his editorial assistant, Anna Elliss, for their patience and support that made this work possible. We are so very grateful for all your understanding!

A Note from Wilma

Very special thanks to my family for their encouragement and to my husband, Sal for his loving support and the many cups of coffee that always came at the right time. ¡Gracias! My thanks also to my two furry babies, who kept me company all those late nights listening to the stories as I reviewed and reread them.

A Note from Audrey

This book is dedicated to my sons, Hopeton and Ian, and to my daughter-in-law, Kimberly. Thanks Ian, for coming to my rescue when I could not think of the right word or phrase. To my co-author Wilma, who encouraged me to take this journey with her, Thanks. And to the memory of my husband Arthur who I am sure is smiling down at me for following in his footsteps and wondering what took me so long.

1
A World of Children on the Move

Children cross borders in varying circumstances and for different reasons.
—UNICEF (2016)

This chapter aims to:

- Define immigration
- Describe the factors supporting immigration
- Explore current views about immigration
- Define who is an immigrant

Key words

- Immigration
- Immigrant children and families
- Immigrant
- Social justice
- Stories

Moving to Other Places

That morning when we visited the local school, the children in the first-grade classroom were listening to a story about moving to other places. In the story, "A piece from home," the child character was struggling to choose what to take with him because they were moving to another country. As the teacher read, one child said, "It is so hard to leave things!" He said it with emphasis while the teacher nodded. Taking a pause in her reading, the first-grade teacher asked, "What would be very special for you to bring?" It did not take long for their answers to pour with all kinds of special items. Some shared what they brought when they moved to a new house, while others thought they could not leave anything behind.

"But sometimes, you need to choose," their teacher added. It was then that she saw a child raising his hand. "Yes, what would you bring?" smiling, the teacher asked. With a concerned face, the six-year-old said, "I saw children on TV, and they didn't have anything." His comment took his teacher by surprise. For a few days earlier, the news had been broadcasting images of migrants coming on foot from distant nations. The first-grade teacher never thought they would be asking those questions. "Well," said his teacher, "sometimes it is awfully hard for some people and they need to move leaving things they love." Another child jumped in saying, "My dad said they are immigrants." Two more hands were waving anxiously, making their teacher realize she needed to address their questions. "Well," she began saying, "Most of us are immigrants. I am an immigrant, too. Want to know about my story?" A resounding yes filled the room as they gathered closer to their teacher.

A World on the Move

Every day, everywhere, people in places near and far are leaving their homelands with a bag full of dreams, while others are pressed to leave because of realities too harsh to endure. That is the ongoing story of immigration that for centuries has driven individuals to move away leaving behind their homelands. That is as well the story that has shaped societies and the destinies of so many, perhaps including you.

In a world constantly on the move, millions of realities continue to be written about the ever-unfolding stories personally shared by many about relatives, neighbors, and friends who became immigrants. Immigration, the movement of people who leave their birthplaces to build their lives in other countries (McLemore and Romo 2005), never ceases. It has transcended time and remains today a major force and circumstance throughout the globe. At the time of writing, almost 300 million are estimated to be immigrants throughout the global community (United Nations 2019a). In the United States, the second most common destination for international immigrants, every year, almost a million immigrants arrive in the nation (Budiman 2020). Nearly 24 percent of students in US classrooms already share an immigrant background (Camarota, Griffith and Zeigler 2017; Dinan 2017).

Numbers may not show it, but thousands of those on the wave of immigration are children. They are children, just like those in the opening scenario. Most of them come with their families and some by themselves. They are also the youngest participants becoming aware about the realities of moving for many reasons. They encounter attitudes and prejudiced responses as they settle in other countries. These experiences are happening in our own neighborhoods and classrooms everywhere. Young children continue to write their new stories as immigrants. Every day is a new experience for a child and with that, new stories will reveal their many life episodes growing up as immigrants.

Of Interest to Everyone

Sometimes it is a story we read, like the one that the teacher was reading to her class, or that we heard someone sharing about their own lives that arouses our interest or brings back memories about ourselves or others who are immigrants. Sometimes it is from what is watched or heard through the media, but children and adults are finding out about the reality of immigration. Accounts about immigrants are constant and opinions are many. Interest in immigration has risen during the past decade, particularly since 2014 when thousands of children came unaccompanied through the borders of the United States, followed more recently by the difficult news of children crossing the seas in their pursuit of hope. Polarizing views and comments about humanitarian efforts all seem to collide as society makes efforts to understand a long-standing issue, that, contrary to what many may think, is integral to society itself (McLemore and Romo 2005). For educators of young children, multiple and necessary questions emerge about immigrants. How much do we know and what is immigration are all questions necessary to answer as society becomes more mindful of their immigrant members.

... But also a controversial topic

An essential social reality and clearly a humanitarian topic, immigration is a highly controversial issue. No different from the past, immigration has inflamed debates that continue today. Polarized views with groundless opinions and bigoted views together with political implications have all compounded to make immigration a topic to be difficult and heatedly argued by many. Derogatory comments and perceptions paired with speculative fear caused many to look away instead of addressing and exploring realities of immigrants in our communities and particularly in our classrooms. Still, it is a topic that demands attention given its constituent role in every society to ensure fairness and social justice for children and their families.

Immigration, a Topic to Address in Our Classrooms

With roots firmly grounded on equity, immigration and the experiences of immigrants are topics demanding attention as children explore diversity in their contexts both personal and of their peers. Conveying its importance, narratives on immigrant experience have defied those that see it as a topic to avoid or they simply look away. But reality cannot be excluded from consideration in our classrooms especially on diversity issues (Robles-Melendez and Beck 2000; Spiegler 2016). Building views that counteract bias and prejudice is a process that starts early in life. This is what makes difficult matters important to explore with young children. Developmentally guided and intentionally planned, we can facilitate discussions addressing children's interest and eagerness to know. Hundreds of children's books, just like what the first-grade teacher was sharing in the opening scenario, are serving as a bridge bringing immigration as a topic to explore in the classroom. Storybooks are a source to dive into challenging realities and topics experienced throughout communities. Altogether, it is a responsible way to guide children in dismissing ungrounded and misleading views while learning about their society.

Rising Immigration in Today's Society

Multiple realities and events including a pandemic, already define the twenty-first century. One of them, clearly, is the increasing presence of immigrants. A rise in immigration was projected to be experienced during the twenty-first century (Martin 2001). Now, a little over two decades later, expectations have been surpassed. Recent years, during the second decade of a still young century, society has witnessed a surge in the number of people migrating from places everywhere throughout the world. It has, at the same time, brought the issue of immigration, as many call it, to the forefront of political and humanitarian discussions (UNICEF 2020).

Many would agree that, immigration is a topic and reality that arouses controversy. Yet, it remains as a fundamental and contributing factor for societal change and growth. Communities across many world regions have seen their transformation happening as people from other places settled in their countries. The vitality emerging from ideas, knowledge, cultures, and experiences they bring continues to benefit places where they settle. Globally, the past decades, since the 1990s, have given place to a gradual change in the demographical makeup of numerous cities. European cities and nations have observed a dramatic change in their demographics as have many communities across the United States.

Driving Forces for Immigration

What leads people to immigrate continues to be a fundamental question in understanding who immigrants are. Millions of immigrants have seen their destinies determined by their own desire and will. Those are the families and individuals setting their own course and moving to other nations. Numerous others, however, are pushed away by the threat of social and political insecurity and changing climate (International Organization for Migration [IOM] 2019). Immigration is a personal experience of great magnitude given its many implications, whether it is a planned or forced decision. Figure 1.1 presents some of the main forces driving people to immigrate.

Stories and accounts about the journeys told by thousands of immigrants have brought to light experiences into the international and national headlines. They have made us more aware about the ongoing presence of immigration.

- Seeking a better life and access to education and educational opportunities for families and children
- Social injustices and discriminatory practices threatening quality of life.
- **Economic challenges**: poverty, unstable employment opportunities, and unemployment
- **Civil conflict and political unrest**: Life-threatening realities emerging out of armed and political conflict in some parts of the world
- **Societal violence**: incivility and gang actions which threaten the quality of life and opportunities for safe livelihood.
- **Natural disasters**: climate changes and increasing intensity and impact of weather events.

Figure 1.1 Some Factors Leading to Immigration.

> **Thinking, and Reflecting … Immigration in the News**
>
> Over the past decade, reports about immigration have been shown and discussed in the international, national, and local news. *What has captured your attention?*
> *What have you learned about immigration?*

Children, They Are Immigrants Too

While reasons vary, for most, whenever we talk about immigration, the image captured is that of adults moving and settling down in other places, but not of children. This time, in the twenty-first century, we all have become aware about the reality of children immigrants, a reality about immigration that, although always present (Klapper 2007), has now presented itself more clearly. This growing awareness about children as immigrants continues, revealing what they experience and the response to them from society.

Today, most immigrant children come along with their families who either come voluntarily or are forced by unimaginable circumstances. The fact is that nearly 14 percent of the global immigrant population are children (IOM 2019). The multiple images and accounts of children crossing the sea and walking endlessly through valleys and borders have uncovered the story of the youngest immigrants. More clearly, we are now seeing children as active participants in the ongoing journey of people seeking a better life and justice.

In the News: Living and Ongoing Realities

We were in the classroom that morning when the teacher in the opening scenario was reading the story, which raised the topic about immigrants, with her first graders. At first, it stunned us to see the children's reactions to the story, especially when one of them raised questions about children and families crossing borders broadcasted over the news. It was much similar to events in 2014, when thousands of unaccompanied children entered the US borders (Shapiro 2014). This time, once again, thousands of children, many of them coming alone, came through the nation's borders during the early part of 2021. At this time, with an increasing number of immigrants coming every day, reports of child migrants continue to call attention to their experiences and to their rights to a childhood with dignity. Since 2003, over 400,000 unaccompanied migrant children have entered through the US borders (Shoichet 2021).

Stories about children, including many who are very young, continue to headline the broadcasts even as we write. Listening to the first graders' concerns came more than just a surprise. It felt like a window was opened, revealing their awareness about such difficult realities. Undeniably, the media has brought the experiences of children closer to everyone. The story simply jumpstarted their curiosity about the events in the news. The discussion that followed uncovered a multitude of angles and personal realities about the reality of migration, so intricately embedded in society.

Consciously Considering ... *Immigration, a Heated Issue*

Over the past decade, immigration has captured the attention of the world. This time, mostly because of the perilous journeys of families and children. Thousands have migrated from places far and beyond our imagination, seeking new beginnings and opportunities. In 2020, the year of the global pandemic, images and news about immigrants crossing the Mediterranean and arriving in Europe or of caravans journeying through Central America continued to be in the headlines of national and international news.

Once again, the reality of immigration has raised controversy. For decades, the topic of immigration has raised a multitude of views and opinions, many of them leading into debates and opinionated ideas. Arguments heatedly pointing to prejudiced and unfair views have failed to acknowledge the reality and contribution of immigrants. They also led to a myriad of opinions and debates not always seeing the needs of people and importance of immigration. Those are still ongoing as everyone seems to have an opinion. Never an easy topic, immigration remains as a difficult subject that many prefer to avoid and consider peripheral to their needs (Suro 2009). Even efforts for immigrants have fallen under the criticism of those with opposing notions about immigration. Although this is a divisive topic, what is at stake here is the life of children and families, not numbers, statistics, and labels.

Immigration, a Constant Reality

The flow of immigrants is an ongoing global experience of our times. Higher levels of immigration have been observed since 1990, reaching its highest number in the present century (Table 1.1). From 258 million migrants in 2017 (UN 2017), reports in 2019 indicated a rapid growth in international migrants, increasing to 272 million (UN 2019a). Projections about immigration indicate its continuing increase in the years to come. Moreover, findings from the Gallup World Poll, conducted over a decade ago (2006–2016), revealed the existence of a trend among people to be either planning or having an intent to migrate (Burrone, D'Costa, and Holmqvist 2018). Indeed, it is a world on the move.

Immigration, as some would say, has become a main denominator, that defines the twenty-first century. During its first two decades, we have seen a marked increase in the number of people who, voluntarily or forced, became immigrants.

Multiple Views and Ideas about Immigration

While immigration evokes multiple opinions even raising controversy, there are many aspects calling for a clearer understanding about this important topic and societal process. Even though immigration is debated, the fact is that future population growth in many parts of the world depends on immigrants arriving and settling down in other countries (Chamie 2016). The United States, one of the main destinations for immigrants, is one of those countries where future population growth is already projected to be linked to immigration (Budiman et al. 2020). Similarly, population increase in many European nations is already considered to depend on the incoming immigrants.

Table 1.1 Global Immigration

Year	Total (in millions)
1990	153
2017	258
2019	272

Source: United Nations 2019b; United Nations 2017.

An Unstoppable Movement

Images in the local and international media have revealed the rising numbers of immigrants moving across and throughout the world nations. This has resulted in the terms *immigrant* and *immigration* becoming more commonly present in the discourse in recent decades. Even during the difficult times during the global pandemic of 2020, immigration had not stopped. Though slowed down, the world still continues to witness an ongoing immigration movement ([IOM] 2019; United Nations 2021). In 2020, Spain recorded over 20,000 migrants from Africa (Johnson 2021). In the United States alone, during the month of March 2021, over 170,000 migrants crossed the southwest border of the nation (Burnett and Rose 2021). Among them, thousands were children, with many arriving unaccompanied (Aguilera 2021). Who are they? Why are they coming? These are all questions continuously being asked now as immigrants' accounts have become publicly shared and discussed.

Who Are the Immigrants?

Defining who is an immigrant begins by considering that the immigrant landscape is as diverse as the places from which they come. There is no single definition describing who is an immigrant or migrant. Many definitions are based on political and government-based criteria (IOM 2019). The term itself embeds multiple realities, some based on voluntary decisions and aspirations, while others reflect a diverse spectrum of difficult and challenging circumstances. Figure 1.2 describes some of the different categories included under the term *migrant*. The

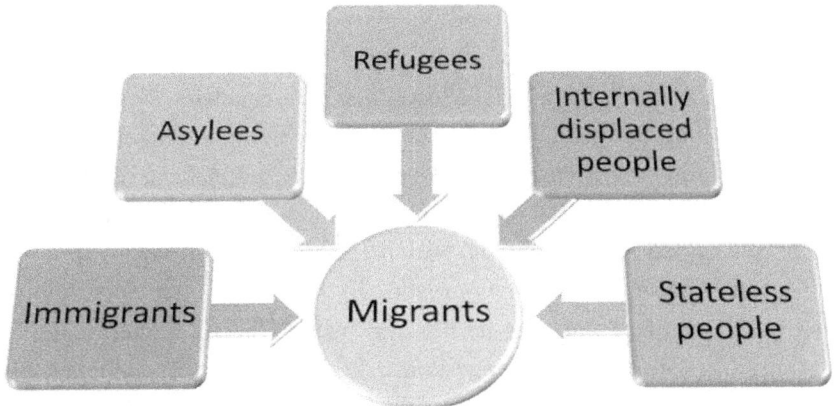

Figure 1.2 *Migrant*, an umbrella term covering multiple realities (United Nations 2018; IOM 2019).

only common element is that they are people who move across borders to settle in places different from those where they were born. From the humblest to the professionals, immigrants represent all socioeconomic and educational levels. Some are poor, while others are from wealthy origins. You will find that some come from rural areas, while others are from large metropolitan cities. Even the multiplicity of languages spoken adds to the diverse profile of immigrants. Linguistically, many may be native speakers or are proficient speakers of English, while others speak a diversity of tongues (Batalova and Zong 2016).

They Are Also Immigrants: Refugees and Asylees

Every minute someone enters another country willingly aspiring to build a future. Yet, over the past decade, the news about the ordeals faced by families and children from many parts of the globe continue to be widely discussed and reported. They unveil the reality of people migrating who are seeking refuge and asylum. Among them, thousands are children who are forced to leave and now adjusting to a new context. Their presence is a continuing reminder of a childhood waiting for society to consider their wellbeing. The call for fairness and opportunities reverberates everywhere. Today's call for governments and organizations to respond remain a pressing issue for sincere and dignified responses to the needs of immigrants (Robles-Melendez and Driscoll 2020).

Forces Motivating People to Migrate

When we read the story *Grandfather's journey* (Say 1997), it reminded us about the many motivations pushing and pulling people to leave their birthplaces. Why do they leave? This is a question commonly and continuing to be asked as we try to determine why people leave their own countries. The fact is that reasons pushing and pulling people to migrate are many. Pulling factors, such as better education and employment opportunities, and pushing realities such as violence, natural disasters, and unemployment, are among those motivating individuals to leave their countries (National Immigration Forum 2019).

Overall, people leave their homelands in search of better opportunities and quality of life. Some may be personal, while others are due to societal circumstances, including changing climates. Seeking a future for children is one of the main reasons families migrate (Burrone, D'Costa, and Holqvist 2018). Aspiration for their well-being is another of the key motivators leading families to migrate. Prompting their desire to leave their countries is also the search for

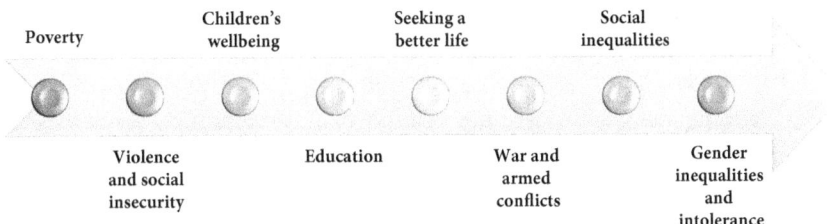

Figure 1.3 Reasons pushing and pulling people to migrate (United Nations 2018).

Thinking and Reflecting ... Motivations

We all have heard stories about people who migrated. Some of us, as immigrants, may have our very own stories Think about your own story or about that of immigrants you know. *What were their main motivations to move?*

---

justice, a factor at the core of many who become immigrants. A list of some of the reasons pushing and pulling people to migrate appears in Figure 1.3.

A Land of Immigrants

Every day, all the time, and through time, someone is making a decision or has already made a decision to cross borders. As a shaping force, we must remember that immigration constitutes one of the main societal factors influencing the character and spirit of a country. This is especially palpable in the United States, when we realize that the nation is home to more immigrants when compared to any other country on the globe (Connor and López 2016; Budiman 2020). Living in the United States, one of the main destinations for world immigrants, one is constantly reminded about the many cultures and multiple places from where we came. Where we came from or where we trace our roots from, all lead to the unending story of migration. Some came long ago, many came yesterday, while others will be arriving even as you read.

Immigration continues today as a vibrant and integral societal experience in the United States. As predicted, by 2050, population growth will be marked by an increased racial and ethnic diversity (National Immigration Forum 2021; Wessel 2021). To a large extent, much of its diversity will be resulting from its increasing immigrant population (Ortman and Guarneri 2009). The fact is that without immigrants, population in the nation would "barely grow" (Wessel 2021, n.p.).

The Immigrant Spirit

There are endless stories continuing to remind everyone about the immigrant ethos defining the nation. We are reminded of this through the pages in *Grandfather's Journey* (Say 1993), where the author tells the story of a young man who came long ago from Japan and made his home in America. We also learn about the brave and determined spirit of Hannah's family in *Hannah is my name* (Yang 2007) as well as that of Marwan (*Marwan's journey*, de Arias 2018), the young boy refugee who, displaced and alone, is seeking a safe place to live. Accounts of recent times continue to remind everyone about the incessant presence of immigrants. This time, stories about children coming across borders with hope, of many escaping war-stricken zones, and others crossing seas, reveal the complexity of the immigration process and how it continues influencing and giving shape to places where we live and to others, close and far away.

Consciously Considering …. *Immigration, a Living Factor in U.S. Society*

An integral process to humankind, immigration continues today in the twenty-first century to define the character of societies not only in the United States but as a reality of the world community. During the past two decades, the flow of immigrants arriving in the European continent and the caravans of migrants moving through Central America are a testimony to the unending efforts of people seeking new places to settle and live.

Classrooms in most communities tell the story of the multiple immigrants who have settled in the United States. In 2018, over 44 million people living in the nation were immigrants (Budiman 2020). Their rising numbers are forecasted to define the immigration phenomenon in the coming years. Just like the child in the opening scenario, thousands of children will also become participants of the immigration experience. By 2050, 34 percent of the population will be constituted by immigrants and their children (Wessel 2021).

Stories of recent times have brought alive the experience of immigration. Over the past two decades, waves of immigrant caravans crossing borders or sailing in frail boats have captured everyone's attention. Their stories reveal the multiple reasons driving thousands to leave behind their countries. Even amid a world pandemic, the ongoing arrival of people from everywhere impels us to understand the enduring nature of immigration (Gramlich 2021; Roberts 2021).

Children, the Youngest Immigrants

Today, the presence of children with ethnic and cultural roots is commonly found in many cities and educational settings in places like Europe and the United States. Immigrants from multiple cultures have settled in continents and nations far from their homelands. Some came as refugees or asylees and are now part of our communities. In fact, it is estimated that about 50 million children have migrated voluntarily or are forced by difficult circumstances to leave their homelands (UNICEF 2016).

Children immigrants are as well an integral part of classrooms and communities throughout the United States. Their presence is a reminder about the ongoing immigrant nature of the nation. Voices of children in a variety of languages other than English are commonly heard in classrooms and school grounds everywhere in the United States. So are, as well, many educators, who are immigrants themselves, teaching in schools throughout the country.

Working in classrooms, we have met so many children of immigrants—some recently arrived and others born to immigrant parents. As we listen to them talk, sharing their feelings and aspirations, they remind us about ourselves, who are immigrants, too. Just like the thousands of children and families who embarked in settling in other countries, our roots also speak about the immigrant heritage that we, the authors of this book, also share.

Weaving Knowledge about Diverse Realities

Beyond leaving one's home, the questions raised by the children in the classroom that we visited showed us their feelings and awareness about difficult events happening to children just like them. Watching the news and hearing discussions and comments by adults, it was evident that immigration was not foreign to many of them. The truth is that there are so many of life realities happening every day, directly or indirectly, that are also a part of children's living experiences. They cannot be ignored as we guide children to learn about society, its diversity and its challenges. Simply, these need to be addressed and explored in our classrooms.

How do we approach topics and realities of immigration in the classroom? Sometimes, it only takes a story, just as we saw with the first graders, to spark interest in exploring and uncovering realities. Now and again this is how we open not just a window but also a door to learn, explore, and build knowledge about topics, even those as challenging as immigration itself (Botelho and Rudman 2009).

How much do we know about children who are immigrants? What do we know about the motivations that brought them or their families to immigrate? What is their experience growing up in our communities? What are some of their successes and challenges faced? These are some of the questions we hope to explore in the chapters ahead. Their answers may not be simple to understand. Whichever these are, they will give us opportunities to build and enhance knowledge about the integral reality of immigration in society.

Immigration Narratives

The narrative of immigration is a living document. It continues keeping alive the experiences of ourselves, our families, friends, and of people vicariously met through stories where we learn about their realities. Shared informally, learned as we read a book or newspaper, or learned through the media, immigrant stories continue as a reminder of their journeys and how they shape and reshape communities everywhere. Still today in the twenty-first century, these stories convey the enduring presence and lived experiences of immigrants. They remain as a living reminder of a world always on the move. People leaving alone, young and old, families and children, together they form the community of immigrants we hear and learn about. With them are their stories revealing their multiple experiences, not just of yesterday but of contemporary times. In the still early decades of the twenty-first century the presence of immigrants is a reality as thousands continue to move crossing borders across the globe. The narrative revealing their experiences continues to be shared in multiple ways.

Every person has something to say. In each of their stories, we learn about the humanity of aspirations, actions, and motivations happening or passed on

---

Thinking and Reflecting ... Considering Immigration

For many, immigration is part of their personal lives, while others may see it as another topic in the news or that we hear about. Take a moment to consider the experiences that come to mind when you hear the term *immigration*. What memories does it evoke? What stories does it remind you of? How personal are these?

to us. We hear about the planned and determined decision of the character in Say's *Grandfather's journey* (1993) to leave Japan, his home country, seeking new adventures as he settles in America. We also learn about the sadness driving many to leave through the images in Sanna's story *The journey* (2016), a vivid reminder about people facing violence and continuing to be pushed to leave their homelands.

Questions abound about immigrants. What brought them, what motivated their journeys, and what makes them endure challenges? These are questions continually being deliberated. Though a process inherent to society, today immigration continues to evoke multiple emotions and opinions, many deeply marked by controversy and misleading views about others. But beyond the motivations, a myriad of realities remains to be uncovered and understood about immigration and about the people who either are forced or willingly set out to find their homes in other lands. Before we look at their stories, it is pertinent to delve more into the meaning and reality of immigration as a process and as a current reality. At the same time, it is relevant to understand the calling that in our contemporary times inspires some to move across borders and others, already immigrants living in other places, to strive for their dreams. A general call for fairness and what is rightfully just remains at the center of what motivates people to immigrate. At the core of immigration is also the need for everyone to be reminded about the inherent dignity and equal rights that humanity has to seek their welfare (UN 1948).

In Search for Social Justice

In all the stories of immigration, we hear a common voice. It is the voice of people seeking justice and equity. A common aspiration: social justice has forever inspired people to journey across borders. It is at the core in the story of immigrants yesterday and today. Across the world society, people continue searching for fairness.

More than just a term, *social justice* is a fundamental and critical concept focused on the rights of individuals. Its essence centers on recognizing the inherent dignity that every person has and their rights to what is equal and fair. Understanding this highly complex idea brings attention to its relationships with diversity and its emphasis on inclusivity (Herbert 2013; Cho 2017). Social justice is for everyone, irrespective of their culture, social status or diverse traits. There are multiple angles in social justice, which altogether portray and underline its relevance in society. At the same time, attention is brought to a spectrum of perspectives defining and indicative of the actions necessary to bringing this concept into a reality (Figure 1.4).

Figure 1.4 Social justice perspectives to bring change.

Seeking Justice, a Narrative that Continues

Multiple dreams, aspirations, and challenges continue through the times pulling and pushing people to migrate. Some strive for educational opportunities to build a future. Others are pushed by harsh political and economic conditions, hampering their desires when they simply want to give their families a better life and to enjoy what they never had. We also find others who were forced to leave due to challenges and discriminatory practices they faced. Still, countless families will leave their lands because of their dreams for a better future for their children. For their children, they will risk everything. This is what we gather when listening to and reading the accounts of immigrant families. Altogether, their stories tell us they come guided by a common aspiration: to find what, in essence, is their right to what is socially fair and just.

Envisioning a Future of Hope

At the core of social justice is the demand for conscious actions to ending and erasing prejudice and unfairness. It is closing and shutting the door to what has held us back from equitably sharing and opening opportunities to everyone. Needed are consciously centered practices and actions (Robles-Melendez and Driscoll 2020). These are transformative and focused on what is right for

> **Thinking and Reflecting ... Social Justice, What Does It Mean to Me?**
>
> Today, social justice is reflective of the aspirations of individuals and organizations in society. The demand to bring this concept into action continues as a challenge. As an educator, think about what you see as essential to bring social justice into action.

everyone beyond any diversity lines. What is right signifies, too, an urgency to address experiences with a mindful and equitable eye on what is needed to provide every child with their rightful opportunities and quality of life. That is perhaps what best illuminates the road taken by thousands that through time have walked, crossed oceans, or flown thousands of miles to find another land where their aspirations can become true. We have heard that same ambition from the many immigrants we have met and taught. Globally, those are reflective of our own families in an increasingly diverse and immigrant-influenced society. That is the story of immigrants who through endless times continue seeking a better life and opportunities.

A Global Aspiration for Equity

Today, voices across society echo a collective aspiration for equity and social justice. At its core, we find the aspirations of people still waiting for the respect and fair opportunities owed to them. They resonate strongly, calling for fairness in a world where countless still yearn for what remains absent and denied for so many. The social justice movement is of a global nature and the call for fairness is heard in so many parts of the world. We see it and learn from the experiences of families and children in communities and classrooms everywhere. Hopeful for respectful consideration, they continue seeking fairness irrespective of social, racial, or cultural diversity.

Social Justice for Immigrant Children and Their Families

The aspiration for opportunities equally present and accessible to everyone, without distinction, is what remains at the core of social justice. Still an aspiration, today, it is zealously pursued by many who understand the need to eradicate so many existing inequalities. Lack of equal opportunities drives many people to leave their homelands, seeking the opportunities they also deserve. One is reminded about the unequal conditions still present reading Buitrago's *Two white rabbits* (2015), where a father and young daughter cross borders in search of a better life, which is a reminder of the thousands continuing to leave behind their homes waiting to find what is socially just for everyone.

The headline news from 2020 to the present continue bringing attention to the ordeal of children and families migrating from places in Asia, the Middle East, and the Americas. To them, the world added the images of thousands of Ukrainian children escaping from the war that is threatening to take their homeland. They have become like an ongoing river of refugees changing the spirit of the world not seen since the Second World War. These children are joining the millions from other regions of the global society who also turned immigrants. The plight for understanding and compassion can be read on the faces of children. It is especially palpable from children, including many coming unaccompanied, telling everyone about realities one would never want to learn about ever again. Driven away by poverty, violence, discrimination, and fear, all seemed to be compounded by the conditions of a pandemic experienced in 2020 and the continuing challenges at the moment that we were writing. Their realities are another reminder of the multiple challenges faced by immigrants and how these also impact children. There are many aspirations and meanings embedded in social justice when seen from the perspective of immigrant children and their families. Their aspirations and struggles are vividly present in society today. This is what drives children in *A journey toward hope* (Hinojosa and Voorhees 2020), coming all the way from Central America, in search of hope. Waiting for equitable opportunities are also the thousands of children, both recently arrived and those born to immigrant parents.

A Difficult Topic but Necessary to Be Addressed

Issues and topics on social justice remain essential to consider and are unavoidable for a society aspiring to address equity and equality. Such is the case of the multiple challenges faced by people of immigration both newly arrived and those living in our communities. As they build their roots in new places, many encounter the challenges of adapting to new cultures and of finding meaning for themselves and their children. Highly polarized and politicized, immigration is not always an easy topic to address but necessary as society across the globe continues to become more influenced by growing immigration.

Equity is an aspiration and a sought-after goal especially in a democratic society. Call for equity and respectful interactions of recent times embody the core for socially just aspirations. How much we know and how well we are aware of the struggles faced by immigrant children whether incoming or long-time residents remain a challenge for educators to respond with fairness. For educators of young children, it becomes essential to delve into their many stories to learn and consider how to address and support children, providing them with what is fair, what is equitable, and what is owed to a child (United Nations 1989; National Association for the Education of Young Children [NAEYC] 2020, 2019).

Stories of Immigration Experiences

Everyone in society deserves and aspires to living in a context characterized by impartiality and fairness. Repeatedly, the message is clear: people are seeking justice and hopefulness. They are also seeking a future of hope for children. This is the narrative loudly resounding through the voices we hear, through the multiple accounts of families and children we have met and taught throughout the years. In all of these narratives, one can palpably feel the challenges experienced by families and the aspirations for fairness and of hope for children. We also hear the same claim in their voices as we read the stories gathered in children's literature telling us about the drama of children leaving their country or born to immigrant parents. It is through those storylines that the image of children as participants stands out, urging us to consider their experience as the youngest immigrants. Literature, we must remember, also serves and becomes a tool for learning and for bringing attention to relevant issues and themes necessary and conducive to supporting a child's own growth and sense about self (Chaudhri and Teale 2013).

The saga of immigrant children continues to be written and it is happening in our own communities. Learning more and uncovering their experiences are triggered by the stories in children's books read and shared with students. On so many occasions, these stories, many based on historical events and others on the lived realities of immigrants from yesterday and today, have led us to explore children's presence and their role as immigrants.

We are all captured by the narratives that people share. It is simply, that stories have power especially in how they present issues and topics that are often avoided. Immigration is one of those that so many, still today, want to avoid because "it is controversial." Throughout this book, the authors hope to use

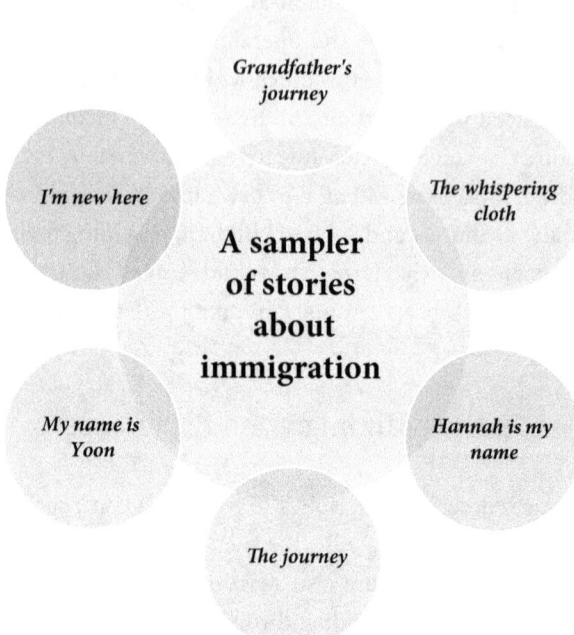

Figure 1.5 Selected stories of children and immigration.

literature to bring attention to the experience of immigration through the eyes of children's storybooks (Figure 1.5). Together, we invite you to examine the needs, realities, and challenges facing young children with immigrant roots.

Windows into the Experience of Immigration and Children

Over the past decade, attention to the lived realities of children who are immigrants has been gaining greater interest. This interest increased in 2014, the year when the United States saw thousands of children, unaccompanied, crossing their borders. More recently, news about children coming in fragile vessels through the waters of the Mediterranean, the Atlantic, and the Caribbean captured everyone's attention. These and many other events have made the presence of children in immigration clearly evident.

At the same time, the news has also shed light on the difficult and unfair circumstances facing many children born to immigrants and living in communities in cities around the globe. More recently, during 2020, movements on social justice and equity and news about the incessant waves of immigrants have made us more keenly aware about the presence of children in immigration.

> **Consciously Considering ... Addressing Immigration in the Classroom**
>
> Difficult topics are so many times avoided or simply left aside. Such is the case of immigration, a topic that draws controversy and a variety of opinions. Yet, it is an issue that cannot be ignored. This is especially a challenge in the classrooms where discussions should be guided to prepare children about realities of today. When addressed in developmentally appropriate ways, issues particularly of social justice nature can be explored in the classroom with young children. One of the premises in anti-bias education, which pursues ways to address unfairness, is precisely that it provides avenues for bringing topics of social justice nature such as immigrant realities into discussion with young children. Social justice is built early and begins with the careful and developmentally oriented planning of activities engaging children in the exploration of issues of interest and related to their experiences. Chapter 7 presents strategies and suggested ways to purposely use children's literature to plan and guide experiences on difficult issues with children.

The multiple images shown across the media also intrigue and create interest about their presence in a process usually observed from the perspective of adults. Ongoing issues—social, economic, and political—challenge children and their families who are immigrants. Echoing their challenges, the literature on immigration has also grown in response to a need to highlight the immigrants' experience. Difficult topics on the nature of immigration and its many circumstances are conveyed through a variety of realities involving children. These narratives serve as a conduit for presenting and bringing attention to challenging experiences (Botelho and Kabakow Rudman 2009; Klefstad and Martinez 2013; Spiegler 2016). They are a wide-open window for young learners to begin exploring and pondering situations unknown to many and familiar to some.

More than Just Stories

The power in storybooks continues to draw and give character to images of children as active participants in unfolding episodes of immigration. Since the past decade, publication of tens of children's books reveal an interest in learning more about the youngest immigrants. Their pages and images invite

> **Thinking and Reflecting .... Avoiding Emphasis on Differences**
>
> Often, we hear comments about accounts of diversity highlighting what is different or that pertains to "others." While it is relevant to recognize the individuality of experiences and characteristics, efforts seem to continue focusing on what is different. Consider for a moment how this type of thinking can be avoided. *How can we prevent the overemphasis on seeing only what is different?*

us to uncover their realities. They also denote the need to know more about who immigrant children are and to learn more about their aspirations and their challenges. Thinking about stories of immigrants, we remember one time when we shared the children's book the *Big umbrella* (Bates 2018) with a group of kindergartners. We were surprised to hear some of the children use the story to talk about immigrants. Their responses were empathetic and evidenced their understanding of the need for protecting others when one child said, "We need to make sure everyone is safe."

It's Not about *Others*: Reclaiming Objectivity

The immigration experience evokes multiple views and opinions addressing diversity. They vividly come afloat through the lens of children's stories about the lives of immigrants. In each of the stories we find opportunities to enrich knowledge and expand thoughts as one uncovers and learns about the many ways diversity presents itself distinguishing individuals and their experiences. In each of these issues of diversity, we find opinions and dilemmas raised by those emphasizing the differences of "others" instead of similarities that define people (Derman-Sparks and Olsen Edwards 2009).

However, when deceptively regarded, these differences will bring us, as many have posited, to face and make efforts to defeat issues of "otherness" (Murdick et al. 2004). Relating with people seen as "others" because of their cultural and ethnic diversity such as immigrant trajectories has been a challenge as the emphasis remains on seeing differences. Conceptualizations based on human and experiential differences have resulted in labeling individuals with diverse cultures, heritage, and ethnic roots as "others." These ideas about seeing people with characteristics different from those of the mainstream as "others" have long divided us and prevented so many from really seeing the sameness in those with stories and heritage differing from their own. It is the lens seeing the "other" that, Delpit (1995) reminds us, continues to alienate individuals in society, labeling them as "different" instead of seeing what is common.

A call for objectivity is vital if we are to learn and deepen our ideas about what makes individuals who they are. Objectively examined, stories bring us closer to face issues and realities of diversity in society. They are windows opening and letting us view different lived experiences. In all, they expand our viewpoints seeing diversity as an inherent trait of humanity as the goal of building a more inclusive society is pursued.

In the stories of immigration, the lived experiences of immigrant children and their families unfold for us to value and learn about. They are not for placing emphasis on differences but rather on seeing and valuing diversity. They are a path to recognizing our relationship to others and the shared humanity that defines us. It is, after all, just like what the character in Mem Fox's story *Whoever you are* (1997) asserts: "And their lives may be quite different but inside they are just like you" (n.p.).

Learning about Child Immigrants

Learning about children is in itself a journey. Uncovering their realities and challenges is pertinent to better understanding their needs and ways to support them. With a focus on children, the chapters ahead explore some of the questions about the young child immigrant through the narratives and imagery in children's literature. In Chapter 2, we will examine further how literature will help us as a tool for exploring and gathering knowledge about the experience of child immigrants, the youngest immigrants.

Reflecting and Beyond

1. What are your views about immigration today?
2. What aspects about immigration do you consider most relevant to explore?
3. As an educator, what are the main responsibilities that we have with young children with immigrant roots?

References

Aguilera, Jasmine. 2021. "The number of unaccompanied children arriving at the U.S-Mexico border doubled from February-March." *Time*, April 8. https://time.com/5953161/unaccompanied-minors-children-march-increase/.

Batalova, Jeanne and Jie Zong. 2016. "Language diversity and English proficiency in the United States." *Migration Policy Institute*, November 11. https://www.migrationpolicy.org/article/language-diversity-and-english-proficiency-united-states-2015.

Botelho, Maria José, and Masha Kabakow Rudman. 2009. *Critical analysis of multicultural children's literature: Mirrors, windows and doors*. New York: Routledge.

Budiman, Abby. 2020. "Key Facts about U.S. immigrants." *Fact Tank*, January 20. Pew Research Center. https://www.pewresearch.org/fact-tank/2020/08/20/key-findings-about-u-s-immigrants/.

Budiman, Abby, Christine Tamir, Lauren Mora, and Luis-Noe Bustamante. 2020. "Facts on U.S. immigrants 2018." Pew Research Center, August 20. https://www.pewresearch.org/hispanic/2020/08/20/facts-on-u-s-immigrants/.

Burnett, John and Joel Rose. 2021. "More than 170,000 migrants taken into custody in the southwest border in March." *NPR National*, April 2. https://www.npr.org/2021/04/02/983937001/more-than-170-000-migrants-nabbed-illegally-crossing-southwest-border-in-march.

Burrone, Sara, Bina D'Costa, and Goran Holmqvist. 2018. *Child-related concerns and migration decisions: Evidence from the Gallup World Poll*. Office of Research. Innocenti working paper. UNICEF.

Camarota, Steven, Bryan Griffith, and Karen Zeigler. 2017. *Mapping immigration's impact on public schools*. Center for Immigration Studies. impacthttps://cis.org/sites/cis.org/files/camarota-pumas_2.pdf.

Chamie, Joseph. 2016. "Prepare for the 21st century exodus of migrants." *YaleGlobal Online*. https://yaleglobal.yale.edu/content/prepare-21st-century-exodus-migrants.

Chaudhry, Amina and William Teale. 2013. "Stories of multicultural experiences in literature for children, ages 9–14." *Children's Literature in Education* 44: 359–76.

Cho, Hyunhee. 2017. "Navigating the meaning of social justice, teaching for social justice, and multicultural education." *International Journal of Multicultural Education* 19(2). https://files.eric.ed.gov/fulltext/EJ1148050.pdf.

Connor, Phillip and Gustavo López. 2016. "5 facts about the U.S. rank in worldwide migration." *Fact Tank*, May 18. Pew Research Center.

Delpit, Lisa. 1995/2006. *Other people's children. Cultural conflict in the classroom*. New York: The New Press.

Derman-Sparks, Louise and Julie Olsen Edwards. 2009. *Anti-bias education for young children and ourselves* (2nd edition). Washington, DC: National Association for the Education of Young Children.

Dinan, Stephen. 2017. Immigrants children numbers growing in public schools. Washington Times, March 15. https://www.washingtontimes.com/news/2017/mar/15/immigrants-children-numbers-growing-us-public-scho/.

Gramlich, John. 2021. "Migrant apprehensions at U.S.-Mexico border are surging again." *Fact Tank*, March 15. Pew Research Center.

Herbert, Jeannie. 2013. "Interrogating social justice in the early years education: How effectively do contemporary policies and practices create equitable learning environments for indigenous Australian children?" *Contemporary Issues on Early Childhood* 14(4): 300–10.

International Organization for Migration [IOM]. 2019. *World migration report 2020*. Geneva, Switzerland. https://www.un.org/sites/un2.un.org/files/wmr_2020.pdf.

Johnson, Christopher. 2021. "More child migrants are arriving alone in Spain's holiday islands ever than before." *CNN World*, February 23. https://www.cnn.com/2021/02/23/europe/child-migrants-canary-islands-spain-intl/index.html.

Klapper, Melissa. 2007. *Small strangers. The experiences of immigrant children in America, 1880–1925*. New York: Ivan R. Dee.

Klefstad, Jill and Kimberly Martinez. 2013. "Promoting young children's cultural awareness and appreciation through multicultural books." *Young Children* 68(5): 74–81.

Martin, Susan. 2001. "Heavy traffic: International migration in an era of globalization." *Brookings*, September 1. https://www.brookings.edu/articles/heavy-traffic-international-migration-in-an-era-of-globalization/.

McLemore, Dale and Harriet Romo. 2005. *Racial and ethnic relations in America* (7th edition). Boston, MA: Pearson.

Münz, Rainer. 2017. "Demography and migration: An outlook for the 21st century." *Policy Brief*. (migrationpolicy.org).

Murdick, Nikki, Paul Shore, Barbara Gartin and Mary Chittooran. 2004. "Cross-Cultural comparison of the concept of 'Otherness' and its impact on persons with disabilities." *Education and Training in Developmental Disabilities* 39(4): 310–6. Retrieved May 11, 2021, from http://www.jstor.org/stable/23880210.

National Association for the Education of Young Children. 2019. *Advancing equity in early childhood education. Position Statement*. Washington, DC: Author.

National Association for the Education of Young Children. 2020. *Developmentally appropriate practice. Position Statement*. Washington, DC: Author.

National Immigration Forum. 2019. "Push or pull factors: What drives central American migrants to the U.S.?" *National Immigration Forum*, July 23. https://immigrationforum.org/article/push-or-pull-factors-what-drives-central-american-migrants-to-the-u-s/.

National Immigration Forum. 2021. *Immigration 2020. For America to thrive*. https://immigrationforum.org/landing_page/immigration-2020/.

Ortman, Jennifer and Christine Guarneri. 2009. *United States population projections: 2000 to 2050*. United States Census Bureau. https://www.census.gov/content/dam/

Census/library/working-papers/2009/demo/us-pop-proj-2000-2050/analytical-document09.pdf.

Roberts, Alex. 2021. "The immigrants are coming! The immigrants are coming!" *Halsey News*, January 17. https://www.halseynews.com/2021/01/17/8000-immigrants-are-making-their-way-north-to-the-united-states/.

Robles-Melendez, Wilma and Vesna Beck. 2000. *Teaching social studies in early education*. NY: Delmar.

Robles-Melendez, Wilma and Wayne Driscoll. 2020. *Issues and challenges of immigration in early childhood in USA*. London: Bloomsbury.

Shapiro, Lauren. 2014. "Surge of unaccompanied children." *Ask FactCheck*, July 18. A Project of the Annenberg Public Policy Center. https://www.factcheck.org/2014/07/surge-of-unaccompanied-children/.

Shoichet, Catherine. 2021. "Why so many kids cross the border alone." *CNN*, March 17. https://www.cnn.com/2021/03/17/us/border-why-children-cross-alone/index.html.

Spiegler, Jinnie. 2016. "Teaching young children about bias, diversity and social justice." *Edutopia*. https://www.edutopia.org/blog/teaching-young-children-social-justice-jinnie-spiegler.

Suro, Roberto. 2009. *America's views of immigration: Evidence from public opinion surveys*. Washington, DC: Migration Policy Institute.

United Nations. 1948. Universal Declaration of Human Rights. https://www.un.org.

United Nations. 1989. *Convention on the rights of the child*. https://www.unicef.org/child-rights-convention/convention-text.

United Nations. 2017. "The world counted 258 million international migrants in 2017, representing 3.4 per cent of global population." *Population Facts*, December 18. https://www.un.org/development/desa/pd/sites/www.un.org.development.desa.pd/files/files/documents/2020/Jan/un_2017_factsheet5.pdf.

United Nations. 2018. "Refugees and migrants: Frequently asked questions." *UN High Commissioner for Refugees*, August 31. https://www.refworld.org/docid/56e81c0d4.html.

United Nations. 2019a. "The number of international migrants reaches 272 million, continuing an upward trend in all world regions." *News*, September 17. The number of international migrants reaches 272 million, continuing an upward trend in all world regions, says UN | UN DESA | United Nations Department of Economic and Social Affairs.

United Nations. 2019b. Department of Economic and Social Affairs, Population Division (2019). *International Migration 2019: Report* (ST/ESA/SER.A/438). https://www.un.org/en/development/desa/population/migration/publications/migrationreport/docs/InternationalMigration2019_Report.pdf.

United Nations. 2021. "Pandemic curbs trend toward ever increasing immigration." *UN News*, January 15. https://news.un.org/en/story/2021/01/1082222.

UNICEF. 2016. *Uprooted. The growing crisis for refugee and migrant children*. New York: UNICEF.

UNICEF. 2020. *UNICEF's agenda for action for refugees and migrant children*. https://www.unicef.org/eca/emergencies/unicefs-agenda-action-refugee-and-migrant-children.

Wessel, David. 2021. "The U.S. in 2050 will be very different than it is today." Peter G. Peterson Foundation. https://www.pgpf.org/us-2050/research-summary.

Children's Books Cited

Bates, A. 2018. *The big umbrella*. NY: Simon & Schuster.
Buitrago, Jairo. 2015. *Two white rabbits*. Toronto, Canada: Groundwood Books.
de Arias, Patricia. 2018. *Marwan's journey*. Hong Kong: Michael Neugebauer Publishing.
Hinojosa, Victor and Coert Voorhees. 2020. *A journey of hope*. Six foot Press.
Milner, Kate. 2017. *My name is not refugee*. Edinburgh, Scotland: Bucket List.
Sanna, Francesca. 2016. *The journey*. London, UK: Flying Eye Books. An Imprint of Nobrow.
Say, Allen. 1993. *Grandfather's journey*. NY: Houghton and Mifflin.
Yang, Belle. 2007. *Hannah is my name*. NY: Candlewick.

2

Children's Literature, a Voice for Social Justice and Critical Consciousness

This chapter aims to:

- Identify the multiple roles of stories.
- Discuss how children's literature serves as a conduit for addressing immigration realities.
- Explain the need for building critical consciousness in early education.
- Recognize the role of stories in addressing social justice issues.

Key words

- Stories
- Children's literature
- Critical consciousness
- Social justice
- Children's rights

All Because of Stories

It was the story we read during our class that made me remember about the stories my parents always shared. But especially it made me think about my mother. She would always have a story to share with messages that have never left me. The day we came to this country, I was so scared not knowing what we would find. A new place, a different language, and a place that did not look to what I knew. That evening, my mother hugged me and said, "Want to hear a story?" I remembered nodding and getting closer to her. As she started, it was like finding a place so familiar that it made me feel safe. Just as she always used to do before, almost every night she would share stories about her growing up and about so many different characters that kept me connected to my heritage. They became well known to me, and through them, today I know, they affirm who I am and my culture. In each story, I could feel again so connected to what made me feel safe. I guess, it was because of that power stories have that all these memories have come rushing back to me. As I read to my students in the classroom where I teach now, I thought to myself how much I would want them to also find those stories that would make them feel at home.

There Is Power in Stories

Everyone has a story they cherish, so personal that it is always kept alive. Sometimes it is a story we heard at home, that was read to us, or that we read. Other times, it is the stories we create as life brings us face to face with more and different experiences. These are the stories that become so special and that we pass on and share with others. Every moment of life seems to be vividly kept in the words of the person telling a story or in the pages of a book waiting for us to read or to be read to others.

It does not matter how they came to us. Stories connect us with times lived, with emotions, people, and events that never leave us. We also remember the moments and especially the persons who shared and brought the stories to us. This is what we hear from the teacher in the opening scenario. She still remembers the stories shared by her mother that gave her that sense of being safe and at home. Even in the most challenging of times, we all seem to go back and remember those accounts narrated to us and that became a part of ourselves. In them, a part of us lives and comes back alive every time we hear or share a story. This is what makes a story such a special and meaningful event (Lukens 2002; Norton and Norton 2011; Laminack and Kelly 2019), giving voice and keeping alive personal experiences and ideals. Their power is undeniable and we are reminded of it every time we think about what stories encompass. Meeting the characters in Margaret Wild's book *The Treasure box* (2017), who take with them a book of stories as they flee from the war, reveals to us, in uniquely special ways, the enduring and intrisic power of stories.

Yesterday and Today, Stories Speak to Us

Regardless of where they came from to us, stories continue to speak to us of memories, events, or realities that are uniquely special to us. That is the power that a story has that, embedded in their phrases or images, keeps conveying to us messages and ideas encouraging or moving us to persevere in the pursuit of ideals. We wonder where their power emanates from when the truth is that

> **Thinking and Reflecting ... Stories and More Stories**
>
> Someone special was the person from whom you always heard stories that are still in your minds and hearts. We invite you to remember who that person was and the story that particularly continues to resonate for you. Who was that person? What was your favorite story?

stories are universal to humanity (Bruner 1986). They are a shared and personal experience commonly familiar because of their ability to bring truth about realities and experiences to the young and old alike. The fact is that stories are an influential and significant experience in a person's life (Stoodt-Hill and Amspaugh 2009; Giorgis and Glazer 2013). It is undeniable the role stories play in connecting us with our families. Traditionally, stories have promoted an invisible, yet strong, sense of connection to our families, our culture, and our unique life experiences. They transcend time and today, in contemporary times, stories continue to weave the thread of emotions and sentiments linking children to their families and to their communities.

More than Just Stories

Stories attract everyone. What they share, uncover, or connect us to reveals that they are more than just simple accounts. In the opinion of Dyson and Genishi, "We all need stories to nourish our selves [sic], to feed mind and heart" (1994, 242). Stories, as they pointed out, are inherent to people's experience, revealing and building a community of views and ideas for those who read or listen to them. We know that many times, stories become a dialogue about realities and circumstances continuing to shape life itself. Whether these are informally shared and passed on by our families or read, embedded in these narratives are glimpses of life, bringing back memories and serving as bridges into experiences familiar and unknown to us. Such are the stories of immigration, ongoing and being written every moment by families and children, right now, in our classrooms and across society. How much do they reveal about the living experiences of children who are immigrants, is what we must ask ourselves. One thing we know is that listening, reading, and critically reflecting on those stories brings us closer to building an understanding about the experiences of immigrant children and families.

Children's Literature, a Journey into Ideas, Ideals, and Life Experiences

From infancy, children's literature accompanies our earliest memories. Characterized by its multidimensionality, in its unique way, children's literature brings joy and awakens our minds while we are learning and uncovering ideas, characters, and places (Lukens 2002; Norton and Norton 2011; Galda, Liang, and Cullinan 2016). There are many definitions of children's literature. Essentially, it is considered as literature directed to children as their main audience. For the purposes of this book, criteria followed to define children's literature stem from Norton (2011), Norton (2013); Galda, Liang, and Cullinan (2016); Giorgis and Glazer (2013); Lukens (2002; 2007); Kiefer (1994), and Yokota (2009). Following their tenets, in this book children's literature is defined as:

- Literature written for children with the purpose of providing enjoyment (Kiefer 1994; Norton and Norton 2011; Giorgis and Glazer 2013) and vicariously building an understanding of different realities (Lukens 2002; 2007). It is literature that engages children in the experiences of society's increasing diversity and global connections (Galda, Liang, and Cullinan 2016).
- Books for children that share and present "a significant truth" (Lukens 2007, 9), such as immigration and social justice issues, in appropriate ways that lead to thoughtful reflection (Giorgis and Glazer 2013).

Literature has a special place in every culture and in humanity. It has allowed us to experience and learn about ourselves and our realities. Undeniably, "literature is the means by which people communicate across cultures and across ages—across all divisions of time and space to gather the collective wisdom of the human experience" (Pugh 1988, 4).

Emphasis throughout this book is on selections from children's multicultural literature given that it is the genre addressing diversity and issues faced by people of different ethnic and cultural backgrounds (Yokota 2009) that more particularly reflect those of immigration.

Children's literature has many goals and roles (Figure 2.1), and to many, literature is what allows children to experience and connect with the past and present and to experience the societal realities, challenges, and emotions of today. Through children's stories young readers learn about diversity, mirroring that of their own and experiencing that of peers personalized through characters that to many become friends and heroes (Lukens 2002; Norton 2011).

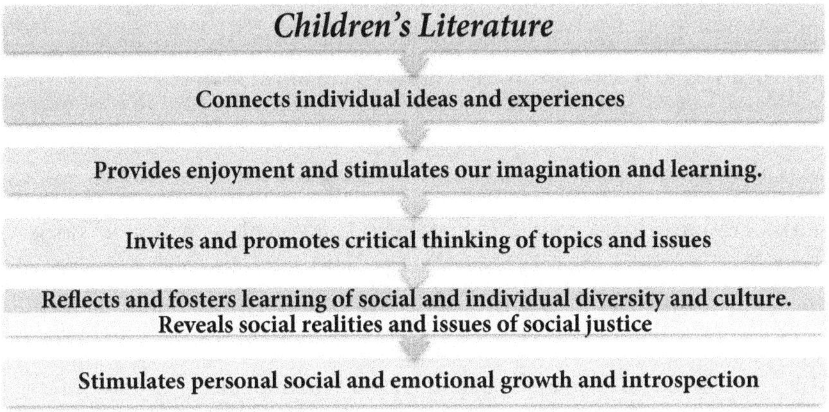

Children's Literature

- Connects individual ideas and experiences
- Provides enjoyment and stimulates our imagination and learning.
- Invites and promotes critical thinking of topics and issues
- Reflects and fosters learning of social and individual diversity and culture. Reveals social realities and issues of social justice
- Stimulates personal social and emotional growth and introspection

Figure 2.1 Multiple roles of children's literature.
Source: Norton (2011); Martinez, Yokota, and Temple (2017).

As a literary area, children's literature is characterized by its multiple purposes, addressing, presenting, and reflecting life itself (Cai 2002; Kiefer, Tyson, Barker, Patrick, and Sanders 2019). Through children's literature, we find a multitude of ideas that propel our imagination or that cement our beliefs and convictions. Our most cherished ideals are often found and reinforced through the pages in a children's book. There are so many occasions where we have encountered the many realities of life glaringly present in a storybook.

Many continue to ask what gives children's literature such magic and significant role for a child and for adults. It is its own nature of a spectrum of topics from the most joyful and fantastic to the most difficult ones, all having a presence in children's literature that imparts a distinctive trait and appeal to readers. Many would agree that it is also how it evokes a myriad of emotions in the reader, individually meaningful given that we each process and make our own "different transactions" with stories (Lukens 2002, xviii). The images emerging from the expressions and phrases in stories tell of actions, events, and ideas delivering a message that speaks to the child as well as to the adult. Literature for children continues to be a powerful didactic tool conveying and leading individuals to learn about themselves and society. Cultural heritage, the accounts and struggles of people, and topics addressing societal unequal realities all find themselves present in children's book titles. Altogether, they play a role in disclosing circumstances defining a continuing search for fairness in society. Many scholars have also highlighted the value of literature as a tool for uncovering and exploring a multitude of sociological realities (Ewick and Silbey 1998; Singer 2011). Children's literature offers, as Sims Bishop (1991) posited, a way to reflect the diverse nature of the world itself.

Learning about Child Immigrants: Using the Lens of Stories

Stories are intrinsic to children's literature. The ingenious nature of stories is well known. From its many literacy roles as well as its cultural and instructional functions, stories have proven to be a compelling vehicle to explore experiences and learn about difficult topics (Norton and Norton 2011; Lukens, Smith, and Miller Coffel 2013). Scholars and educational practitioners agree that children's stories are also a way to learn about and examine realities of children with diverse roots and experiences (Dyson and Genishi 1994; Cai 2002; Cardenuto 2012; Kleftstad and Martinez 2013; Ada 2016; Henry and Robles-Melendez 2019). They provide a special lens into the multiple worlds and experiences of individuals, bringing us closer to learning and meeting experiences from many realities, some familiar and others unknown to us (Cai and Sims Bishop 1994; Singer 2011; Norton 2013). The journey of immigrants is one of those realities that continue to be shared and explored through the telling and reading of stories. Immigration and children have been a topic explored in many of the genres encompassed in children's literature. Topics about immigration have been more specifically embedded into multicultural literature, literature dedicated to examining issues of diversity, culture, and social justice.

Children's Literature, an Opportunity to Learn and to Raise Awareness

A book and a story, they both are doors that open our imagination and our own thoughts. We all would agree that the variety of possibilities embedded in a storybook is endless. This is, what in our practice as educators, we have learned and experienced working with children in the classroom and working with college students preparing to become teachers. One of the many possibilities that stories provide is to learn and reflect on issues of today (Yokota and Kolar 2008). Living in the increasingly diverse and more globally connected society of our times, we are reminded that everyone deserves respect and fairness. We have learned, how with a story, the mind is prompted to inquire and question realities that are problematic and difficult to conceive from a stance on issues such as fairness and justice.

Recent decades have also made us witness the difficult moments experienced in society because of a gradual rise of discrimination and prejudiced behaviors and actions. Among those caught as targets of these behaviors are immigrants, whose voices are yet to be heard to erase the misinformed positions still rising in many parts of the world. In many instances, opening the discussion is not an easy thing to do. We have personally experienced it and have also realized the potential and power of a story, which opens the door to begin and continue conversations about the diverse experiences of our times.

An Invitation

This book is an invitation. It is an invitation to use the power of stories to build our consciousness about standing realities of biased actions and prejudiced responses, this time directed, in particular, to immigrants. Our focus is on children and the invitation is to learn and raise our awareness about their immigrant experience through the multiple narratives coming to us through children's literature. The growing number of books addressing a broad selection of immigration topics provides a tool to examine and explore immigration from the perspective of the child. This time, children's literature is serving as a tool in the praxis of understanding and building our consciousness about immigration and children. Through the next chapters, stories will help us appreciate and consider milestone moments in the life of young children who are immigrants. The invitation is open for readers to join us.

Critically Looking and Reading Children's Stories

We all agree that there are many ways to read a story. It is known also that there are many dimensions that a story unveils and discloses, and that every time we read them again, new perceptions and messages emerge. Using a critical perspective to examine narratives in stories leads us to unwrap and find messages and realities that call attention to and speak about struggles and challenges facing individuals and society. Critically examining stories or critical literacy has been described as a way to look at realities going beyond the words and guided by perspectives anchored in addressing what is socially just (Vazquez, Janks, and Comber 2019). The need for reading with an intention to question and bring to discussion realities present in our world has risen today as society, cognizant of inequities, calls on everyone to stop the silence and search for responses leading to actions for the sake of fairness.

Inspired by the work of Paulo Freire and his milestone work prompted by the publication of *Pedagogy of the oppressed* (1970), critically reading takes us to uncover realities opening the conversation to reveal the "hidden voices" (Wallenstein 1987, 35) in what is read. This is what emerges when reading leads us to taking a conscientious focus about the challenges and issues facing people in society (Vazquez 2004; Yokota and Kolar 2008; Janks 2013), whether it is local, national, or global. Critically reading is to take a walk across the plot and characters and open the curtain to find the realities posed in a story. Unpacking the messages found in a story book calls us to consider and learn about what they reveal and to hear those hidden voices. Stories, after all, are means to convey ideas and experiences, sometimes very difficult ones, in subtle but clearly intentional ways. They are as well tools to continue unveiling and bringing to attention a myriad of inequities and disparities still present today. Critical literacy is one of the avenues providing ways during early childhood to begin building a conscience about societal inequities. Stories have the power to inspire and empower children to gain an understanding about themselves and about peers and the circumstances they face. This is how education can consciously promote fairness and equity in our students.

Responding to Stories

Every time that a storybook is read, a sharing of ideas and sentiments unfolds. Some have pointed out that stories have special ways to touch your emotions and evoke certain feelings. These are many of the ways in which we respond to stories, denoting the variety of transactions made with what is read. How one responds lies in the way the message is presented leading one to feel that it speaks to you. Literature scholars have long pointed out that reading or listening to a story evokes a response, which describes how the reader reacts to the contents and topics addressed (Norton 2013). According to the reader response theory that Rosenblatt (1978) proposed, readers may respond efferently when they look and gather information from a text. Responses could also be aesthetic, which Rosenblatt described as being those when readers make a personal connection with what is read. Making it personal and establishing connections (Fialho 2019) is also what reveals how children construct meaning from what they read. Creating a space where their comments are welcome, invites children to share their thoughts and encourages them to build on their ideas and views.

Becoming Mindful about Societal Challenges Begins Early

Some may argue why we are using stories to address such a complex topic. There are, as well, many purposes and goals for selecting stories one reads or that are shared with children. Reading critically enhances the value of a story and moves us into becoming mindful about experiences and circumstances that remind us about ongoing inequalities in our society. How to respond and mindfully consider what these inequities are begins early in life. In developmentally and individually appropriate ways, leading children to consider and inquire about the challenges of peers and families near and far starts during the early years (Vazquez 2004; Robles-Melendez and Beck 2019; Derman-Sparks and Olsen Edwards 2020).

In our own teaching experience, we have chosen stories to open conversations about difficult and controversial topics. One of those times was when we shared *Crow boy* (Yashima 1976), a story reminding us about the need for recognizing and understanding individual diversity. Inviting the students to look more deeply into the story and to place themselves in the boy's classroom led to a frank conversation on the hurtful and damaging impact of prejudice. We also remember the voiced determination of students who stood up for their peers after reading and delving into issues of social unrest and conflict displacing people depicted in Sanna's narrative about refugees in *The Journey* (2016). Undeniably, the power embedded in the lines of a story can move us to recognize inequities. Just as Freire keenly pointed out, in reading the words, we can also read the world's realities.

The powerful way that stories have driven us to reflect on existing experiences denying others of what is rightfully theirs is undeniable. They are windows, mirrors, and sliding glass doors, asserted Sims Bishop, to look into experiences and events of diversity helping to open our minds to the reality of society. Stories are also influential and arouse our sense of fairness and empathy bringing attention to realities in society, a reason that inspired us to explore the lived experiences of immigrant children conveyed through the lens of children's literature on immigration. The invitation is open for you to join us in exploring the voices that will bring us closer to understanding the experiences and realities of immigrant children.

Critically Reading: Taking a Social Justice Stance about Immigrant Children

In times where society has heard claims for equity and dignity, it has become more clearly evident that we must lead our children to mindfully become aware about the call for social justice. Leading a generation into understanding the

> ### Thinking and Reflecting ... Addressing Difficult Topics
>
> Children's literature offers opportunities to address and engage in the discussion of issues sometimes considered to be very difficult. Take a moment to reflect on stories you have read or that you have shared that addressed difficult or controversial topics. What prompted you to select them? Which ones would you recommend?

rights that everyone has to enjoy the same respect and understanding begins early in life. As educators, critically selecting and sharing readings to unwrap realities and spark their inquiry is fundamental if we are to address society's inequities. Many agree that, in very compelling ways, stories expose us to realities and play an influential role in our social and emotional development (Marriott 1998; Yokota 2009; Lukens, Smith, and Coffer 2013). This is where one realizes the role and value of children's literature designated as multicultural. Intrinsically, it embodies a repertoire of topics and issues essential to learning about as children grow up and socially become constituents of society. Key to their formation is providing experiences that will denote and reflect their communities, their realities, and those of their peers (Robles-Melendez and Beck 2000; Gonzalez, Moll & Amanti 2005)). Instilling in the child a sense about fairness is central to developing the attitudes and spirit for justice in society, and this begins during the early childhood years. Intentionally selected with children's developmental needs in mind, children's literature is an avenue leading the child to exploring and learning about societal realities. Each story becomes a door leading children into the experiences of themselves and those of their peers. As they travel through places, meeting characters and circumstances, their sense of reality broadens. With that, perspectives on fairness and justice also begin to emerge.

Multicultural Children's Literature, an Avenue into Diverse Realities

Today, as we write, narratives shared about diversity are opening doors into experiences of a society continuing to struggle with issues of social justice. The world of children's literature, and especially multicultural literature, engages us in exploring and learning about the realities, experiences, and situations of people with diverse roots and backgrounds. Scholars agree that because of the magnitude of the goals pursued in multicultural literature, it is difficult to have a single definition that can precisely encompass its goals (Cai and Bishop 1994; Cai 2002). Rudine Bishop affirmed the need for multicultural literature saying, "We need diverse books because we need books in which children can find themselves, see reflections of themselves" (Reading Rockets 2021). Multicultural literature has also become the gateway to present and learn about the stories and lived experiences of peers and families not only far away but those living in our own communities.

The struggle and cry for people's equal rights found its voice through multicultural literature. Influenced by and emerging out of the Civil Rights Movement, multicultural literature addresses topics pertaining to the experiences of people from diverse cultures and the marginalized groups in our society (Lukens, Smith, and Coffer 2013; Norton and Norton 2013; Norton 2013). Through its pages, stories about equality, fairness, and social justice issues continue to come alive, calling for greater mindfulness about their realities. Shared in ways that speak to the young and the adult, stories provide an avenue where children can see themselves while exploring and uncovering the diversity and cultural experiences of families, friends, peers, and adults (Bishop 1991; Ada 2016). Because of the role it plays in presenting and disclosing issues of diversity, multicultural literature is a crucial teaching tool for children (Martínez, Yokota, and Temple 2017). Beyond the setting and the plot in a story, children's books bring to us complex circumstances demanding attention, awareness, and action. Immigration is one of those topics that continue to be regarded as controversial by many and avoided by others.

Taking a Closer Look: Multicultural Literature and Immigration Topics

Multicultural literature is a path waiting for the reader eager to explore issues and topics addressing diversity, culture, and social justice. Exploring the experiences of immigrants has been addressed in multicultural literature. Earlier publications during the 1970s began examining the experiences of immigrants as shown by Weiner's *Small hands, big hands* (1970). This story continues to resonate today as society becomes more mindful about prejudice and lack of acceptance toward diversity. Calls for tolerance during the 1990s led to an increased number of publications focusing on multiculturalism. Among these is *My name is Maria Isabel* (Ada 1995), another story that dives into the experiences of children with immigrant heritage and their experiences growing up in a different culture. Experiences of immigrant families are revealed in Bunting's *A day's work* (1994), where we learn about the child's agency supporting and helping his grandfather to secure a job. Since then, and more recently, the topic about immigration has become more specifically addressed by numerous publications for children.

Children as Immigrants in Children's Books

Immigration has been the focus of interest of many authors, particularly since the last decades. Stories like Say's *Grandfather's journey* (1989), Choi's *The name jar* (2003), Jimenez's *La mariposa* (2000), and Bunting's *A day's work* (1997) made the presence of immigrants strongly evident as their protagonists dealt with different societal challenges. They also reinforced the presence of children as immigrants and further accentuated the diversity of issues they faced growing up. Immigration, as have been shared earlier, is a complex process with a multitude of different issues. A variety of issues related to immigration have been addressed in children's books published in North America, Europe, and other parts of the world. While they provide a variety of perspectives and take place in diverse settings and are seen from multiple angles, the experience of immigration is the common factor linking them together. Their topics place emphasis on issues of individual, cultural, and political nature.

The recent immigration wave and the simultaneous crisis experienced since early in the 2010 decade has seemingly influenced many of those books authored during recent years. Many of them have also centered their stories on the experience of the child. They have contributed to making their experience more visible and are especially appropriate to be shared with children. Bringing their stories into the classroom, reinforces one of the main characteristics of children's literature. They serve as an avenue to engage children in learning more about themselves and to learn about the experiences of their peers and adults (Crippen 2012). More on how to use stories of immigration will be addressed and discussed in Chapter 7, where we explore ways to introduce these as part of classroom teaching practices for young children. Selecting those that we are exploring to learn more about child immigrants, led us to choose those where the presence of children was evident not just as characters but as protagonists.

Consciously Considering .... *There Is Power in Stories Shared*

Powerfully, stories continue to be a vehicle in which values, principles, and aspirations of a cultural group are conveyed in unique ways. Regarded by UNESCO (2003) as an intangible cultural heritage, oral narrations are an influential factor as individuals begin to develop a sense of connection with their heritage. They also provide an influential link to a group's achievements and struggles.

Shared and passed on from generation to generation, narrations and stories maintain the collective memory alive and actively present for its members. In many cultures, they remain today as a fundamental element bonding their members. It is as what Bridges Smith (2004) stated about the Xhosa in South Africa who have a tradition of storytelling. The author reported that the common cultural heritage reflected in their stories became a "unifying force" during the difficult time of the apartheid. Similarly, stories of immigrants and about immigration serve as a vehicle connecting and exposing the events and emotions of people who went across borders. Whether immigration accounts are personal or are those of family members, pieced in a mosaic of multiple narratives we see the realities, events, and challenges faced.

Why Stories?

"Once upon a time ..." the familiar phrase continues to remind us about the many stories that started to be shared and passed on from one generation to the next. What was shared and continues to be shared reflects the experiences of humanity in its many dimensions. For children growing up, the power of stories continues to embody a myriad of opportunities where they learn and uncover realities of themselves and others. Through the narratives shared by families and of those learned at school, children begin to uncover the multiple dimensions of life's circumstances and happenings. As they read, stories take children to experience the narratives of their own family life, to learn about those of peers and neighbors, and of people and places distant and close to them. Realities of life, of people's actions and events, and of cultures all make their presence clear when reading stories. We each know what we learned that caught our interest or the character we met that still motivates and impresses us, and of places calling us to come. That is the magic of stories that turn themselves just as Sims Bishop

> ### Thinking and Reflecting ... Meaningful Stories
>
> We all have a special story that reminds us about our own story or heritage. Take a moment and think about that special story. Who did you learn it from? What made it special to you? What image does it convey about you and your heritage?

(1990) described them, into windows, mirrors, and doors into our own world and that of people we meet and of experiences demanding our attention.

Multiple Roles of Stories

The enjoyment as well as emotional experience of stories is an undeniable trait. Beyond serving as a source of enjoyment, stories play a significant role in children's lives. The power of a story is seen as one playing multiple roles (Figure 2.2). Stories are more than just a narration. They are instrumental for children and adults, as they build their aspirations and make them face challenges and life's issues. Moreover, stories play a meaningful role for children especially as they learn about their own realities and begin to learn about that of their peers. Emotionally, the role of stories continues to be a major factor in supporting how we perceive and process experiences (Alexander, Miller, and Hengst 2001).

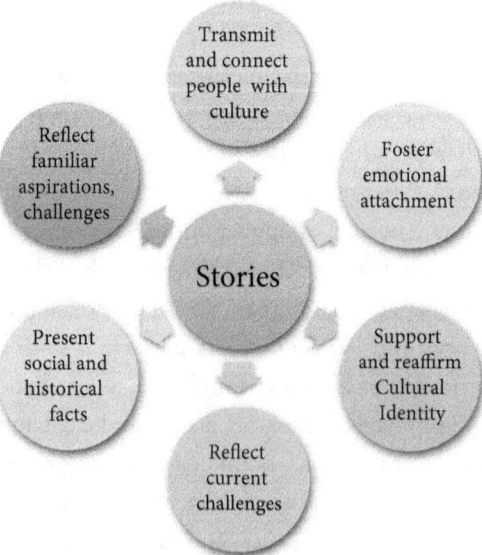

Figure 2.2 Multiple roles of stories.

Stories Are a Door into One's Culture

Stories have long served and continue today to convey one's culture and heritage. It is in the intimacy of a shared time, where young children begin to learn about their heritage. Through the many forms of oral traditions, folktales, nursery rhymes, chants, and accounts turned into family and community stories (Nasiruddin 2013), children begin learning about their heritage and begin to meet characters and historical trajectories. The moments when stories and traditions are shared whether at home or by significant others become a gateway into the cultural world of a child.

Whether stories are shared at home, in the neighborhood, by family members, or significant others, they all link children to their culture. Stories play a role in what is called enculturation, a key process happening in early childhood where children learn about their culture. Shared orally, narratives, whether through stories or other linguistic forms, are a catalyst to learning values, practices, and beliefs of one's culture. In every culture, families and adults share messages about practices and long-held values through the engaging language of their folklore and oral traditions.

> **Thinking and Reflecting ...** *Oral Traditions and Enculturation*
>
> We learn about practices and social conventions held in the culture that we belong to through folktales or stories that we hear at home. What ideas or practices from your culture do you remember learning through stories shared at home? Which of those stories are still shared with children?

They Are a Rich Fund of Cultural Knowledge

From childhood, stories shared orally or read to us are a factor scaffolding the child's emerging sense of attachment, emotionally connecting us to our culture (Alexander, Miller, and Hengst 2001; Erickson 2018). Crossing generations, the shared retelling of *nanas* or nursery rhymes, of lullabies, and stories passed on by families continue to resonate with all the emotions that later, even as adults, keeps connecting us to our heritage. They are part of those very personal funds of knowledge (González, Moll, and Amanti 2005) people bring wherever they come to live. In her book, *Marwan's journey*, de Arias (2018) reminds us how in stories we bring the personal presence of our heritage when the young boy says, "I walk and my footsteps leave a trace of ancient stories, the songs of my homelands, and the smell of tea and bread, jasmine and earth" (n.p.). It is, too, a reminder of the individual and very personal culture that we continue to bring wherever we go, keeping us close and tied to culturally affirm who we are. In the classroom, this is experienced every day, just as we see Kanzi, a young Egyptian girl in *The Arabic quilt* (Khalil 2020), who proudly shares her special family treasure.

Expressed through stories are the aspirations, challenges, and struggles defining the underpinnings of people's heritage and culture. Through the voice of the storyteller, learnings for a lifetime are shared with children presented in ways to be always remembered. Embedded in the narratives shared are tales of actions and behaviors from characters representative of a culture along with the group's ideals, morals, and societal conventions deemed essential. In the narratives, the wisdom of a culture is passed along and carried through life. It is, simply that, "culture lives in stories" (Smith 2020, n.p.), and they are part of those personal belongings we bring wherever we go and continue to treasure (González, Moll, and Amanti 2005).

For some of the immigrant parents and early childhood teachers whom we met, stories from their childhood remained as vibrant as when they first heard them. No matter how far you are, a story keeps you feeling attached to your family's roots. This is what was heard from immigrant parents from Peru whom we met and who still remembered and continue to share the same stories told to them by their families. Similar comments were shared by another parent from Vietnam who was interviewed by the authors. She mentioned that she continues to remember the morals in the stories learned from her grandmother and is now passing them on to her own children.

Stories also make us relive special childhood moments with our own families. This is what we experienced in *Grandma's records* (Velazquez 2004), where the grandson remembers those shared times from his childhood while visiting his grandmother and learning through her about his own cultural musical traditions. The story conveys the pride felt about his culture and the special emotional connections to his grandmother. Other times, there are stories that drive us to understand the experiences of refugee children like the young girl we meet through Kobald's story *My two blankets* (2019) when families are left with no option but to leave what they know.

> **Thinking and Reflecting** ... Cultural Characters
>
> Every culture has characters that represent their values and ideas. Whether they are from legends, myths, or history, we learn and meet them through stories shared at home, in the classroom, and from adults. Take a moment to remember one of those characters that you learned or read about in stories. What values or principles from your culture does the character represent?

Sharing Stories, a Way to Convey Life Happenings

Never forget your roots for they are the very soul of who you are.
—C. Martinez (school teacher)

Everyone has a story to share or knows a story that became so dear and special to them. They are so special that they continue to be passed along to our children, sharing with them what is integral and unique to who one becomes. The fact is that we all have a story we cherish because of its personal and meaningful message to us. They speak to us in ways that help us "make sense out of life" (Lukens, Smith, and Miller Coffel 2013, 5). In each one, we keep the messages continuing through time to remind us about our most personal experiences and aspirations. More than just stories, they are narratives encompassing experiences, aspirations, and challenges where life itself is revealed in unique ways to those listening or reading them. Through them, we may find ourselves reflected and validated as individuals (Sims Bishop, 1990; Norton and Norton 2011; Forest, Garrison, and Kimmel 2015). Whether shared informally or read from a book, stories are a living record of ideas influencing the reader in multiple ways, taking us to reflect, consider, and broaden our views and ideas. A reflection of the times and of its major events, a look at the children's book section will reveal the challenges, issues and topics reflective of an era.

Turned into stories, these narratives embody ideals, experiences, and life events. Seen through the eyes of those who experienced them or learned about them from others, their messages resonate through time. Even the most difficult issues and topics are conveyed through stories helping individuals to reflect and reaffirm beliefs and ideas. They also guide us to question and inquire about realities that are individually and societally relevant. Many times, it is through a story that our eyes are opened to issues calling for social justice actions. Drawing us to critically consider issues demanding action, stories remain as a powerful vehicle for individual and personal growth (Swindler Boutte, Hopkins, and Waklatsi 2008). They are also influential in getting us to walk outside our own realities, and learn about the experiences and challenges of people not only beyond our borders, but also within our own communities. In times when difficult issues take place, children's books provide a means to address these in ways that help children in making sense about challenging circumstances. Through its images and storylines, they are invaluable resources bringing children to process realities in ways that are developmentally sound.

Stories of Immigration: Making Experiences of Immigration Visible

Stories of immigrants and their life-changing efforts continue to take shape every day. Current immigration waves have led many to become aware about their presence. Still raising controversy, it has, at the same time, raised in many an interest in learning more about immigrants. Even as we write, images from the media continue to display the saga of many children and families venturing across the sea and land. Whether planned or not, immigration continues as an experience with multiple implications for their protagonists. A thousand questions abound about their experiences and especially the reasons that brought them or their families to other countries. Eyes are also on the many children living in our communities both recently arrived and on those born to long established immigrant families. In so many ways, they have brought attention to immigration, whether it is shrouded in controversy or not, they have made their presence more clearly visible (Robles-Melendez and Driscoll 2020).

Thinking and Reflecting ... Stories that Open Our Eyes

There is always a story, we would agree, that opens our minds to a variety of realities and experiences. Those are the stories that for many become their own. We invite you to take a moment to reflect and consider which one has been that story that, still today, you remember for its powerful way "to communicate with you".

As we write, society throughout the world continues to experience multiple challenges—social, political, economics, and the continuing threat of a pandemic—forcing many to seek other places to start their lives for them and their families. Their realities have shed light on those who migrated and settled recently or years ago in our own communities. As we listen and learn about the experiences of immigrant children today, accounts on the media are serving as bridges leading society to center their attention and learn about the youngest immigrants. Though their participation is noted through the historical annals, presently, children have now become more clearly visible as characters in the long-standing episode of immigration (Robles-Melendez 2019). Many new additions to children's literature have contributed to accentuate their presence. Even as we were writing, a variety of new book titles continue to emerge addressing immigration from the eyes of childhood.

Children's Stories Bring Us Closer to Learn about Immigration Experience

Children's literature has become a powerful channel for people to express and give voice to the experiences of child immigrants. Literature continues to be not only a conduit for enjoyment but also one leading to uncover and present difficult realities and circumstances (Botelho and Rudman 2009; Norton 2013; Martínez, Yokota, and Temple 2017). Today, children's literature deemed as multicultural is of special impact not only on the young child but on adults, too. The spectrum of themes addressed in multicultural children's books reflects the multidimensional realities found in our society. These realities are uncovered to the reader through the plot and characters of stories, playing an important role in exposing inequities and visibly revealing to readers socially challenging realities that demand action (Cai 2002; Singer 2011). Their perspectives on the experiences of people from diverse cultures, unveil to readers, conflicts emerging from biased and discriminatory practices. They are, in our view, bridges that connect us with experiences and lived realities many times ignored or unknown to many. Stories are also avenues, widely presenting side by side issues and circumstances present in society. Reading with intention to uncover the experience of individual diversity, children's books provide opportunities to question the social and cultural realities reflected. These are stories that call for addressing what Takanishi (2005) refer to as leveling the playing field for children of immigrants.

Stories Illuminating the Experience of Immigrant Children

Children's literature scholar Rudine Sims Bishop (1990) asserted that stories are windows allowing us to look into episodes and life's moments. Botelho and Rudman (2009) remind everyone that, wide open, stories lead us to discover and deepen our understanding of realities sometimes unfamiliar or intricately reflective of our experiences. They are a window we continue to open to explore and learn about immigrant children. In our own experience, they have become avenues we continue to use to traverse worlds we know and those yet to be known. We remember the expressions and comments from many of our students whenever we shared stories about immigration. For some, they set off opportunities to ask questions that, as they candidly said, otherwise would have been difficult to ask about. After reading *Maria Molina and the Days of the Dead* (Krull 1994), one of our authors recalls the comments from some of her students who wondered about rituals and practices continuing to be followed. The discussion led to explore and inquire about their meaning and about commonalities with the student's own cultural practices. Not only do stories share insights of lived realities but they also become a bridge into the day to day acculturation experiences of young immigrant children.

Learning about the experiences of young immigrant children is ongoing. For early childhood educators, these are stories continuing to happen in their classrooms and communities. There are many and different sources to learn about their lived experiences and stories. Here, we turn to explore their lived experiences through stories from children's literature. Because a story is an invitation to learn more, we delve into those that continue to open our eyes and hearts into the journeys of immigrant children growing up in our classrooms and communities.

Using the perspective of children, we look into what these stories reveal about children and their experiences. What do they tell us? How much do they reveal about what it means for children to leave their country? What challenges do they

---

Thinking and Reflecting ... Books as Avenues to Explore Diverse Realities

We all have favorite children's books that have taken us to explore, learn, and meet new realities. Take a moment to think which children's book has been especially meaningful to you to learn about issues of diversity. What made that book so special? What did you uncover through the story?

face as they grow up in a different culture? These questions and our need to learn more drive us to use the lens of stories from children's books to unpack their realities.

There is much to be learned about young child immigrants, many questions that still need to be answered. As educators and advocates for children's equitable rights, finding answers to these questions is relevant and necessary to ensure they find what is needed for them to thrive. In searching and gathering answers, we come to consciously build an understanding about children's needs, reflecting on their influence in our society and communities and seeking ways to equitably and responsively provide support for their successful development (Crosnoe 2013; Adair 2015; Abo-Zena 2018; Robles-Melendez and Beck 2019).

On the Bookshelves

In recent years, many of the titles published have placed attention on the experiences of immigration. Stories such as *The journey* (Sanna), *The Day War Came* (Davies), and *Dreamers* (Morales 2018) are now emerging strongly as reminders of what it means to be an immigrant child, especially seen through the experiences of child immigrants. These stories have become a source to unveil and to learn about the realities faced and continuing to unfold in society. Intended for children, in so many ways, these books are communicating, not only to children but also to adults, the multifaceted challenges faced. But what is more relevant, they are opening our eyes and making us conscious about their experiences. Because of the special lens they give us, in the chapters ahead, we explore experiences of young child immigrants using the narratives in a selection of children's books.

Building Our Consciousness: Social Justice and Children's Rights

We are here! Can you see us? This is the cry that so many times we have heard from immigrant children and people we know. It is a cry for acknowledgment that immigrants are a continuous reality in society, wherever we are in the world. Their presence cannot be hidden or tossed away but rather needs to be appraised to value more clearly what they represent and how much they contribute to a nation's communities. It is a call for building consciousness about immigration not only as a process but as a human and personal experience defining so many people.

After sharing with her graduate students the story *My name is Yoon* (Recorvitz 2003), one of our authors remembered the reaction and comments from one of her students. In a tone that reflected frustration, she shared how many times she had to clarify to people what her name was. Born to immigrant parents, she commented that it felt like they wanted to make her be who she was not. Her comments made us aware of how often, many times unintentionally, we rob people of their own identities. This and so many other experiences make us realize how evidently critical it is to consciously understand the crucial realities that people experience. This also makes us mindful about the imperative for equity. While much has been gained, equity, in our current society, still remains remote and absent for so many. Bringing attention to these many realities is what begins the process of addressing inequities. Holding distorted views and prejudiced responses to immigrants is one of those realities calling for and demanding fairness not only in our nation but in so many parts of the world.

Social Justice and the Young Immigrant Child

Every child deserves the same opportunities and conditions to blossom and enjoy the magical years of their childhood. Reality, however, has shown us that for many, that is a dream many times too distant from them. To open doors and bridge those differences is what social justice calls us to do for children, for every child. For many children of immigrants, the aspirations for equal and same experiences continue to drive efforts for those who are consciously advocating for their rights.

In *Carmela full of wishes* (de la Peña 2018), the painful experience of family separation resonates as we hear the voice of the child wishing her father would be back again with them. Just as so many other children who have found their families separated, the story highlights how immigration continues to impact childhood experiences. The search for equal and consistent equitable opportunities and experiences is continuous. This is one of the main aspirations in education, to uphold the principle of equality. Equality is what drives the need and the reason for social justice efforts. Still today, for many, experiences and equal opportunities are still uneven or absent. This anchors the need for building awareness about realities in our communities and society and demanding action. More importantly, they accentuate the need to provide what is the same and equal (Freire 1970; Takanishi 2004).

Conscious awareness about the conditions and circumstances faced by others is at the heart of social justice. At its core is the acknowledgment of undeniably existing disparities justifying the need for determining equitable practices and opportunities (Bankston 2010). Social justice is a multidimensional concept, not easy to define given its broad implications rooted on fairness. Social justice is a fundamental idea anchored on the recognition of the individual rights that everyone possesses and the need for respect. As a first step, achieving social justice for children begins as we become cognizant about the many existing inequities children experience and their implications on the life of a young child (NAEYC 2019). Second, central to achieving social justice for children of immigration is how consciously we move into action, making decisions to end the existing disparities in a child's experiences. Third, we need to consider, how we ensure the presence of social justice components owed to children (Figure 2.3).

Today, efforts for social justice constitute a call to ensure every child enjoys the same experiences and opportunities regardless of their individual cultures or diversity. Current experiences demand that we be mindful about continuing discriminatory practices, prejudice, and lasting and damaging stereotypes still prevalent in our society. The call for equity continues. The call becomes even more urgent for educators everywhere. In our global society, it is essential that we become determinedly aware about the unequal realities experienced by thousands of children who are immigrants, growing up and present in our

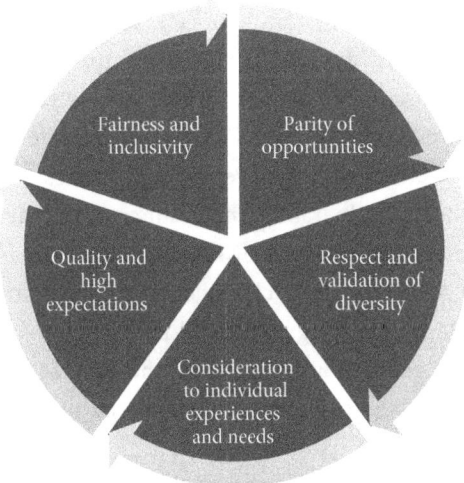

Figure 2.3 Key components of social justice for immigrant children.

Source: Herbert (2013); Mevawalla (2013); Robles-Melendez and Driscoll (2020).

classrooms. Children cannot wait; they need support and quality experiences now. Conscious awareness about the needs of a child is a mandate for all educators and especially for early childhood educators. This is what will ensure that equity is not denied.

Remember, Children Have Rights

> ... the United Nations has proclaimed that childhood is entitled to special care and assistance.
> Preamble, Convention on the Rights of the Child (United Nations 1989)

Whenever we read or learn about some of the circumstances facing children of immigrants, we all must remember that every child is entitled to conditions and experiences supporting their potential and successful development. Equity is, in fact, owed to every child regardless of their diversity. Aspirations for children's safe and successful development continue to guide efforts of educators and advocates everywhere. Striving to ensure children's well-being starts when we reaffirm our belief that every child has rights. They are owed support but also respect for their rights. The milestone Convention on the Rights of the Child (CRC) (United Nations [UN]1989) reaffirmed the integrity of childhood and defined the fundamental rights that every child has. This is powerfully stated every time we remember that every child has the right to grow and develop.

Challenges of current times demand greater attention to children's rights. This is especially critical as discriminatory rhetoric continues to undermine the integrity of children's experience. Growing up, all children have a right to be in environments where they are valued, supported, and cared for. They have a right, just as Article 2 of the CRC declares, to be in places where the diversity that defines their identity is recognized and respected. As declared in the CRC, their inherent vulnerability makes it crucial to understand the need to safeguard children. Misleading views and unequal experiences continue to threaten children of immigration, clearly calling for our attention and action. With consideration to the integrity of children, affirmed in Article 3 of the CRC, society is obliged to make decisions and take actions that are always in the best interest of the child. In education, the pursuit of children's best interests should be always paramount. Growing awareness about the needs of immigrant children is a call to ensure their best interests are upheld and protected. In the next chapters, issues facing immigrant children will be addressed.

Becoming Consciously Mindful about Child Immigrants

"No llegué ayer, pero como si lo fuera. Aunque nací aquí, me siguen viendo como de afuera." [I didn't arrive yesterday, but it seems like I did. Though I was born here, they still see me as an outsider.]

—Comments from a ten-year-old child

Getting to know about the experiences and expectations of children who are immigrants is precisely the intent of the authors of this book. As educators, and particularly as those working with young children, it is vital to know not only the meaning but also the ensuing implications for both those recently arrived and for children born to immigrant parents. It is a fact that the immigration experience permeates through generations. Concerned and interested in presenting the saga of immigration seen through and from the eyes of children, we chose children's stories from picture books because of their unique appeal to portray and engage readers in uncovering the diverse realities of immigration. They are also a means of leading us to become mindful about the challenges they face.

Children's Books, a Bridge into The Experience of Immigration

Stories, whether read to us informally or formally, become real to us as we hear accounts that connect us with family events and experiences. In the saga of immigration, children's books on immigration are a bridge, linking us with the narratives recorded about the experiences of families, friends, and people who ventured out seeking a future. They also convey the experiences of those who during their childhood set out across other borders. Such is the case in Levinson's story *Watch the stars come out* (1985), where the grandmother shares with her granddaughter "a special story" that connected the child with her family's immigrant background so engaging that she wants to continue listening to more special stories. We also witness it in *A different pond* (Phi 2017), where the child learns about his father's nostalgia and longing for the homeland he was forced to leave, becoming a refugee. Countless generations in so many places have also experienced similar moments, listening to stories about the journeys of their parents, grandparents, and relatives that brought them to where they live now. Others are now creating and starring in their own stories of immigration. Those are the stories happening and unfolding in front of us throughout places in our world communities. These stories also reveal the many-sided issues of child immigrants.

These are issues continuing to call for fair and equal opportunities for children to successfully grow and develop and succeed (Crosnoe 2013; Adair 2015).

Selecting Children's Books about Immigration

Today, there are a growing number of titles, particularly picture books, which share and provide opportunities to learn about immigration and immigrants. It is, however, not an easy task to identify book selections focused on the experience of children with immigration. Many more have been published in recent years, and even at the time while writing this book. This is evidence of the interest in addressing the experience of immigration from the perspective of childhood. We found a variety of titles, that were mostly categorized under "multicultural stories," which added to the complexity of the selection. This is something that Botelho and Rudman (2009) had noted before when they denounced that, irrespective of their diversity traits, all stories about diverse cultural groups are lumped together within the larger cluster of multicultural literature. Choosing those that more closely reflected experiences of children with immigration led us to establish specific parameters.

To guide the story selections addressed in this book, we opted to choose picture books with stories appropriate for young children (ages three to eight) related to immigration with children as protagonists, and where experiences were presented from their perspective as a child. Opting for stories for this age group responded to the fact that we wanted to focus on stories that could be shared in early childhood classrooms. Building a sense about social justice issues and anti-bias responses begins early and literature provides a valuable tool to embark on achieving this goal (Yokota and Kolar 2008; Norton 2013; Ada 2016). We also selected stories with themes and topics more closely related to the experiences of young children and their families.

Reasons Guiding Our Selections

Because of the complexity of immigration, stories selected included that of children crossing borders. Also considered were books about immigrant children born to immigrant families. Stories addressing the variety of reasons for immigration were the focus of our selection, including planned and also forced immigration as in the case of child refugees and asylees. In terms of language, stories published both in English and Spanish were selected. We also chose stories taking place during the twentieth and twenty-first centuries. Selections were limited to those published from 1980 through 2021.

Choosing Stories

Choosing stories to consider followed suggestions and criteria from various children's literature scholars (Cai 2002; Yokota 2009; Norton 2011). We selected stories addressing immigration where the following points were met:

- Children were the protagonists.
- Stories were told from the perspective of a child.
- Stories presented accurate representation of current immigration situations.
- Stories reflected unbiased views about immigrants.
- Illustrations were free of biased representations or inaccuracies.

Guiding the analysis of the story narratives were the lenses of social justice, of consciousness, and of the rights of children. Through these lenses, as you will find in the chapters ahead, we delve into the realities of immigration seen through the eyes of children (Figure 2.4).

Bridges and Avenues: Children and Immigration Experience

It is well known that stories are also invitations welcoming us to become more mindful about stories of immigration demanding attention and action. These are stories that also have the power to impact our understanding, as the brain processes what is heard or read, making us connect with the circumstances and emotions emerging from stories that even have the power, as reported, "to

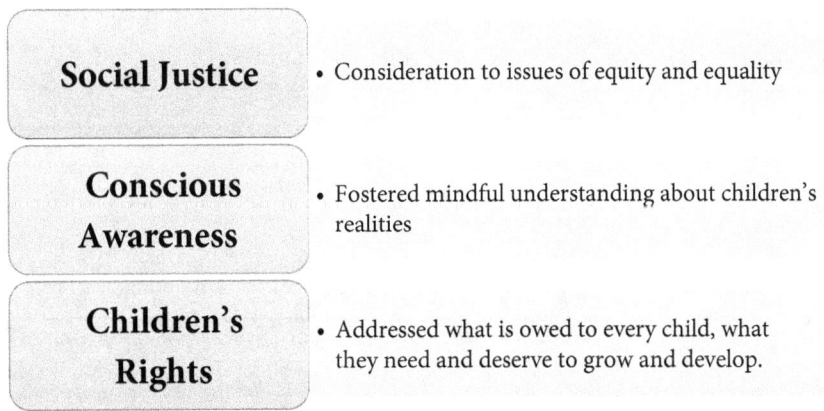

Figure 2.4 Exploring experiences of immigration for children: Three focal lenses.

influence over our attitudes and behavior" (Renken 2020, n.p.). For educators, understanding the experiences and realities of children is a continuous call. Only as we deepen our knowledge can we come closer to comprehending their everyday experiences, challenges, and aspirations. This time, the call is urgent, with society getting to learn about immigrant children and their multiple encounters that challenge and threaten in many instances their development and integrity.

We all cross bridges, bridges that defy what separates and keep us apart, sometimes more often than what we may even realize. Many bridges exist to connect realities no matter how different these may be. We also drive through avenues leading us to find and meet those roads that detail the experience of those we know and of those we are yet to meet. Bridges and avenues are precisely what we take to more closely learn about the realities of children who are immigrants. This time, the stories from children's literature are the bridges and avenues we take, connecting and leading us to know and learn about children and the immigration experience. They are also what you are invited to follow in the coming chapters. This journey will take us to explore the experiences of childhood turned into immigrants, their lived experiences in the context of their homes and in the classroom.

Reflecting and Beyond …

1. Think about the children's stories that have become personal or special to you. What made them become special?
2. Children's books are a powerful tool in the classroom. How do they support children's sense about self and others?
3. Review the children's book selections in your classroom or in your school library. How many reflect the children's cultures? Do any address immigration experiences?

References

Abo-Zena, Mona. 2018. "Supporting immigrant-origin children: Grounding teacher education in critical developmental perspectives and practices." *Teacher Educator* 53(3): 263–76.

Ada, Alma Flor. 2016. *A magical encounter. Latino children's literature in the classroom* (3rd edition). Mariposa Transformative Education Services.

Adair, Jennifer. 2015. *The impact of discrimination on the early schooling experiences of children from immigrant families*. Migration Policy Institute. https://www.migrationpolicy.org/research/impact-discrimination-early-schooling-experiences-children-immigrant-families.

Alexander, Kristin, Peggy Miller, and Julie Hengst. 2001. "Young children's emotional attachment to stories." *Social Development* 10(3): 374–98.

Banskton, Carl. 2010. "Social justice: Cultural origins of a perspective and a theory." *The Independent Review* 15(2): 165–78.

Bishop, Rudine. 1990. "Mirrors, windows, and sliding glass doors." *Perspectives* 6(3): ix–xi.

Botelho, Maria and Marsha Rudman. 2009. *Critical analysis of children's literature. Mirrors, windows and doors*. NY: Routledge.

Bridges Smith, Colin. 2004. "Telling stories: Past and present heroes." *Frontiers: The Interdisciplinary Journal of Study Abroad*. https://files.eric.ed.gov/fulltext/EJ891490.pdf.

Bruner, Jerome. 1986. *Actual minds, possible worlds*. Cambridge, MA: Harvard University Press.

Cai, Mingshui. 2002. *Multicultural literature for children and young adults. Reflections and critical issues*. Connecticut: Greenwood Press.

Cai, Mingshui and Rudine Sims Bishop. 1994. "Multicultural literature for children: Towards a clarification of the concept" (Chapter 5) (57–71). In A. Dyson and C. Genishi (eds.). *The need for story: Cultural diversity in the classroom and community*. Urbana, IL: National Council of Teachers of English.

Cardenuto, Nancy. 2012. "Sharing stories, sharing cultures. Towards the equitable exchange of children's stories." *Multicultural Education*, winter: 40–2.

Crippen, Martha. 2012. "The value of children's literature." *Oneota Reading Journal*. https://www.luther.edu/oneota-reading-journal/archive/2012/the-value-of-childrens-literature/.

Crosnoe, Robert. 2013. *Preparing the Children of Immigrants for Early Academic Success*. Migration Policy Institute. https://www.migrationpolicy.org/research/preparing-children-immigrants-early-academic-success.

Derman-Sparks, Louise and Julie Olsen Edwards. 2020. *Anti-bias education for children and ourselves* (2nd edition). National Association for the Education of Young Children. Washington, DC.

Dyson, Anne and Celia Genishi. 1994. *The need for story: Cultural diversity in the classroom and community*. Urbana, IL: National Council of Teachers of English.

Erickson, Elizabeth. 2018. *Effects of storytelling on emotional development*. Retrieved from Sophia, the St. Catherine University repository website. https://sophia.stkate.edu/maed/256.

Ewick, Patricia and Susan Silbey. 1998. *The common place of law: Stories from everyday life*. Chicago, IL: Chicago University Press.

Fialho, Olivia. 2019. "What is literature for? The role of transformative reading." *Cogent Arts & Humanities* 6(1). https://doi.org/10.1080/23311983.2019.1692532.

Forrest, Danielle, Kasey Garrison, and Sue Kimmel. 2015. "The university of the poor: Portrayals of class in translated children's books." *Teachers College* 117(2): 1–40.

Freire, Paulo. 1985. *The politics of education. Culture, power and liberation*. MA: Bergin & Harvey.

Freire, Paulo. 1970/2013. *Pedagogy of the oppressed*. London: Bloomsbury.

Galda, Lee, Lauren Liang, and Bernice Cullinan. 2016. *Literature and the child* (9th edition). CA: Cengage.

Giorgis, Cyndi and Joan Glazer. 2013. *Literature for young children. Supporting emergent literacy, Ages 0-8* (7th edition). MA: Pearson.

González, Norma, Luis Moll, and C. Cathy Amanti (eds.). 2005. *Funds of knowledge: Theorizing practices in households, communities and classrooms*. Mahwah, NJ: Erlbaum.

Henry, Audrey and Wilma Robles-Melendez. 2019. "The power of stories." Paper presented at the European Early Childhood Research Association. September, Thessaloniki, Greece.

Herbert, Jeannie. 2013. "Interrogating social justice in the early years education: How effectively do contemporary policies and practices create equitable learning environments for indigenous Australian children?" *Contemporary Issues in Early Childhood* 14(4): 324–34.

Iwai, Yuko. 2015. "Using multicultural children's literature to teach diverse perspectives." *Kappa Delta Pi Record* 51(2): 81–6.

Janks, Hilary. 2013. "Critical literacy and research." *Education Inquiry* 4(2): 225–42.

Kiefer, Barbara. (1994). The potential of picturebooks. From Visual literacy to Aesthetic Undertsanding. Boston, MA: Pearson.

Kiefer, Barbara, Cynthia Tyson, Bette Barker, Lisa Patrick, and Erin Sanders. 2019. *Charlotte Huck's Children's literature: A brief guide* (3rd edition). NY: McGraw-Hill.

Klefstad, Jill and Kimberly Martinez. 2013. "Promoting young children's cultural awareness and appreciation through multicultural books." *Young Children* (November): 74–81.

Laminack, Lester and Katie Kelly. 2019. *Reading to make a difference. Using literature to help students speak freely, think deeply, and take action*. NH: Heinemann.

Lukens, Rebecca. 2002. *Critical handbook of children's literature* (6th edition). Boston, MA: Allyn & Bacon.

Lukens, Rebecca. 2007. *Critical handbook of children's literature* (8th edition). Boston, MA: Pearson-Allyn & Bacon.

Lukens, Rebecca, Jacquelin Smith, and Cinthia Miller Coffer. 2013. *Critical handbook of children's literature* (9th edition). MA: Pearson.

Marriott, Stuart. 1998. "Culture, identity and children's literature." *The Irish Journal of Education* xxix: 9–20.

Martinez, Miriam, Junko Yokota, and Charles Temple. 2017. *Thinking and learning through children's literature*. MD: Rowman and Littlefield.

Mevawalla, Zinnia. 2013. "The crucible:Adding complexity to the question of social justice in early childhood development." *Contemporary issues in early childhood* 14(4): 290–9.

National Association for the Education of Young Children [NAEYC]. 2019. *Advancing Equity in Early Childhood Education. Position Statement.* National Association for the Education of Young Children. https://www.naeyc.org/sites/default/files/globally-shared/downloads/PDFs/resources/position-statements/advancingequitypositionstatement.pdf.

Nassirudin, Qurratulain. 2013. "Nursery rhymes and the social-construction of gender roles." *Journal of Educational and Social Research* 3(4): 77–84. https://www.mcser.org/journal/index.php/jesr/article/viewFile/426/443.

Norton, Donna. 2011. *Through the eyes of a child. An introduction to children's literature* (8th edition). MA: Pearson.

Norton, Donna. 2013. *Multicultural children's literature: Through the eyes of many children* (4th edition). Boston, MA: Pearson.

Pugh, Sharon. 1988. *Teaching children to appreciate literature.* ERIC Digest 1. https://files.eric.ed.gov/fulltext/ED292108.pdf.

Reading Rockets. 2021. *Transcript from an interview with Rudine Sims Bishop.* https://www.readingrockets.org/books/interviews/bishop/transcript.

Renken, Elena. 2020. "How stories connect and persuade us: Unleashing the brain power of narrative." *NPR.* https://www.npr.org/sections/health-shots/2020/04/11/815573198/how-stories-connect-and-persuade-us-unleashing-the-brain-power-of-narrative.

Robles-Melendez, Wilma. 2019. Conoceme! Empoderando a los educadores del nivel infantil para apoyar la herencia e identidad cultural de los ninos immigrantes en el nivel preescolar. Paper presentation at the Annual Conference of the National Association for the Education of Young Children. Nashville, TN.

Robles-Melendez, Wilma and Vesna Beck. 2000. *Teaching social studies in early education.* NY: Delmar Publishers.

Robles-Melendez, Wilma and Wayne Driscoll. 2020. *Issues and challenges of immigration in early childhood in the USA.* UK: Bloomsbury.

Rosenblatt, Louise. 1978. *The reader, the text, the poem: The transactional theory of the literary work.* Carbondale, IL: Southern Illinois University Press.

Sims Bishop, Rudine. 1991. "Evaluating books by and about African Americans." In M. V. Lindgren (ed.). *The multicolored mirror: Cultural substance in literature for children and young adults* (pp. 31–44). Fort Atkinson, WI: Highsmith Press.

Singer, Amy. 2011. "A novel approach: The sociology of literature, children's books, and social inequality." *International Journal of Qualitative Methods*, 20, 4: 307–20.

Smith, Amy Lynn. 2020. *Can storytelling catalyze culture change?* UNCH Innovation Service. https://medium.com/unhcr-innovation-service/can-storytelling-catalyze-culture-change-22dc1965cdfc.

Stoodt-Hill, Barbara and Amspaugh Linda. 2009. *Children's literature. Discovery for a lifetime.* MA: Pearson.

Swindler Boutte, Gloria Swindler, Ronnie Hopkins, and Tyrone Waklatsi. 2008. "Perspectives, voices, and worldviews in frequently read children's books." *Early Education and Development* 19(6): 941–62.

Takanishi, Ruth. 2004. *Leveling the playing field for immigrant children. Supporting immigrant children from birth to eight.* Foundation for Child Development. https://www.fcd-us.org/assets/2016/04/LevelingPlayingField.pdf.

UNESCO. 2003. *Oral traditions and expressions.* https://ich.unesco.org/en/oral-traditions-and-expressions-00053.

United Nations. 1989. *Convention on the Rights of the Child.* https://www.unhcr.org/uk/4aa76b319.pdfconvention.

Vazquez, Vivian. 2004. *Negotiating critical literacies with young children.* NY: Routledge.

Vazquez, Vivian, Hilary Janks, and Barbara Comber. 2019. "Critical literacy as a way of being and doing." *Language Arts* 96(5): 300–8.

Wallenstein, Nina. 1987. "Problem-posing: Freire's method for tranformation." In I. Shor (ed.). *Freire for the classroom: A sourcebook for liberatory teaching* (pp. 33–44). Portsmouth, NH: Heinemman.

Yokota, Junko. 2009. "Learning through literature that offers diverse perspectives: Multicultural and international literature." Chapter 7. In D. Wooten and B. Cullinan (eds.). *Children's literature in the reading program: An invitation to read* (pp. 66–73). International Reading Association. Virginia.

Yokota, Junko and Jacqui Kolar. 2008. "Advocating for peace and social justice through children's literature." *Social Studies and the Young Learner* 20(3): 22–6.

Children's Books Cited

Ada, Alma Flor. 1995. *My name is Maria Isabel.* NY: Atheneum.
Bunting, Eve. 1994. *A day's work.* NY: Clarion Books.
Choi, Yangsook. 2003. *The name jar.* NY: Dragonfly Books.
de Arias, Patricia. 2018. *Marwan's journey.* NY: Michael Neugebauer Publishing.
de la Peña, Matt. 2018. *Carmela full of wishes.* NY: Penguin Books.
Goode, Diane. 1985. *Watch the stars come out.* NY: Puffin Books.
Jiménez, Francisco. 1998. *La mariposa.* Darby, Pennsylvania: Diane Publishing Company.
Khalil, Aya. 2020. *The Arabic quilt. An immigrant story.* ME: Tilbury House.
Kobald, Irena. 2014. *My two blankets.* Houghton Mifflin Harcourt.
Phi, B. 2017. *A different pond.* North Mankato, Minnesota: Picture Window Books.
Recorvitz, Helen. 2003. *My name is Yoon.* NY: Farrar, Strauss and Giroux.
Velásquez, Eric. 2004. *Grandma's records.* NY: Bloomsbury USA Children.

3

We are Immigrants: Children Crossing Borders

A child is a child, no matter why she leaves home, where she comes from, where she is, or how she got there.

—UNICEF (2020)

This chapter aims to:

- Examine the goals and aspirations driving families to leave their homelands.
- Identify social justice factors forcing families to embark on the journey of immigration.
- Consider the experience of immigration through the voice of children.
- Reflect on the emotional dimension of immigration.

Key words

- Immigration
- Relocation
- Planned migration
- Forced migration
- Emotional response
- Trauma

A visit from my uncle

My uncle Deme, a tall and kind man, and his children would always call us for New Year. Long before I was born, he had moved to another country. I learned about him from the stories and the photos that my mother always shared. This time, as I remember him, my memories were of the stories he shared about the place where he went to live. He left hoping to make a better life, something my abuelita *would always repeat*. "Se fue buscando una vida mucho mejor para sus hijos que la de aquí" *(he left seeking a much better life for his children than here). It was through his letters that I came to know him and the cousins that I only met in the photos he used to send. Whenever he wrote, he would write promises he would come to visit. I finally met him and a cousin that one time when he came to visit my* abuelita. *I was nine years old and was so impressed by all he shared about the tall buildings of the city where he lived. He would always say that they would never compare to the hills and beaches* en nuestra tierra *(in our homeland). That day I remember how he told my mother,* "Cómo me gustaria quedarme *(how much I would like to stay)."* Aqui soy quién soy *(here I am who I am), he said with an expression that still today is so vividly remembered. He never returned but I never forgot that comment. It was years later, when together with my children, I also left my homeland that I understood my uncle's nostalgic comments.*

Seeking Dreams

It was in preparation to read a children's story about immigration that we asked our students to share their thoughts about immigrants. Our goal was to learn about the perspectives our students had on the meaning and implications of immigration. One of our students, an immigrant herself, decided to share the story about her uncle that opened this chapter. It was through his experiences, she remarked, that she came to learn about immigration, not knowing that one day she would become an immigrant, too. She candidly shared that through her uncle's and cousin's calls and letters, she began to learn and experience the surprise encounters of people learning to navigate in a different culture and about the struggles, sometimes quietly experienced, of immigrants. Her uncle, as she pointed out in her story, was also the first one to set a trend in her family to leave and settle in another country, not an uncommon experience among immigrants (Suárez-Orozco and Suárez-Orozco 2001). Many others in her family followed, which included her, too. What drove them was their desire to find a dream especially for their children. "Buscamos un sueño," we are seeking a dream, she added as the discussion unfolded. The search for a dream remains today as a driving motivation for so many who every day decide to move and cross borders.

Moving, an Experience with Many Dimensions

Moving is one of those experiences that for many, we have in common. The reality is that the reasons behind moving may be so different and the experience even more so for those who once moved to another place. Beyond packing and choosing what to take, memories of the places where we once lived always remain and are carried with us in our minds and hearts, just like the grandmother in *Grandma's records* (Velázquez 2001), who became emotional as she listened to her special song evocative of her homeland. The fact is, as we have heard people say, one never leaves for we remain emotionally connected to the place we came from. Critically reading stories of immigration, we sense the longing and loving memories in the voices of those who moved and settled in lands they now live. Say in *Granparent's journey* (1995), conveys this as the main character reminisces about his country of origin. We also hear the voice of the child in some of the stories of immigration also hoping for the places they left behind (Winter 2007; Park and Park 2001).

A myriad of expectations and endless questions are not uncommon while people once prepare to leave. No less are the emotions experienced as one learns that moving is in sight. For some people, emotions intensify especially when moving is an unexpected reality forced by reasons beyond one's control. Moving or relocation to another place to live is a major experience for anyone. But it is particularly so for children, whose known world is suddenly changed and, where what they know is left behind (Kelly and Lamb 2003). We feel the uneasiness of eight-year-old Jangmi, the young girl from Korea whose parents are moving to the United States in the story *Goodbye, 382 Shin Dan Dong* (Park and Park 2001). Jangmi shares her sentiments and reveals how she cried goodbye to her home and tells us, "I loved my home right here! ... I didn't want to leave my best friend" (n.p). Who cannot help but feel for her when perhaps we experienced moments like hers.

Many may see residential and community changes as another routine part of life experiences. However, the fact is that moving and relocating, whether within one's own country or across borders, signifies a multidimensional experience with many implications. Moving is a multidimensional experience, revealing its impact on an individual's emotions, culture, language, and social positioning (Figure 3.1). Considerations about moving bring to light the influence that this experience has on an individual's well-being (Clair 2019).

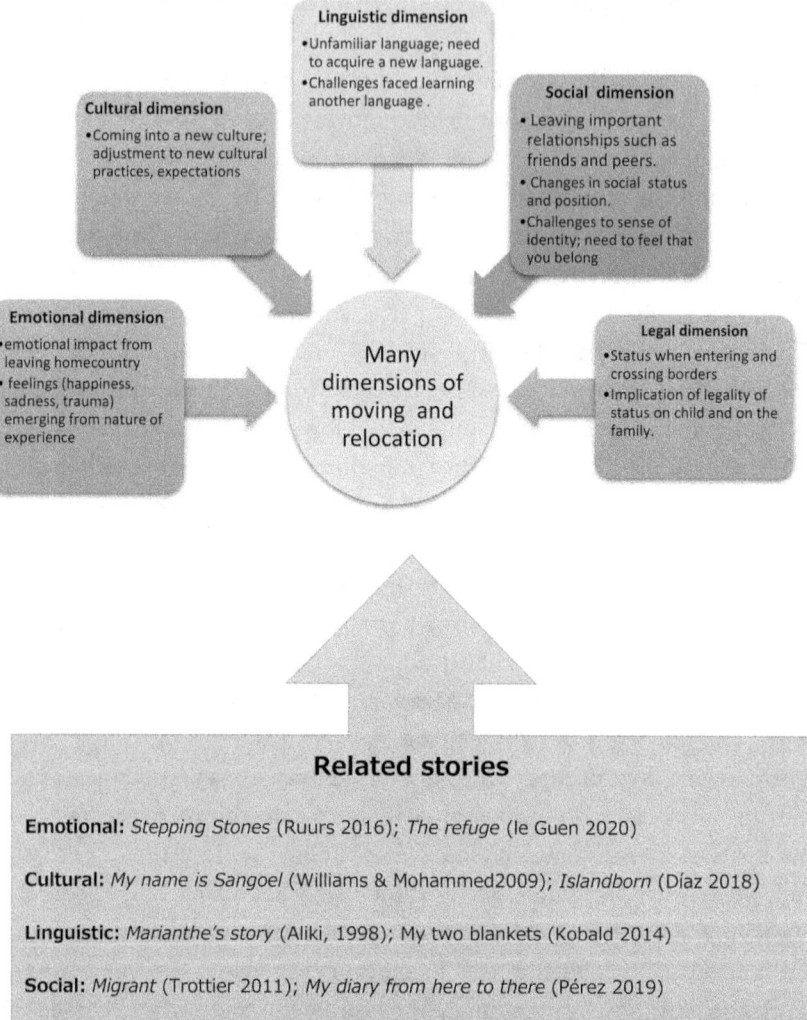

Figure 3.1 Moving is a multidimensional experience.

Children and the Experience of Moving

"Tim is very nervous. He's moving to Calabash" (Wagner and Eriksson 2012, n.p.). This is how the authors of *Tim's big move* begin their story about a young child learning from his parents that they are moving to a new place. Worried about the uncertainty of what he will find, the story reminds us about the experiences that for most may be a familiar one. Many people may remember moving to a new home during their childhood. Who could forget, especially during childhood, that moment when we learned that we were leaving behind the place we had called our own? The place where everything felt like it belonged to us and that we belonged? That special friend or simply the special corner of the house where we would play and fantasize during our childhood days.

A bundle of questions emerge as the moving day approaches. Ingeniously expressed in the story by Tim's furry friend as they prepare to move, they reveal the landscape of feelings evoked by the move seen through the eyes of the young child. In fact, it reflects so many of those feelings and questions that children—and adults, too—experience once they have learned about an upcoming move. Through their questions, one perceives the uncertainty as the child's known world comes to end and a new one is to begin. Developmentally, during the early childhood years, disruptions experienced from residential mobility may become a difficult and challenging reality to process for young children as the environment, routines, and people they know change (Shonkoff 2010).

It's More than Just Changing Places

For many, moving is simply another of those events we may experience during our life. Yet, it is more than just leaving and relocating to another place, especially if you are a child. What makes moving such an impacting and worrisome experience is the fact that it implies changing many dimensions of a child's life and routines. Leaving the place where one lives is an experience that evokes many different emotions. Moving is an emotionally impactful event as one is leaving those special relationships that make one feel safe and cared for. Many children will feel the excitement of going to a new place and country just like Hannah, the young girl character in *Hannah is my name* (Yang 2004), who likes the place where they now live even though it is very different from their home in faraway Asia. She thinks that the elevator in her building "looks like a lion cage" (n.p.). Yet, for many, even when the move has been planned and is welcomed, it can make them feel apprehensive as realities are altered. As families plan and move to other countries, we hear the apprehension in the voices of children as in

> ### Thinking and Reflecting ... What Would You Miss?
>
> One of the authors of this work who moved to another country experienced the longing for the closeness to the sea. If you have moved or plan to move, what would you miss from the place where you lived?

Angelina's island (Winter 2007) and in *Goodbye, 382 Shin Dang Dong* (Park and Park 2002). For both, the uneasiness comes from the friendships and relatives that are staying behind. Even the weather they are familiar with is missed by both girls in these stories. The fact is that it is not uncommon to hear immigrants talk about how they miss the climate and the familiar landscapes of their homeplaces. Those connections emotionally built as we interact with places and its people are what make moving such a powerfully emotional experience.

Special Places, Special Connections

Environments are a powerful force connecting people to places in so many ways. Connections are also built with the places where we live. We all know that a place is more than just a geographical location. We develop strong bonds with the geographical characteristics and the nature scape of the settings where time is spent as we grow up. Whether it is through internal migration or crossing borders, individuals are emotionally linked to the community we called home. In *A different pond* (Phi 2017), we experience the strong linkages the father still feels for his country. He shares them with his son as together they go fishing during the early hours of the morning. Similarly, we meet the grandmother in *Grandma's records* (Velazquez 2001), who, listening to the music from her homeland, brings back those strong connections.

The sentiments and memories that keep us attached to a place are invisible but strong. So are the feelings that link children to the place they know and call home. Conveyed by the many emotions that most of us may have had at one point in our lives, moving signals a new beginning and a new way to be seen and considered. Just remember how it felt if you were once the new kid in your classroom or in the neighborhood. We asked our students how they had felt after moving, especially during their childhood. Their comments revealed a variety of different feelings and emotions. One person commented she felt like she would never be the same. She was six year old at the time and still remembered how she would ask her parents why they had moved and shared that, still today, she would miss her classroom and being with her friends.

Where Are We Going? Facing Change

Change is always a challenging experience. Even when it is already an expected experience, it is still a devastating experience especially when it comes to

> **Thinking and Reflecting ... Moving Away**
>
> For most of us, moving is one of the experiences we share in common. There are many emotions and feelings embedded in this experience. Take a moment to remember that time. How did you feel when you learned that you were moving to a new place? What memories do you still have about the place where you lived?

leaving behind what we know. Seen through the perspective of children, studies have shown that change is an experience that is challenging to process and understand. Psychologically, change threatens children's sense of control and security. This explains the resistance some may show, or the apprehensive behaviors others may exhibit. Leaving the place where one lives is more than just changing locations. Whether long planned or suddenly learned, moving implies change (Darling 2010; Coulton, Theodos and Turner 2012). In many cases, it is a life-changing experience. Change, whether planned or not, always brings questions and makes one feel hesitant about what is yet to come. For children, change is an experience that takes them away from what is known from where they feel safe and in control (Berk 2015; Kostelnik et al. 2015).

Emotional Experiences: Moving to Other Countries

The year 2020 registered a crude reality in many ways. Beyond the pandemic, 36 million children were reported as migrants (UNICEF 2021). Numbers kept rising and in 2022, with new challenging events, including armed conflicts and devastating natural events, many more were pushed away from their homes. Implications are clear especially as we consider the needs of children. From the nursery room to the primary grades, many are recent immigrants or children born to immigrant families who are attending schools throughout the global society. In 2019, over 24 percent of children under age five in the United States were immigrants (Migration Policy Institute 2019).

Stories have the power to bring memories and experiences, making them present once again. Reflecting on the story *I dream of Popo* (Blackburne 2021), brought back conversations with children and adults remembering those special relationships with grandparents. Similar to the young Taiwanese girl who missed being again with her Popo [grandmother], after her family moved to another

> **Consciously Considering ... Children's Well-being**
>
> The well-being of children is a major concern driving efforts to ensure their successful development, learning, and future. Major events and experiences are known to impact and influence one's life. These are even more influential during childhood, particularly the early years because of their impact on a child's overall well-being. "Children have a right to wellbeing as children" (OECD 2009) is more than a statement but a reminder about the goal and responsibility society has for its children. Indeed, a big move is a new beginning, but the fact is that, whether moving just a block away or to another country, changing residential locations remains as one of those experiences emotionally loaded for young children and adults alike (Jelleyman and Spencer 2008; Shonkoff 2010). Narratives on the topic of moving provide a wide avenue to explore the impact of changes seen through the lens of children. They make us aware about how moving to other places is an emotionally charged experience for children.

country, those we met also kept fond memories about their grandparents. So many of the children we met in classrooms we visited came from places close and far away. Some were born here or came as infants and recollections were those learned from their families. Others, preschoolers and primary age, remember the pets they left behind or the friendly faces of relatives and adults they still long to see again.

Moving to another country, as thousands did and continue to do even today, evokes so many different emotions, especially as you cross borders. A thousand questions, many left unanswered is what many children experience as they leave the place they call home. Even when it is an expected event, it is not unusual for a child to feel excited, fearful, or apprehensive. A sense of loss is not uncommon for those relocating to other places. These are the same feelings author Jeri Watts conveys through the young boy character in the story *A piece of home* (2016), who, stepping into his new school, struggled to understand why his family left Korea. Watts' narrative reveals the emotional battle of the young boy who now feels "different" in a place he is still trying to figure out. The boy's feelings are further accentuated as he remarks about his grandmother noticing her eyes used to sparkle before and that now "her eyes don't gleam—not at all" (n.p.).

Emotional Connections: The Yearning for the Places We Leave

What makes a place special? There are many reasons and we all may have a special one that links us to the place where we live or once lived. Emotional connections to a place are built by people in the places they live. They are invisible lines anchoring people's roots to the places where they live. Strong sentiments make us feel connected, whether it is a house, location, or the relationships we had, make us feel the emotional impact of losing these when we move. Those connections are also what contribute to the quality of life that we experience, giving special meaning to life (Choi and Oishi 2020). They are as well what support the individual well-being of children and adults. Whether it is a short distance away that one moves or to a different country, moving is a complex experience that impacts people beyond just changing your residential address. What is relevant to know is that changing places where we live is a factor influencing our well-being (Stokols and Shumaker 1982; Hartig and Lawrence 2003; Shonkoff 2010; Oishi and Schirmmack 2010).

Leaving behind Special Relationships: Relatives, Friends, and Peers

There is nostalgia and a longing that immigrants feel as they leave behind their home countries. Sometimes, quietly felt, other times openly expressed as we see by the expressions of children like Jangmi, the eight-year-old girl that Park and Park (2001) poignantly portrayed in *Goodbye, 382 Shin Dan Dong*, struggles with the idea of leaving her home and her friend. Even though her parents tried to make her feel excited about her new home in another country, she is reluctant to accept that her home will be now in another place. Not an uncommon response, moving is an experience that challenges a child's sense of stability during a very vulnerable developmental time (Shonkoff and Garner 2012). We hear in her voice the emotions felt by many children whose families migrate. For them, even though they may build new linkages in other places, the places they lived always will be kept as cherished memories.

We hear the same strong emotions and feelings from children who struggle with the reality of having left their country. In Nuño's *The map of good memories* (2016), we meet another young girl, Zoe, who this time is a child forced to leave with her family because of the threats from war conflicts. In the story, the memories and feelings about her homeland are kept alive as she reminisces about those special places with memories that "made her happy." A map of memories, of moments no one can take away will brighten her days even when forced to leave behind her country. Such is the power of memories that connect us to the places that make us feel we belong. In Zoe's words, we hear what repeatedly is also voiced by those who leave their homelands, "the map of a city she was sure she'd return to one day" (n.p.). Even if years pass, for most, the hope to return remains with immigrants. That emotion of the homeland left is what we read from the images of the grandmother in *Grandma's records* (Vazquez, remembering a special song).

Others forced to leave unaccompanied to escape from dangerous situations, also feel the loss of their environment and relationships. The memories and longing of children for the places they are leaving behind are revealed in the poems of Jorge Argüeta (2016). In his poetry, he conveys the experience of unaccompanied children walking through the trails in Central America and Mexico enroute to *el norte* (the north) as they seek peace and safety. With them, together with their dreams, are also the memories of their families and places where they lived.

An Emotional Experience

Regardless of the reasons, moving and relocating during the early years carries significant impact particularly during a time when emotional attachments are being built. Emergence of emotional bonds with significant people is one of the social and emotional milestones taking place during the early childhood years. These are affected when relationships with families and significant others are interrupted and distanced. Developmentally, attachment is built with those with whom children regularly interact (Bowlby 1973; Kostelnik et al. 2015). Leaving adults and family members who normally are part of the child's world impacts the child's emerging sense of emotional connections. Transplanted into other contexts, young immigrant children feel the loss of those with whom they felt emotionally safe and connected. Recognizing their anxiety and struggles is essential to mitigate the struggles as they transition into a different context and culture. Immigration in itself is a stressful reality with one of the stressors being the loss and separation from familiar and cherished relationships. For some, like young Angelina in *Angelina's island* (Winter 2007), those first moments and time will make them yearn for their special relationships, now far away. Angelina's sadness and feelings of loss is felt when we hear her say, "I miss my grandma all the time. I talk to her in my dreams" (n.p.). Her nostalgia is also for her homeland, wanting to feel again the warmth of the air of her Caribbean island.

> **Consciously Considering … Feelings and Emotions**
>
> In an informal conversation with a group of five-year-old children, we found that it was that sense of not knowing what to find that made them feel hesitant about moving away, even if that was nearby. Some recalled previous experiences and shared their frustration at losing the space where they enjoyed playing. We also heard from some of the children how they missed their friends and relatives. "*Me hacen falta mis tías*" (I miss my aunts), one of the children said who had not seen them since her family moved. Unquestionably, leaving what is known and who you know, relocating and moving to new places, whether near or far away, influence and alter a child's sense of stability (Robles-Melendez and Beck 2000; Berk 2015). We must remember that, after all, for people, a place means and signifies much more than just a geographical location (Ellen and Turner 1997). Emotional and cultural ties bind us to the locations familiar to us where one finds meaning in the daily experiences and interactions that make us feel we belong.

Beyond the change in terms of physical location, moving is like being uprooted and planted again to start life in a different context, even if that context is familiar or within your own town or country. It is even more impactful when the changes take people away from their homelands. Many we met and interviewed shared that, even when things go well, the melancholy and longing are unavoidable. The uncle in the opening scenario to this chapter clearly revealed his nostalgia for his town. His self-consciousness about the place he left behind was an affirmation of the relationships still kept vibrantly present and relevant to him. Despite the many years that had passed, he was still connected to the place where he had lived.

Crossing Borders

Borders are more than just a designation that politically and geographically separate people from places and other realities. They are also borders of profound psychosocial and cultural character. They become lines that distinctively define locations where people's lives every day give life to the culture that defines their interactions, whether socially, politically, or ideologically. Together, they represent a composite of people's diversity in all its many different traits

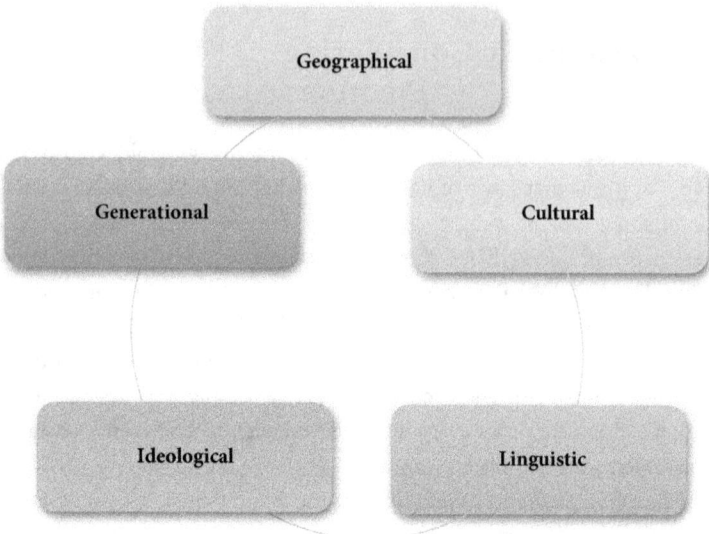

Figure 3.2 Borders are of many kinds.

(Figure 3.2). They designate principles, social and culturally profoundly rooted hopes, aspirations, and ideals for a future yet to be attained. They are milestone experiences many may cross in life. Whether planned or compelled by difficult realities, embedded in everyone are cultural borders, markers that delineate the intimate values, ideals as well as realities and expectations we carry as members of a group. One thing is certain: people set out across borders driven by their dreams and hopes.

People crossing borders has been a theme addressed in many children's stories. We remember the first time we read with our graduate students Eve Bunting's story *How many days to America* (1989). It sparked a multitude of emotions. The story, set in an unidentified country facing political challenges, narrates the journey of a group of families and their children who escape in search of freedom in a somewhat improbable set of events. Written during a time of violent political conflict in some Latin American countries, the story weaves together many of those events and brings attention to the reality of immigrants. Reactions to the story brought up a lot of comments and personal remarks. Many connected the plot and the setting with events familiar to them either because of people they knew or because they were reminded about very personal events. Some shared personal experiences including that of their own relatives, and of neighbors. Others reflected on the danger faced and the determination

> **Thinking and Reflecting ... Borders We Cross**
>
> Throughout our lives, there are many borders that people go across. Besides the geographical lines defining countries, borders are markers of experiences and of transitions. Consider some of the borders that you or someone you know have crossed in the past. What were the reasons leading you/them to cross them? What were the implications, culturally and personally, of the borders crossed?

of immigrant families and children in their classrooms. Through the years, the universality of the aspiration for a safe place reflected in this story still resonates, communicating a need that remains today driving immigrants to other borders across the world.

In today's global community, borders continue to be crossed and sought to be crossed by many who see their aspirations for themselves and their families beyond their own lands. Perhaps more intensely evident during these first two decades of the twenty-first century, people are continually coming across borders driven by a complex number of reasons. Together with them are children who, as their families set on the path, also become participants in the journey of immigrants. Invisible lines with profound meaning, borders when crossed, become defining moments in the lives of so many adults and children (Adair 2015). Unaware about the significance of the places left behind, just like adults, children are also protagonists in the journey of immigration, an event marking and shaping their childhood and future life experiences.

Opening the Door: Into the Experience of Children and Immigration

Rudine Sims-Bishop (1990) posited that books are like doors we open to enter into a realm of the diverse realities people experience, reflective of our own and exposing readers to those unfamiliar to them, while stories are a magical door leading us to uncover and revisit in some cases a spectrum of different realities both known and unknown to us. Reading through the pages of a book is like crossing borders. Critically reading into the many children's literature books on immigration, we also cross borders; this time stories take us across borders of time and place while crossing cultural borders where we enter to learn about people's ideals, aspirations, and values (Dietrich and Ralph 1995; Corliss 1998). Intentionally seeking to uncover their realities, we come to learn about the experience of people becoming immigrants and living as immigrants. We see books also as avenues, which lead us to learn, this time, about the experience of children as immigrants. Throughout the catalogue of children's book stories, we come to experience and explore the multiple situations and motivations pushing and pulling others to migrate. Vividly presented, narrations and illustrations in children's books take us along with characters, some based on actual accounts and historical realities, to where the saga of immigration is unveiled.

Crossing borders, despite the many challenges to encounter ahead, is journeying into the beginning of many dreams. This is what we hear in stories we read like that of Yaccarino based on his own family immigration experience. It is also what we gather from narratives and anecdotes shared by families, relatives, passed on, or read. They are accounts of struggles, determination, and of hope for the future being made from tireless efforts of parents for their children and families, too. This is one among the many

---

Consciously Considering … All for Children

Comments drawn from conversations with our own students reaffirm what many scholars of immigration have stated: that decisions to migrate are commonly grounded by the desire to build a future for their families and children (Suárez-Orozco and Suárez-Orozco 2001; Tizmann and Fuligni 2015; Robles-Melendez and Driscoll 2020). Some of the students to whom we spoke came as children, while others were the children of families that migrated and established their homes generations ago.

"*Fue lo mejor*" (it was the best) was the answer we heard from a graduate student who herself came as a child. She did not hesitate to add that she would always remember all the efforts her parents made. No different was the response of several other students, who also felt the same way, thanking their parents for "giving us a future." One shared about her father who migrated first and how they waited for that moment when they finally joined him over two years later. "He did it for us and will always thank him," she added reminiscing the moments lived. Talking with immigrant parents, we also learned about the sacrifices made as they left their countries and set on an uncertain journey. Once again, their children and families were the main reason that drove them to leave.

messages gathered through the children's stories on immigration that we discuss ahead. Leaving behind what they knew in search of a dream, while others, with no other options, families and children determinedly continue to cross borders seeking a better future (Crosnoe 2013; Valdez, Valentine, and Padilla 2013; UNICEF 2020).

Stories, a Kaleidoscope of Perspectives about Immigration

Many authors of children's books have written about the experience of crossing borders. These stories serve as bridges into the immigrant experience revealing how people were guided to leave their homelands, some, as we have shared earlier, forced by aspirations or by circumstances in hopes of finding a better life (Corliss 1998). As a topic, it has attracted many to record the children's experience, some emerging out of their interest, what they have witnessed, and others narrating their very own accounts. At the same time, they serve as an avenue allowing children who are immigrants to learn about their own stories, where they can see themselves, and reaffirming their own role as immigrants in society.

A number of children's books on immigration disclose the true stories of people who came or were forcibly driven to cross borders. They provide a window into the variety of challenging and difficult reasons that led individuals to migrate (Dietrich and Ralph 1995). With a resurgence of immigration in the current times, many of these immigrant children's stories have recently resurfaced to remind everyone about the experience of children in immigration. In recent times, especially since the 2014 arrival of unaccompanied immigrant children, many authors have become mindful about the need to tell and highlight the reality of children turned into immigrants. Since then, they have added to the catalog of stories many more accounts reflective of challenging circumstances pushing people, including children, to find other places to live. Overall, children's books have become tools helping readers to delve into and learn about a process already turned into a very difficult and controversial topic and issue (Bowen and Schutt 2007; Yokota 2009). Interest into the everyday experiences of immigrant children is also thematically addressed in many stories. They provide insights into the day-to-day experiences of children and families where cultures come to meet. They also allow us to further delve into the experience of becoming an immigrant from the perspective of children. It is through the thematic lines of children's books on immigration, discussed in the next section, that we set out to explore and learn about the children's experiences.

> **Thinking and Reflecting** ... Children Becoming Immigrants, Some Voluntarily
>
> Becoming an immigrant as a child lies in the hands of families. Many have posited that children involuntarily become immigrants. Yet, recent years have shown that many children, mostly those in their teens, are voluntarily crossing borders (Hovil et al. 2021). Take a moment to consider the many reasons why children are leaving to become immigrants. Which ones today are pressing children to leave their homelands?

Defining Moments for Children

The moment one embarks into a new adventure may implicitly mark a defining moment in our lives. So is the case of immigration, which, in itself, is a major defining moment for children. Becoming immigrants is like being uprooted and planted again, remarked one of our colleagues, who came as an eight-year-old child to live in the United States. In her mind are still alive the moments she learned her language was not the language they welcome or that people would understand. Some of us, immigrants too, may remember peers and neighbors who lent a hand as we started to navigate through daily experiences. Writing this chapter brought to us memories of children who in the past and even today are forced into becoming immigrants. They are in our classrooms just as some of those we know who themselves were immigrants decades ago. Many of them will not have any recollections of arriving in other lands because of their young age. Others may still remember what they left, relatives and places, and even a favorite pet. Those moments that marked the beginning of their new selves as immigrants are happening every day in our present society.

Crossing Borders with Hope

Some of the immigration narratives vividly reveal the meaning of that moment borders are crossed and the subsequent events that marked the lives of children and their families. This is what is learned from Morales' *Dreamers* (2018), where she shared her own true story, coming with her infant son as she leaves her country and crosses the border into the United States. In her own words, she reveals how it marked the beginning of a different life: "we enter a new country carried by hopes and dreams, and carrying our own special gifts, to build a better future" (n.p.). Similar to the endless numbers of immigrants arriving yesterday and today, Morales crosses the border bringing with her not only her child but also a world of dreams and aspirations together with her many talents. In the story she authored, we come to learn about the thousands of children, infants themselves, who arrived in new lands and became immigrants. This is an unending story, continuing to reveal determined efforts all guided by the hopes of parents and families for their children who will be the new generation.

We also learn about the experience of crossing from Mills, who shares another true story of a father and son who set out to cross the border in *La frontera: El viaje con papá/My journey with Papa* (2018). This time, the child is aware about the journey about to begin as he leaves with his father. They embark on a journey crossing the US border seeking opportunities they cannot find in their own land. Guided by their will to do better and the determination to overcome whatever challenges that may lie ahead, stories of immigrants crossing borders disclose a multitude of realities and the yearning for a better life and a future. Reading Mills' story as well as the illustrations we learned about the father and son journeying through inhospitable territory. Their travel makes us conscious of the ordeal of unauthorized immigrants crossing through the perilous border into the United States. Once again, their story conveys the reality experienced by children brought along by parents hopeful to give their young a future. This is a story that continues to happen today just as we were writing. Their saga, whether happening in North America or in the Middle East with the thousands risking their lives to arrive at the European borders, demands everyone to become aware about the unfair conditions surrounding and threatening the possibilities and prospects of a better life for children and their families.

Armed with the desire to find a better life for the family, we also learn about the journey of Hannah and her family, in this case, a young girl who crosses international borders as she and her family travel from Asia to the United States to begin a new life in Yang's *Hannah is my name* (2004). Based on Yang's own experiences arriving as a child from Taiwan during the 1960s, the story vividly reflects the desire for freedom that drove her family to move continents away. In the story, she reveals that her parents came particularly to give their daughter a future in a place where "a girl is free to be anything she chooses" (n.p.), which the mother tells her daughter as she wonders why they came. The story leads us to experience the difficulties faced as the family waits to make their status official waiting for the arrival of their "green cards.[1]" Despite the hardships faced as Hannah's parents struggle, their resilient attitude keeps them hopeful and determined.

We Need to Leave: Refugees and Asylees Seeking a Place to Live

The experience of refugees and asylees has always been present in society. It continues today, especially bringing attention to the thousands of children whose own survival is at stake every day. They are demanding attention from society about their rights, reminding everyone that the threat to their lives is still a reality in many places throughout the world. So many children today still struggle to survive ongoing political challenges, poverty, insecurity, and natural disasters that have intensified in recent years. They challenge everyone to consider what is being done to ensure their rights as children are considered. This time, the principle of best interest of the child set in Article 3 of the Convention of the Rights of the Child (United Nations 1989) demands everyone's sincere efforts and attention.

Children's literature has served as an avenue taking readers into the stories and lived experiences of those who are forced or displaced from their homelands. According to UNICEF (2021a), nearly 33 million children were considered displaced in 2020, a reality raising concerns for their future and well-being. Forced by circumstances, they get on the immigration path, fleeing realities unimaginable to be experienced by children. Reading the pages of stories like Garay's *The long road* (1997) and Buitrago's *Two white rabbits* (2015), we experience together with children and their families the danger and courageous decisions as they escape in search of safety. Narrated from the perspective of the child, in these two stories, we experience the longing for what is left behind like the pet doggie, Pinto, that in Garay's story the boy continues to miss.

The beginnings of a new life are marked every time a family moves and crosses borders. These are also moments defining the life of children. Propelled by multiple reasons, as already pointed out, we enter into the reality of people forcibly leaving and crossing borders as demonstrated by stories from authors like Ruurs (2016), de Arias (2016), and Sanna (2016). Their stories convey the painful reality of families and their children having no options to overcome challenges and survive. Portraying the reality of refugees, in both stories, we are faced with their experience even at the time of writing where thousands continue to escape from a multitude of pressing situations including the pandemic of 2020 and a war in 2022 that had already pushed over four million to find refuge in neighboring European nations.

Through Sanna's story, *The journey* (2016), we hear the voice of the child narrator, who already realizes that home is no longer a safe place to live: "last year our lives changed forever … The war began. Every day bad things started happening around us and soon there was nothing but chaos (n.p.)." Visually,

Ruurs' story *Stepping stones: A refugee family's story* (2016) captures the mind and soul through its images. The stone figures not only tell the story but are a reminder about their culture and traditions they also carry with them as they move across land and sea. Meantime, the storyline seen through the perspective of the child denotes the shock and expectation of what is to come.

Harrowing experiences trying to cross borders into freedom have been the focus of many children's immigration stories. Experiences of those seeking refuge or asylum expose how many are forced to go across borders. Choosing those where children are main characters and where their voices are heard, as one reads them, we participate together with the characters in their dramatic escape from life-threatening and harsh circumstances. Seeking the cover of the night or navigating seas and rivers, as they go along, they convey the fear and urgency driving people to find ways to leave, all to save themselves. Using the perspective of the child as protagonists, these stories convey the experience of a migration forced by harsh and dangerous circumstances.

The journey (Sanna 2016) is one of those stories where images dramatically expose the dangerous conditions. Viewed through the child character's experiences, we hear the child say, "The war began. Every day bad things started happening around us and soon there was nothing but chaos" (n.p.). Evidently different from those who voluntarily leave their home countries, Sanna's story helps us to experience the emotionality and danger faced as the child together with her mother and sibling "leave at night to avoid being seen" (n.p.).

Social violence and insecurity have also moved authors to capture and voice the difficult realities experienced in current society. Their stories have opened a new avenue drawing attention to what is pressing and leading many families including children, who coming alone, also escape from their home countries. Poet Jorge Argüeta in his book *Somos como las nubes/ We are like the clouds* (2016) calls it "the odyssey" of countless children and young people risking everything trailing through difficult places while seeking for a safe place to live. His poems, which bring readers closer to the epic journey of children from Central America, reveal the inner thoughts of children taking on the uncertain road following a dream for a safer place. Reading the stories of children forced to leave, one cannot avoid thinking about the impressions such experiences leave in a child's mind and soul. Puzzled by the way they leave and entering into unknown trajectories, we are driven to delve into some of the children's responses and reactions through stories narrating their impromptu journeys from which they now emerge as immigrants. In *Two white rabbits* (2015), author Jaime Buitrago takes us along to experience the journey through the eyes of the young girl walking together with her father as they leave their country. "Where are we going?," we hear her asking as they continue journeying though not sure where they will be next. Buitrago also takes us to experience the uncertainty of those traveling sometimes by land, others crossing waters, and other times simply walking. Father and daughter in this story are a reminder about the thousands of people forced to migrate from difficult realities just like those in the Central American caravans similar to the characters we met in Sanna's (2018) story escaping from conflict-ridden areas in other continents.

Do We Need to Leave?

How would you feel learning that you are leaving your hometown? No doubts that it would bring many questions to your mind. It would especially make you wonder why. If you are a child, leaving may be a particularly major challenge. Some may even resist the idea or even try to stop their family just like what the young child in Harper's *I like where I am* (2004) tries to do. He likes his home and his school and cannot accept that they are leaving for another town. Resisting the idea that they are leaving is not an uncommon reaction for a child who feels home is where he presently lives. This sense of frustration is not uncommon especially when you feel that they are taking away the place you feel is your own. His reactions throughout Harper's emotion-filled story evoke those of immigrant children, who similar to him, find out they, too, will be leaving and moving to a place he does not know. Relocation is never an easy change for a family. Leaving a place we know is more than just a shift in the space where we live. For children, it implies a dramatic transition and change in their lives. It is even more when one considers that, for a child, decisions about moving, whether within one's homeland or across other borders, are not in their hands and rest with the adults.

What to Bring, What to Leave

We all have things we cherish that carry so many meaningful memories of times lived. Young children also have special items they love, which bring them comfort as they play, carry, or use them. Objects and items play a key role in marking special and milestone experiences. They also connect us with people we care and feel emotionally attached to. Moving is a time where many experienced the dilemma of choosing what to bring, what to leave. Deciding what to take is as hard as what you leave behind. Some immigrant children that we spoke with told us about the many things they missed and longed to have or see again.

In Levitin's *A piece of home* (1996), the young boy is faced with a great predicament as he gets ready to move away. Though his family had long been planning to immigrate "to America," now that the move is coming, he struggles trying to think what to bring, especially when his Papa said, "only one special treasure" (n.p.). Faced with having to make a decision, it reminds us about the challenging reality of leaving what one knows and have cared for. A difficult experience for adults, it is even more so for a young child being challenged to choose what to bring.

With differing circumstances, deciding what to bring is also what the child in *Far from home* (Parker Rubio 2019) is forced to do. Awakened one night by his parents, he hears them say, "We have to leave home" (n.p.). "We have to go right now" (n.p.). This time, he had to choose only one toy to bring. One can feel the pressure and heavy emotional demand on the child, who like many in recent decades suddenly find themselves leaving what they knew.

And Now, What Will Happen Next?

Even greater transitions and changes are experienced when children find themselves crossing borders. Planned or forcibly leaving their homelands, many children turned into immigrants, wonder and question the reasons for their move. In conversations with adults who arrived as children, some still lament having left their relatives and their school friends. The longing for the home left behind and for that special place filled with memories and friends is palpably conveyed by Amada, the girl child character in *My diary from here to there/Mi diario desde aquí a allá* (Pérez 2009). Writing in her diary, her words uncover her anxiety and despair saying to herself, "Am I the only one who is scared of leaving our home, our beautiful country and all the people we might never see

---

To Think and Reflect ... Learning that You Are Moving

Perhaps you experienced moving to a new place during childhood. What were some of your memories about the time when you found out that you were moving? What emotions did the news about moving evoke in you? Possibly, you have worked with children who have relocated from other communities. How did they react? What are some of their comments, questions?

again?" (n.p.). Through the story, we come to witness the trauma it brings her to leave behind the place where she feels at home. The reality of leaving arouses a multitude of emotions and makes a child question the reasons behind such decisions. Revealed through the narrative in stories like Pérez, the fear and concerns of the immigrant child are revealed. Feeling apprehensive, many will wonder why they need to leave their world behind.

Decisions to leave one's country is never a simple one. Multiple factors influence decisions to migrate. The reasons, however, may be as diverse as the places we left and those where we came to live. Just as discussed earlier in Chapter 1, individual circumstances guide decisions to leave. In some cases, migration is planned and anticipated, while for some, conditions experienced lead or force people's decision to move (Figure 3.3). In planned migration, factors such as social and economic opportunities continue to encourage many to migrate.

Current immigration throughout the world's regions has shown a continuous rise motivated by both individual plans and forced by challenging circumstances. Planned migration happens all the time. Reasons are multiple and range from opportunities for better life conditions to considerations for the family's future. Still, even when decisions to migrate are anchored by aspirations and opportunities, they continue to be a major change in the life of a child.

Am I an Immigrant?

Surprise, intrigue, fear, and expectation are not uncommon emotions for children finding themselves becoming immigrants. Those were the reactions of the young girl and boy in de Regil's story *A new home* (2019). Both are leaving, interestingly to each other's respective countries, and wonder why they are moving. We hear them say to themselves, "I'm not sure that I want to leave my

Figure 3.3 Reasons to migrate.

Source: Robles-Meléndez and Driscoll (2020); United Nations (2020).

home" (n.p.). Presented from the perspective of the two children moving to other countries, the story reflects the feelings that many children would experience trying to understand why they must move, especially to a country different from their own. This is perhaps where children begin to question not only why they have to go to another country but also what will that country have that will make them feel they are at home again. Consciously or unconsciously, feelings of being an outsider are not absent from the minds of people crossing borders. This is, in fact, what prompts the need to consider the social and emotional impact that this experience has on children.

Transitions, an Emotional Experience

A new place to live brings a multitude of changes that when seen through the eyes of children, we can realize the enormity of the experience. This is what many of our students shared as we talked about moving. Sharing comments about their own experiences and those of the children they teach, they all agreed that it was a transition difficult to understand. While there was excitement, they all pointed out to the stressful experience no matter the reasons for leaving the place where they lived. Transitions as we know are part of life. They call for adjustments to one's lifestyles and routines. From the perspective of the early years, transitions are a demanding task facing a young child. Transitions entail not only a cognitive challenge as one processes and tries to make sense of a new reality, but they are also emotionally charged experiences (Landy and Osofsky 2009; Fields, Merrit, and Fields 2017).

Moving, changing the context where one lives, represents a major change and adjustment for children. Psychosocially, the early childhood years represent a time where some changes may influence the child's emerging sense of trust and feelings of safety (Berk 2015). Experiencing stability in their environments, daily routines, and interactions highly contribute to feelings of safety and security (Levine and Munsch 2016). The place where one lives is tied to emotions and feelings of belonging and safety. A child's sense of connection and relationship is constructed following referents in the places they live. Familiar people, relatives, the house where they live, their surroundings, all are used by children to build their sense of place and belonging (Lin and Barton 2010; Epstein 2009; Read 2007).

A sense of place is also aligned with the relationships children have built that give meaning to them. The familiar sounds and voices of relatives, neighbors, and even their pets, all contribute to supporting and making the place feel like theirs. Whenever changes are experienced, disruption in their otherwise stable

> **Think and Reflect ... Connections and Relationships**
>
> Connections are built through all the different relationships that a child has at home, in the neighborhood, and at school, for those already attending early experiences. If you were planning to move, think about the relationships that you have that were meaningful to you. Which ones would you miss the most? Which ones do you think would be most meaningful to you?

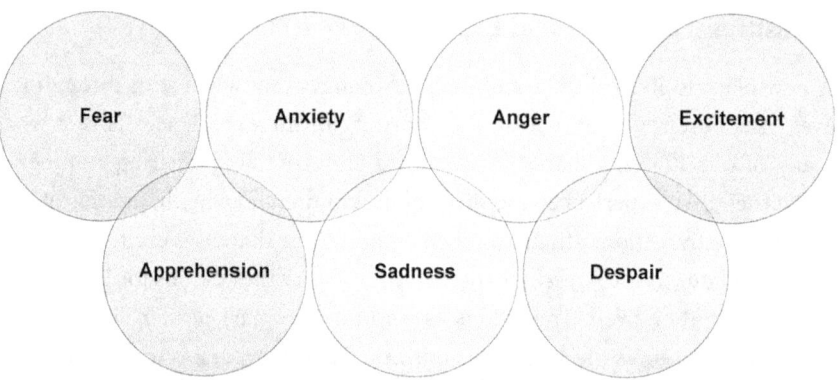

Figure 3.4 Transitions—children's emotions and feelings.

reality happens. We hear this sense of loss in *My two blankets* (Kobald 2014), where we learn about the despair and sadness that the young girl feels after war forced her and her aunt to leave their country. At the opening we read how the child laments all the changes she now faces, which even made her aunt stop using her nickname Cartwheel. She comments, "Everything was strange. The people were strange ... Even the wind felt strange" (n.p.).

During childhood, it is not uncommon to observe how big changes and transitions may evoke a variety of feelings in a young child. These may go from excitement, anticipating an event, to feelings of sadness, anxiety, frustration, and anger (Figure 3.4).

Children's reactions to the experience of moving have been the topic of interest for many authors. Their narratives provide an avenue leading us to delve into the myriad of emotions experienced by children. Gathered through the narratives in a selection of stories that were examined, one can listen to the voices of children as they learn they are moving away from the place where they belong and call home.

Growing Consciously Aware: Those Forced Transitions

Preparing a child for a transition is always imperative. Just as transitions are planned in the classroom to ease the impact of activity changes, they are also needed when leaving a place. However, there are many times when circumstances, given the urgency or need to move, may narrow or deter time to talk about reasons for relocating. Current times, and the past decade have revealed the pressing conditions leading thousands of children to leave with their families. Those are moments where the gentle and caring voices of families ease the difficult experiences just as those we hear of the mother in *My name is not refugee* (Milner 2018), who talks with her young child about what is to come. Throughout the world's regions, many have and are experiencing serious and difficult situations threatening their lives (United Nations 2021).

Uncertainty and Emotional Moments

Thousands of children are still today forced to leave, sometimes without a clear notion of where they are headed. The fear, surprise, and a thousand other emotions reflected on their faces are what is perceived through the emotional tone of Marwan in *Marwan's Journey* (de Arias 2018), a child escaping from violent conflict that as he says "swallowed up everything" (n.p.). Alone, he walks with others who also escape and painfully, we learn about the uncertainty of their destination, "… and I don't know when I will get there, or where I am going" (n.p.). While writing this chapter, thousands of children and their families saw themselves forced to flee because of dangerous conditions in their countries. A devastating earthquake in Haiti forced families and children to seek refuge and asylum (Shakil 2021; UNICEF 2021). Thousands of Rohingya children and families from the northern part of Myanmar and millions more from Ukraine were still seeking refuge as we write this book.

Emotionally, moving is a transition into a different reality where, for children, the sense of control is no longer affirmed. It also implies losing that feeling of safety and comfort that ties us to a place we know. Just the thought about what is left behind will sadden you and bring despair knowing what you will no longer have or see. This is the feeling conveyed by the child in *Far from Home* (Parker Rubio 2019). He is forced to choose only one toy as his family leaves in the middle of the night. Meanwhile, he also wonders when he will be able to see his grandparents again. Even in planned changes, one must remember that relocating disrupts the routines of children's daily lives (Shonkoff 2010).

In Search of a Place to Call Home: Compelling Reasons, Captivating Stories

Providing an avenue into the diversity of issues facing society, many authors of children's literature have addressed a number of the challenges of our times, where most reflect long-standing issues. In particular, a growing number of books published in the recent decade have addressed the difficult issues driving many to leave their places of birth. Through their pages, we learn about current challenges as well as those in the past about political, social, economic, and environmental issues driving and forcing thousands of children and their families to search for a place they could call home.

The driving force of finding a better life that historically motivated generations is the story ongoing today. It is a story of generations, making us aware about their struggles and aspirations and how they toiled to pave the way for their families. That is precisely what we find when reading *All the way to America* (2011), where through its colorful illustrations, Dan Yaccarino tells us the story of his own family, coming with hope "in search of opportunities" (n.p.). Clearly postulated are the sacrifices made by immigrants and how they built what generations later enjoy. Reflectively considered, Yaccarino's story invites us to ponder who the immigrants are both from a personal stance and from a societal point of view.

In *Kalak's journey* (2016), author Quintana Silva presents the circumstances faced by a family of storks that, "lived in a part of the world where the nests were old … and there was never enough food for everyone." (n.p.), that forced them to find a better place. Using a family of storks as characters, the storyline is reflective of what today makes people choose to leave and "fly off to another part of the world" (n.p.). Moved by the thought of finding a better place to build a better nest and be happy, are similar aspirations continuing to guide many who leave their homelands.

Bringing these issues to the forefront, authors and illustrators present them with compelling texts and illustrations. Figure 3.5 includes some selected titles of stories addressing social challenges, violence, and armed conflicts that today still are motivating migration, both planned and forced.

Emerging with clarity through many stories, are children who, together with their families, are protagonists in the search to find a safe place to settle and begin life again. They are stories where the voice of children emerges strongly sharing their aspiration and feelings as they find themselves leaving their homeland. One of those cases is that of the young child in *Far from home* (Parker Rubio

> **Stories of immigration addressing key reasons driving and forcing children and famillies to migrate**
>
> • *Seeking a better life and work opportunities*
> - *Marianthe's story* (Aliki 1999)
> - *All the way to America* (Yaccarino 2011)
> - *El viaje de Kalak [Kalak's journey]* (Quintana Silva 2018)
>
> • *Social insecurity and violence*
> - *The long road* (Garay 1997)
> - *Somos como las nubes* (Argüeta 2016)
> - *How many days to America: A thanksgiviong story* (Bunting 1988)
>
> • *War conflict and violence*
> - *Far from home* (Parker Rubio 2019)
> - *The day war came* (Davies 2018)
> - *Stepping stones: A refugee family's journey* (Ruurs 2016)

Figure 3.5 Selected stories of immigration: Key reasons driving immigration for families and children.

2019). Forced by the unsafe reality of their homeland, the parents leave in the middle of the night with their young child, who grapples to understand as he clutches the only toy he is able to carry with him.

No less difficult and urgent is what forces the mother in *Lost and Found* (Kuntz and Shrodes 2017) to escape with her children. In this case, what is narrated is the true story of a family seeking safety. Still, even when children are informed, for many, leaving not just the place where they live but what is known becomes a challenging experience. After all, the place where we live matters in many special ways to each one (Ellen and Turner 1997; Vergeront 2013). Moving and relocating presents the challenge of finding oneself again in a place you can feel you belong. A sense of place develops gradually as the child once again begins to build relationships: cognitive, affective, and cultural, that give meanings to a person's life (Matthews 1992; Lim and Barton 2010).

Making Sense out of the Experience of Moving

Coming across the thematic line of stories is the social and emotional impressions and impact of the immigration experience. For instance, we are touched by the intense emotional need to have a friend that Lubna, a young refugee girl, feels that made her figuratively transform a pebble into a friend (*Lubna and pebble*, Meddour 2019). Powerfully presented, the story is a revealing snapshot about the social and emotional needs children have, whether they are refugees or whether they came with families who planned to migrate to other places. Placing attention on their well-being, we are reminded that children have developmental needs that require mindful consideration.

Developmentally, for children, a sense of security emerges from those supportive relationships with families, friends, and people they know. It also comes from everyday routines, being familiar with the space where we live or interact, and even from the familiar paths surrounding the places we call home (Copple and Bredekamp 2009; Kostelnik et al. 2012). These are, as well, components influencing our emotional sense of feeling safe. Knowing where one is and what to expect gives feelings of being in control. Built over time, feeling safe is constructed through interactions with people as familiarity with places and people grows (Derr 2002; Read 2007). Leaving behind familiar places and those we know is what perhaps helps explain why transitioning into a new setting oftentimes makes us feel apprehensive and fearful. This may help us to understand the many questions that the girl in McCartney's story *Where will I live?* poses as she comes to live a new place. They also answer why children who recently moved and relocated may feel lost in a place where their cognitive, social, and affective feelings are different from the context where they now find themselves (Lim and Barton 2010). For children to, suddenly or not, find themselves in a different place is an emotionally dramatic experience leading to feelings of being lost.

Building a sense of a new location develops over time. It builds as interactions and familiarity with the new location grow and expand. For young children, as connections are built, they begin to make sense of their new reality and start building feelings that will gradually make them feel they are in a place familiar to them. These connections emerge as children experience their new environments especially as they develop relationships with peers and adults. It is through their experiences with people, routines, and overall interactions in their new contexts that children start to make sense about the realities of their new settings. This is what we learn from many stories like Kobald's (2014), when the young refugee finds a friend.

Finding Self in New Contexts

Interactions with people, both adults and peers, strongly play a role in how children begin to feel socially and emotionally connected to new environments.

The same is observed in young immigrant children (Kostelnik 2015; Warsi 2017; Sibley and Brabeck 2017; Carter, Katharine 2020), who may find themselves in a context unknown to them. This is what we see in some of the stories about young immigrants crossing borders. Levine's story *I hate English* (1989) presents the shifting feelings of young Mei, a Chinese child whose family immigrated to New York. She struggles at first, unable to see herself fitting in a new school where especially the language is different. From her initial rejection where her feelings of being lost are clearly conveyed, she begins to feel more accepting of the new place where her family settled. Familiarity with her school and the caring response of her teacher gradually make Mei Mei make sense of her environment and feeling that it is also where she belongs. This is also reflected by José, a young boy in *The long road* (Garay 1997), where after moving as a refugee to North America, with time, he gradually begins to feel that "The strange faces in the classroom became familiar" (n.p.).

The physical environment plays a role, too, in making us feel emotionally connected. The climate, the natural landscape, and the overall community structure and architecture all contribute to feelings of emotional well-being. Familiarity with what is known and present in our contexts are elements children relate to and use as referents. They also contribute to feelings of belonging and of connectedness (Eva 2017; Robles-Melendez and Beck 2019). Author Jeanette Winter (2007) reveals the sense of disconnect that a child feels living in a climate and landscape dramatically different to what was known to her. In her story, *Angelina's island*, we hear that the young immigrant child coming from Jamaica feels like a stranger living in a city. "But this not home, it doesn't sound like home, it doesn't look like home (n.p.)," she says, disclosing her struggle and resistance to being in a place that she cannot feel connected to or where she belongs. Conveyed through the dramatic illustrations in her wordless book *Here I am* (2015), author Patricia Kim (2015) allows us to experience the challenge felt by the young boy who finds himself living in a bustling city environment. The vivid illustrations communicate to readers the strong emotions the young child experiences. Confusion and disbelief seem to be the feelings as the young boy tries to understand the place where he now resides. Though wordless, the images capture the strong sentiments portrayed in each of the story illustrations. These are emotions not uncommon for children, whose decision to move lies in the hands of the adults. Psychologists and child development professionals have pointed out the struggle children experienced trying to understand why they leave (Carter 2020). This is especially concerning when, sadly, many immigrant children find themselves exposed to unwelcoming attitudes and become the victims of discrimination (Adair 2015; Brown 2015).

Moving and Children's Well-being

The well-being of children is paramount in all efforts and drives what the Convention of the Rights of the Child refers to as acting *in the best interest of the child*. Research has also identified changes in residential location as a factor influencing an individual's well-being and more specifically on children (Cortos, Theodos and Turner 2012; Murphey, Bandy, and Moore 2012; Clay 2019). Well-being is a complex and multidimensional concept that, overall, describes the quality of life people experience (Lipman, Anderson and MacIntosh 2009; Statham and Chase 2010; Federal Interagency Forum on Child and Family Statistics 2021). Key to defining an individual's level of general welfare are the physical, social, and emotional conditions experienced that promote and contribute to a person's well-being (Marotz 2019; Sorte, Daechel, and Amador 2020). Many are the stories that narrate the challenges children faced trying to make sense about their new environments.

Crossing borders and moving into a different context, where culture, language, and social expectations are different, is an enormous and trying experience for children to process and make sense out of. What continues to place a child's well-being at risk is the nature of the variety of experiences children may encounter. Immigration is a mosaic of realities with some more difficult than others. But altogether, according to psychology experts, it is a stressful experience influencing children's social, emotional, and educational development (Carter 2020). Psychologists also posit that the impact of what is experienced by children is not always clearly evident. This calls for attention to how they respond to the challenges faced as they struggle to adapt and adjust to new circumstances. Addressed by several authors, adjustment challenges continue to draw concerns for families and teachers. One of those stories is *A piece of home* (Watts 2016). Here the author narrates the experiences of young Hee Jun, a young Korean boy who wrestles with trying to adjust to living in the United States, where a job opportunity brought his family to live. Behind he left his friends, his house, and the places he knew and where he "was not extraordinary, not different, … just me, like so many others" (n.p.). The narrative aided by the illustrations conveys the anxiety and emotions felt by the boy, who, like many other immigrant children, battles to adjust and states, "*I am different*" (n.p., emphasis added). Being responsive to the feelings of children and helping them to feel they belong is essential. With understanding and support, gradually, as the story reveals, children will begin to feel no longer as strangers but that they belong.

Concerns about the children's psychological well-being have been voiced by many professional organizations (Okazaki, Haarlament, and Liu 2019), who join in bringing attention to their needs. Reflecting on many of the characters from the literature on immigration, we are made aware and urged to understand the pressing need to support the social and emotional well-being of children who are immigrants. Responding positively to their needs, we must remember, is society's responsibility.

Change brings about the need to rebuild feelings of trust, which emerges as children make sense of their new environments. As children begin to regularly experience routines, their confidence builds. Developmentally, it is known that interactions with peers and adults together with stable routines gradually contribute to building a sense of security about a new context (Kostelnik et al. 2015; Sorrels 2015). Forming new friendships and beginning to master a new language, among other things, are experiences contributing to rebuilding that sense of trust lost as children experience the challenges faced relocating, moving or seeking refuge in safer countries. Many story characters guide readers to experience the emotional challenges felt as they readjust to new settings after leaving their own homelands. Some of those story characters are listed in Figure 3.6, where each bring alive the sentiments experienced as they adjust to their new realities.

Building Our Consciousness about Child Immigrants

We could not ignore that, at present, society has experienced a wave of children who, driven by difficult and dangerous circumstances, have taken their destiny in their hands and have left their homes. They are crossing borders in hopes of

Lubna *(Lubna and pebble)*	**Deo** *(The banana leaf ball)*
• *Loneliness, using a pebble to establish a relationship; need for companioship and a friend to trust.*	• *Alone and struggling to adjust to life living in a refugee camp after losing his family to conflict.*

Characters revealing the socioemotional challenge of immigration

Maria Isabel *(My name is Maria Isabel)*	**Hannah** *(Hannah is my name)*
• *Struggling for her name not to be changed.*	• *Feeling fearful waiting for her family's status to become official*

Figure 3.6 Emotional impact of moving: What we learn from some story characters.

finding a safe place to live and thrive. The thousands of children who arrived unaccompanied during 2014 into the US borders was a marker telling everyone about the desperation that pushed so many children to leave. Today, sadly, the numbers have surpassed those of 2014 and continue to grow at the borders of many other continents.

When one reads and reflects on *The map of good memories* (Nuño 2016), one cannot avoid thinking about the many children forcibly leaving just as the protagonist in this story who "because of the war she had to flee with her family and take refuge in another country" (n.p.). Globally, thousands of children have been leaving their hometowns escaping from places where the absence of hope and of a future permeates. Reports from UNICEF (United Nations 2022) revealed that in 2022, 37 million children had been forcibly displaced. It was also reported that about 30 percent of those migrating through the Central America-Mexico corridor were children, half of them coming unaccompanied (Amnesty International 2021). Many of them were forced out or displaced due to war, conflict, or violence, factors that remained behind the thousands of children continuing to leave from places everywhere around the world. Their situation raises many concerns particularly when considering their well-being, given the vulnerability that childhood implicitly places on children. The emotional impact on children of the violent and threatening conditions forcing children to leave has been captured by many authors. Among them is Nicola Davies, who leads us to experience the horror faced by the child when "a voice of thunder" changes the world she knew in *The day war came* (2018). The images in the story lead us to experience how a typical day is transformed, as war suddenly erupts, an experience sadly repeated and, today, is a lived reality of so many children. As victims of political and ideological unrest and violence, children continue today to be marked by the horror of losing what they knew and of their sense of security and safety. Whether in continents close to each of us or far away, the stories remain as reminders of the conscious need for understanding about their experiences as their childhood is marred by uncertainty and violence.

Narratives from stories about refugees and asylees, such as Garay's *The long road* (1997), convey the emotions and challenges faced by children confronted with the reality of finding themselves in a different place. In Garay, who illustrated his own story, reveals the shocking moments experienced as the character, José, escapes with his mother, hiding in the dark of the night until they finally reached the border into safety. We live his struggles, as he is challenged, living in a place where Spanish is not spoken, while he learns English.

Argüeta, in his book *Somos como las nubes/We are like the clouds* (2016), catches the voice of children from Central America migrating alone, forced by dangerous conditions in their country. Though the book is more appropriate for upper elementary children, his poems reflect the ongoing saga of children who similarly in other parts of the world are venturing to go across borders. In his poetic narration, Argueta conveys the sentiments and fears of children coming unaccompanied. We can feel the trepidation of the unaccompanied boy who begins to imagine what will happen as they get close to the border area.

Many are the experiences and adjustments for a child turned into an immigrant. As they adjust to their new reality, we seek to explore what happens as the child immigrant encounters life in a new context. The ongoing day-to-day realities of young immigrants especially as they come to experience school are what we will delve into and explore in the next chapter.

Beyond the Stories: Getting to Know Children

Every time we read a story about immigrant children, a new element is added to the number of factors demanding society's conscious attention. The lived experiences of a child are a tapestry of happenings, all adding to the reality they live and are a part of, during the most vulnerable years of their life. Rogoff, Dahl, and Callanan (2018) remind us of the need for consideration to children's lived experiences as essential if we are to understand who they are and the life trajectories they have followed. She and her colleagues reflect on what educator Jerome Bruner had earlier posited about the need for reflection to mindfully and consciously consider the challenges experienced. Who the child is, calls for learning about the uniqueness of his/her "lived experiences." What Bruner brought to everyone's attention, and which Rogoff highlights, is precisely what we also wanted to emphasize, this time about the children of immigrants. We need to consciously learn and know about what they experience that reveals their own stories with the successes and challenges faced. The realities many experience as immigrants are a constant plea for justice. Their own diversity and cultures

---

> **Think and Reflect** ... Children's Literature and an Agenda for Social Justice
>
> Children's literature is known for all the difficult and challenging topics it continues to address. In your consideration, what are some of the social justice issues that you consider children's stories are raising? Why are these considered to be critical for education?

have made them the target of unfair comments and actions (Suárez-Orozco and Suárez-Orozco 2001; Adair 2015). The fact is that the reasons that drove their families to arrive and settle in other lands, demand honest consideration all in the hopes for a future and better life.

Increased presence of immigrant children demands our attention. Addressing their wellbeing begins with a thourough knowledge about their realities and lived experiences. In a century where the world has come to experience and learn about the unfortunate circumstances of thousands and thousands of children (UNICEF 2021), forced to leave their homelands, society is summoned to understand and respond to their needs. This is not just a headline in the evening news or on the morning paper. Each of the faces of children that we have come to meet, some smiling despite the severity of their circumstances, others telling a story without words just as we look at them, they are all a reality waiting for the world to respond. They also embody a social justice agenda by itself. It is the agenda for finding what is in the best interest of the child, as the United Nations postulated through the signing of the Convention of the Rights of the Child (1989).

Reading through the children's literature about immigrants, the door is opened to further consider and become mindfully aware about immigrant children. We remind you that children's literature is known for the many serious and difficult issues that it addresses in ways unique to engage the child and adult alike. Lukens, Smith, and Coffel (2013) noted this characteristic about books for children remarking it is a way to bring attention to controversial topics and issues such as immigration that often times, people want to avoid. Erasing those sentiments must begin if we are to bring socially just attention to all children and families, who leaving their homelands, bring with them hopefulness and motivation to start once again.

Reflecting and Beyond

1. What are some of the impressions and thoughts children experience when moving to other places?
2. Identify at least two stories you would share with children who are moving or have recently moved.
3. Think about the reasons pulling and pushing families to leave. Which ones do you consider as most pressing?
4. Locate one of the books mentioned in this chapter and identify the emotions experienced by children as they become immigrants.

Note

1 Green cards are the official permanent resident card allowing immigrants to live and work in the United States.

References

Adair, Jennifer. 2015. The impact of discrimination on the early schooling experiences of chidlren from immigrant families. Washinbton, DC. Migration Policy Institute.

Amnesty International. 2021. *Facts and figures: Deportations of unaccompanied migrant children by the USA and Mexico*. June 11. https://www.amnesty.org/en/latest/news/2021/06/facts-figures-deportations-children-usa-mexico/.

Berk, Laura. 2015. *Infants and children: Prenatal through middle childhood* (8th edition). Boston, MA: Pearson.

Bowen, Dorothy and Melissa Schutt. 2007. "Addressing sensitive issues through picture books." *Kentucky Libraries* 71(1): 4–7.

Brown Spears, Christia. 2015. *The educational, psychological, and social impact of discrimination on the immigrant child*. Washington, DC: Migration Policy Institute. https://www.migrationpolicy.org/research/educational-psychological-and-social-impact-discrimination-immigrant-child.

Carter, Katharine. 2020. "Helping children through the emotional toll of immigration. Counselor uses nondirective play therapy to help immigrant clients open up." *American Psychological Association*, January 31. https://www.apa.org/members/content/immigration-emotional-toll.

Choi, Hyewon and Shigehiro Oishi. 2020. "The psychology of residential mobility: a decade of progress." *Current Opinion in Psychology* 32(April): 72–5.

Clair, Amy. 2019. "Housing: An under-explored influence on children's wellbeing and becoming." *Child Indicators Research* 12: 609–26. https://doi.org/10.1007/s12187-018-9550-7.

Copple, Carol and Sue Bredekamp. 2009. *Developmentally appropriate practice in early childhood* (3rd edition). Washington, DC: National Association for the Education of Young Children.

Corliss, Julia. 1998. *Crossing borders with literature of diversity*. Norwood, MA: Christopher Gordon.

Coulton, Claudia, Brett Theodos, and Margery Turner. 2012. "Residential mobility and neighborhood change: Real neighborhoods under the microscope." *Cityscape* 14(3): 55–89.

Crosnoe, Robert. 2013. *Preparing the children of immigrants for early academic success*. Washington, DC: Migration Policy Institute.

Darling, Nancy. 2010. Moving is tough for kids. *Psychology Today*, July 11. https://www.psychologytoday.com/us/blog/thinking-about-kids/201007/moving-is-tough-kids.

Derr, Victoria. 2002. "Children's sense of place in northern New Mexico." *Journal of Environmental Psychology* 22(1-2): 125–37.

Dietrich, Deborah and Kathleen Ralph. 1995. "Crossing borders: Multicultural literature in the classroom." *The Journal of Educational Issue of Language Minority Students* 15. Boise State University. https://ncela.ed.gov/files/rcd/BE020474/Crossing_Borders.pdf.

Ellen, Ingrid and Margery A. Turner. 1997. "Does neighborhood matter? Assessing recent evidence." *Housing Policy Debate* 8(4): 833–66.

Epstein, Ann. 2009. *Me, You, Us: Social-emotional learning in preschool*. Ypsilanti, Michigan: High Scope.

Eva, Amy. 2017. "How teachers can help immigrant children feel safe." *Greater Good Magazine*, April. https://greatergood.berkeley.edu/article/item/how_teachers_can_help_immigrant_kids_feel_safe.

Federal Interagency Forum on Child and Family Statistics. 2021. *America's children: Key national indicators of well-being, 2021*. U.S. Government Printing Office. https://www.childstats.gov/pdf/ac2021/ac_21.pdf.

Fields, Marjorie, Patricia Merrit, and Deborah Fields. 2017. *Constructive guidance and discipline: Birth to age eight* (7th edition). MA: Pearson.

Hartig, Terry and Roderick Lawrence. 2003. "Introduction: The residential context of health." *Journal of Social Issues* 59(3): 455–73.

Hilpern, Kate. 2015. "Moving and how children can be affected." *Huffpost UK*, August 14. https://www.huffingtonpost.co.uk/2014/08/14/moving-house-and-how-children-can-be-affected_n_7334248.html.

Hovil, Lucy, Mark Gill, Iolanda Genovese, Olivia Bueno, Josiah Kaplan, and Ramya Subrahmanian. 2021. *Reimagining migration responses: Learning from children and young people who move in the Horn of Africa*. Florence: UNICEF Office of Research—Innocenti.

Jelleyman, Tim and Spencer Nick. 2008. "Residential mobility in childhood and health outcomes: a systematic review." *Journal of J Epidemiology and Community Health* 62(7): 584–92.

Kelly, Joan and Michael Lamb. 2003. "Developmental issues in relocation cases involving young children: When, whether, and how?" *Journal of Developmental Psychology* 17(2): 193–205.

Kostelnik, Marjorie, Kara Gregory, Anne Soderman, and Alcie Whiren. 2015. *Guiding children's social development and learning* (8th edition). CA: Wadsworth/Cengage.

Landy, Sarah and Joy Osofsky. 2009. *Pathways to competence: Encouraging healthy social and emotional development*. MD: Paul Brookes.

Levine, Laura and Joyce Munsch. 2016. *Child development from infancy to adolescence. An active learning approach*. CA: Sage.

Lim, Miyoum and Angela Calabrese Barton. 2010. "Exploring insideness in urban children's sense of place." *Journal of Environmental Psychology* 30: 328–37.

Lippman, Laura, H. Kristin Anderson Moore, and Hugh McIntosh. 2009. *Positive indicators of child well-being: A conceptual framework, measures and methodological issues*. Innocenti Working Paper No. 2009–21. Florence: UNICEF Innocenti Research Centre.

Lukens, Rebecca, Jacquelin Smith, and Cynthia Miller Coffel. 2013. *Critical handbook of children's literature* (9th edition). MA: Pearson.

Marotz, Lynn. 2019. *Health, safety, and nutrition for the young child* (10th edition). CA: Cengage.

Matthews, M. 1992. *Making sense of place: Children's understanding of large-scale environments*. HY: Rowman and Littlefield.

Migration Policy Institute. 2019. *Children in U.S. Immigrant Families*. https://www.migrationpolicy.org/programs/data-hub/charts/children-immigrant-families.

Molborn, Stephanie, Elizabeth Lawrence, and Elisabeth Downing Root. 2018. "Residential mobility across early childhood and children's kindergarten readiness." *Demography* 55(2): 485–510.

Murphey, David, Twana Bandy, and Kristin Moore. 2012. "Frequent mobility and young children's well-being." *Child Trends Research Brief*. Publication #2012-02. https://www.childtrends.org/wp-content/uploads/2013/06/2012-02ResidentialMobility.pdf.

OECD. 2009. *Doing better for children*. Paris: OECD.

Oishi, S and U. Schimmack. 2010. "Residential mobility, well-being, and mortality." *Journal of Personality and Social Psychology* 98(6): 980–94.

Okazaki, Sumie, Jessy Guler, Miriam Haarlammert, and Sabrina Liu. 2019. "Translating psychological research on immigrants and refugees." *Translational Issues in Psychological Science* 5(1): 1–3. http://dx.doi.org/10.1037/tps0000188.

Perreira, K.M. and I.J. Ornelas. 2011. "The physical and psychological well-being of immigrant children." *The Future of Children* 21(1): 195–218. http://www.futureofchildren.org/futureofchildren/publications/journals/article/index.xml?journalid=74&articleid=546.

Read, Marilyn. 2007. "Sense of place in child care environments." *Early Childhood Education Journal* 34(6): 387–92.

Robles-Melendez, Wilma and Vesna Beck. 2000. *Teaching social studies in early education*. NY: Delmar.

Robles-Melendez, Wilma and Vesna Beck. 2019. *Teaching young children in multicultural classrooms: Issues, concepts, and strategies* (5th edition). CA: Cengage.

Robles-Melendez, Wilma and Wayne Driscoll. 2020. *Issues and challenges of immigration in early childhood in USA*. London: Bloomsbury.

Rogoff, Barbara, Audun Dahl, and Maureen Callanan. 2018. "The importance of understanding children's lived experience." *Developmental Review* 50, Part A: 5–15. https://doi.org/10.1016/j.dr.2018.05.006.

Shakil, F. M. 2021. "Afghan refugee crisis poised to explode." *Asia Times*, September 17. https://asiatimes.com/2021/09/afghan-refugee-crisis-poised-to-explode/.

Shonkoff, Jack. 2010. "Building a new biodevelopmental framework to guide the future of early childhood policy." *Child Development* 81(1): 357–67.

Shonkoff, Jack and Andrew Garner. 2012. "The lifelong effects of early childhood adversity and toxic stress." *Pediatrics* 12(1): 232–46.

Sibley, Erin and Kalina Brabeck. 2017. "Latino immigrant students' school experiences in the United States: The importance of family–school–community collaborations." *School Community Journal, 2017* 27(1): 137–57. Available at http://www.schoolcommunitynetwork.org/SCJ.aspx.

Sorte, Joanne, Inge Daechel, and Carolina Amador. 2020. *Nutrition, Health, and Safety for Young Children: Promoting Wellness*. Boston, MA: Pearson.

Sorrels, Barbara. 2015. *Reaching and teaching children exposed to trauma. Gryphon house*. Lewiswille: North Carolina.

Statham, June and Elaine Chase. 2010. *Childhood wellbeing: A brief overview*. Briefing paper 1. Childhood Wellbeing Research Centre. https://assets.publishing.service.gov.uk/government/uploads/system/uploads/attachment_data/file/183197/Child-Wellbeing-Brief.pdf.

Stokols, Daniel and Sally Ann Shumaker. 1982. "The psychological context of residential mobility and well-being." *Journal of Social Issues* 38(3): 149–71.

Suárez-Orozco, Carola and Marcelo Suárez-Orozco. 2001. *Children of immigration*. Cambridge, Massachusetts: Harvard University Press.

Titzmann, Peter and Andrew Fuligni. 2015. Immigrants' adaptation to different cultural settings: A contexttual perspective on accuturation: An intoduction for the special section on immigration. International Journal of Psychology, 50(6): 407–12.

UNICEF. 2018. *Children on the move. Key facts and figures. Data Brief*. file:///C:/Users/WSM/Downloads/Data-brief-children-on-the-move-key-facts-and-figures-1.pdf.

UNICEF. 2021. *Massive earthquake leaves devastation in Haiti*. Appeal. https://www.unicef.org/emergencies/massive-earthquake-devastation-haiti.

UNICEF. 2021a. *Child displacement*. September. UNICEF Data.

UNICEF. 2020. *Migrant and refugee children*. https://www.unicef.org/migrant-refugee-internally-displaced-children.

United Nations. 1989/2021. *Convention on the Rights of the Child*. https://www.ohchr.org/en/professionalinterest/pages/crc.aspx.

United Nations. 2022. A record 37 million children displaced worldwide: UNICEF. *UN News*, 17 June. httpd://un.org/en/story/2022/06/1120642.

Valdez, Carmen, Jessa Valentine, and Brian Padilla. 2013. "Why we stay: Immigrants motivation for remaining in communities impacted by anti-immigration policies." *Cultural Diversity Ethnic Minority Psychology* 19(3): 279–87.

Vergeront, Jeanne. 2913. Place matters. Museum notes, July 13. https://museumnotes.blogspot.com/2013/07/place-matters.

Warsi, Sadia. 2017. Welcoming refugee children in early childhood classrooms. Young Children, 10(5).

Yokota, Junko. 2009. "Learning though literature that offers diverse perspectives: Multicultural and international literature." In D. Wooten and B. Cullinan (eds). Children's literature in the reading program: An invitation to read (pp.66–73). Virginia: International Reading Association.

Children's Books Cited

Argueta, Jorge. 2016. *Somos como las nubes/We are like the clouds*. Toronto, Canada: Groundwood Books.
Arias, Patricia. 2018. *Marwan's journey*. NY: mineditionUS/Penguin Random.
Buitrago, Jairo. 2015. *Two white rabbits*. Toronto, Canada: Groundwood Books.
Bunting, Eve. 1988. *How many days to America*. NY: Clarion Books.
De Regil, Tania. 2019. *A new home*. NY: Candlewick.
Garay, Luis. 1997. *The long road*. NY: Tundra Books.
Harper, Jessica. 2004. *I like where I am*. NY: Putnam.
Kim, Patricia. 2015. *Here I am*. NY: Picture Window.
Kobald, Irena and Freya Blackwood. 2014. *My two blankets*. Boston: Houghton Mifflin Harcourt.
Kunz, Doug and Amy Schrodes. 2017. *Lost and found cat. The true story of Kunkush's incredible journey*. NY: Crown Books.
Levine, Ellen. 1989. *I hate English*. NY: Scholastic.
Levitin, Sonia. 1996. *A piece of home*. NY: Dial Books for Children.
Milway, Katie. 2017. *The banana leaf ball*. Toronto, Canada: Citizens Kids.
Meddour, Wendy. 2019. *Lubna and pebble*. NY: Dial Books.
Morales, Yuyi. 2018. *Dreamers*. NY: Neal Porter Books.
Nuño, Fran. 2017. *El mapa de los buenos momentos*. Madrid: Cuentos de Luz.
Park, Frances and Ginger Park. 2001. *Goodbye, 382 Shin Dang Dong*. Washington, DC: National Geographic Society.
Parker, Rubio, Sarah. 2019. *Far from home. A story of loss, refuge, and hope*. IL: Tyndale House Publishers.
Pérez, Amada. 2002. *My diary from here/Mi diario de aquí y acá*. CA: Children's Book Press.
Say, Alan. 1993. *Grandfather's journey*. NY: Houghton Mifflin.
Vazquez, Eric. 2021. *Grandma's records*. UK: Bloomsbury.
Wagner, Anke and Eva Eriksson. 2012. *Tim's big move*. NY: NorthSouth.
Watts, Jeri. 2016. *A piece of home*. NY: Candlewick.
Winter, Jeannette. 2007. *Angelina's island*. NY: Frances Foster Books.
Yang, Belle. 2004. *Hannah is my name*. NY: Candlewick.

4

Growing Up as the Youngest Immigrants: Through the Eyes of Children

This chapter aims to:

- Explore the challenges facing immigrant children during the early childhood years.
- Identify some of the cultural challenges faced by young immigrant children.
- Discuss some of the experiences children and families encounter as they adapt to a different culture.
- Examine some of the factors supporting children's ethnic identity.

Key words:

- Immigrants
- Culture
- Acculturation
- Ethnic identity

Missing them so much

Every week in the first-grade classroom, children would choose a book to read and talk about. That morning, one of the children brought a book from home that she wanted to share. "It's one of my favorite books," said her teacher a bit surprised as the six-year-old girl gave him the book. Showing the group the story, Nonni's moon *(Inserro 2018), teacher Mr. Vazquez quickly asked her, "Why did you pick this one?" "It reminds me about my grandmother," she said with sadness in her voice. "I miss her a lot," added the girl who only a couple of months earlier had joined the class. "Let's read it!" her teacher said, with the child assenting and her classmates following saying, "Yes!" Mr. Vazquez opened the book and started to read the story.*

It soon caught the interest of the class. Listening to their teacher read made the young students feel the sadness of Beanie, the young girl migrant longing for her grandma living in a distant country.

As he read the last page, one of the children could not wait and jumped saying, "Why didn't she come, too?" Not surprised at the question, Mr. Vazquez did not hesitate to say, "There are times when you are not able to come, even if your family leaves." A few hands started to wave also wanting to comment, with more than two relating to the story and saying how much they also miss someone from their family. "You know," Mr. Vazquez began to say, "I still miss my aunts so much." The eyes of the children opened big as they listened to their teacher talk. "Let's think about what else to do that will keep them in our minds. That would also help our friend here. Ideas? What would you do?" A flurry of ideas and suggestions started to pour as children shared what they would do.

Immigrant Children, a Continuing Story

Every time we read stories of immigration, we are reminded about the story of immigration continuing to repeat itself everywhere in the world. For so many of us, it is our very own story, whether from childhood or now as an adult. Coming to other places filled with dreams and hopes for a better future, this story connects us with the generations of immigrants whose presence and diverse cultures continue to transform our communities. It is also a narrative that unpacks the story of children of immigration, one unending and happening everywhere, in places far and near to us. Stories about a childhood growing up in other cultures and places also speak to us about the challenges faced. It reminds us about the many things they leave behind, not only their home but a culture, and those special relationships just like the young girl in the opening vignette, who longs to see her grandmother. Finding a voice in a story revealing her sadness, the young first-grader brings a storybook to share with everyone how much she misses her grandmother.

Immigration, with its hope and challenges, is also an ongoing reminder about families and about their children, those who came and of those born in the countries they now call home. We are also prompted to remember the thousands of children who came during their childhood and became immigrants. Continuing to happen, every day, in communities throughout the globe, countless immigrant children are growing up and building their stories.

Their faces and voices tell us about the kaleidoscope of cultures and experiences they represent and the stories they continue to write.

Glancing into the Realities of Immigrant Children

Stories abound, telling the saga of ongoing experiences children traverse as they grow up in nations that they now call home. Authors of children's literature have and continue to be inspired by the many accounts of immigrant children's lived experiences. Once again, in this chapter, we explore how children experience immigration using the special lens provided by children's books. Some storylines may sound familiar to us because they are tied to and relate to the commonality of experiences of childhood. They are a reminder to everyone that every immigrant child, just as every other child, shares one thing in common, that they are simply children. Childhood also brings a multitude of realities that shape and give a unique character to each one. This is what we ought to consider about children of immigration.

How much do we know about immigrant children, growing and becoming in our communities and everywhere else in society? There is much to know and even more to uncover beyond the context of this book. In the pages ahead in this chapter, we take some glimpses into their experience growing up. Through those snippets that children's literature on immigration provide, we continue to consciously build knowledge about their experiences and challenges still faced today.

Children of Immigrants in Our Communities

Immigrant children, whether born in their homelands or born in the places where their families now reside, as they grow up, share many similar experiences and challenges. As immigrants, they embark on the task of negotiating and navigating cultures that may differ strikingly from theirs. For many, it will be finding themselves with the challenge of practices, routines, and languages that differ from their own (Gonzalez, Moll and Amanti 2005; Garcia Coll 2012; Adair 2015). Navigating through the tasks of adjusting to new cultural realities while growing up brings children to face cultural, societal, and legal challenges (Figure 4.1). It is through these experiences that children's dynamic and determined character reveals itself (Suárez-Orozco and Suárez-Orozco 2002; Garcia-Coll 2012).

Children's Lives, a Mosaic of Diverse Experiences

A mosaic of experiences is what we find in communities where immigrant children live. Countless are the experiences that are written every day by children of immigrants. They are an assortment of happenings, some common to childhood, others difficult and challenging to what is socially fair and just for the children. Reading through the many children's stories on immigration, a number of traits clearly emerge describing the mosaic of events and circumstances of young children. Some of their experiences allow us to learn about their interests and individual agency, particularly in moments when they find themselves challenged in difficult context and situations where their resilient spirit is revealed. Many of their lived experiences also call attention to events still demanding social justice for children and their families. They are clamoring for society to respond to them. As their stories take shape, we learn how children navigate through cultures and landscapes that, so often, are diverse from those of their own. These are experiences that will mark their lives as immigrants.

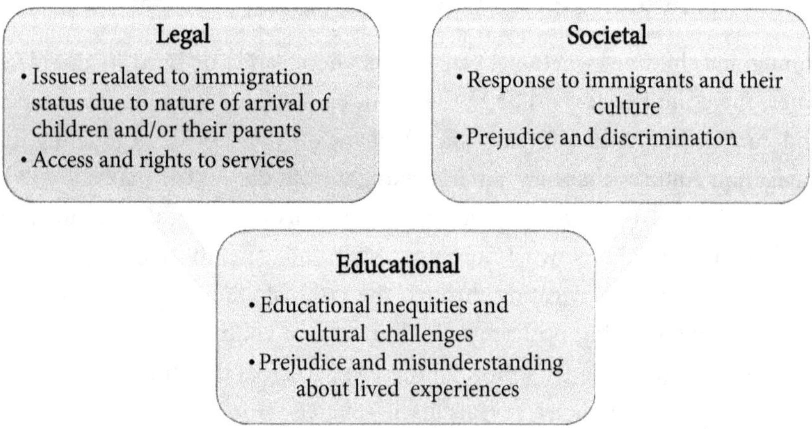

Cultural
- Different cultural expectations, practices, routines, values, principles
- Different language and linguistic differences

Legal
- Issues realated to immigration status due to nature of arrival of children and/or their parents
- Access and rights to services

Societal
- Response to immigrants and their culture
- Prejudice and discrimination

Educational
- Educational inequities and cultural challenges
- Prejudice and misunderstanding about lived experiences

Figure 4.1 Challenges facing children of immigrants.

Consciously Considering ... *Valuing Children as Children*

During one of our classes, one of the authors remembers that as the discussion about immigrant children was ending, one of the students observed, "They are just children, simply children!" She is right. They are children bringing their vibrant energy to our communities and allowing us to know about their journey. How they meet the challenges of growing up in contexts new or different to what they know, and where, sometimes, they are not welcomed, that is the story that keeps writing itself every day. One thing is clear, and it is that the immigrant presence in neighborhoods and classrooms bring the vitality and richness of their heritage to our society. In each child of immigrants, the future continues to reveal itself as we uncover, value, and support their potential. They are children, confident of society's support. It is their trusting attitude, waiting and counting on adults to help them, that also raises our consciousness about the unending call for understanding of their many realities (Suárez-Orozco and Suárez-Orozco 2002; Adair 2015). Those are the experiences and happenings embedded in each of their stories immigrant children continue writing today. Many are the challenges, but many more are the strengths that children bring. They move forward beyond challenges from society and systems not yet open to embrace their diversity. These acts of prejudice and rejection, regardless of what they are, simply deny and violate children's rights already universally recognized (Vaghri, Tessier, and Whalen 2019).

Opening a Book, Learning about Immigrant Children's Realities

Stories are just a mirror of lives.

—Anonymous

Children's literature has always served as a bridge into different realities. This time, through stories, we come to learn, explore, and gain perspectives on the lives of immigrant childhood. Some of their stories will bring us close to home, while others from afar will open our minds and hearts to the unending journey of children turned into immigrants.

Stories have the magical power to introduce children and adults to people familiar to them and also to those still to know. Through the pages in storybooks, we open a door (Sims Bishop 1990), leading us to learn and walk into the "wider world beyond" (Yokota 2009, 66). Using the power that storybooks have, this time, we open them with intention, to experience and consider the realities of immigration seen through the eyes of children. We urge you to think about those concerns that may grab your attention, and to consider the implications they have for young children and their well-being.

When meeting Hannah, the young Taiwanese girl who moved to San Francisco (California) in *Hannah is my name* (Yang 2004), we see how she manages life in a new country with a language that is not her own and where even her name is now different. Reading her story, we learn how she also eagerly awaits together with family for the "green card" that will allow her dad to work without any fear. As a window into the life of immigrant families and children, through her story, we learn about experiences reflective of those of thousands of children taking place every day.

Consciously Reading to Uncover Children's Realities

Consciously aiming to learn about immigrant children, stories give us a glimpse into their experiences. Sims Bishop (Fink 2016) firmly believed that every time we open and read a story, we open windows to a diversity of life experiences and events. With the window wide open, we explore realities sometimes unknown to us, sometimes familiar, and other times, personally experienced by us. This time, whenever we open a window, it is with the purpose of consciously, and purposely determined, to inquire and look into the lived reality of children merging into cultures distant from what is known to them. Mindfully doing so as posited earlier, stories of immigration become avenues that awaken our understanding about the existing realities of children. The storyline and illustrations, consciously read against the backdrop of children's rights (United Nations 1989) and moving beyond the words (Freire and Shor 1987), open up to reveal and demand attention to what children do, what they need, and to what is still left undone for them.

Reading the different titles of children's books addressing immigration, readers find a catalog of topics and challenges defining the experiences that are faced by immigrant children. Their stories are clearly interconnected and individually and collectively reveal the challenging experiences of immigrant children (Figure 4.2). Stories highlighted in this book are but a selection of the many titles opening the window and leading readers to delve into the narratives of immigrant children.

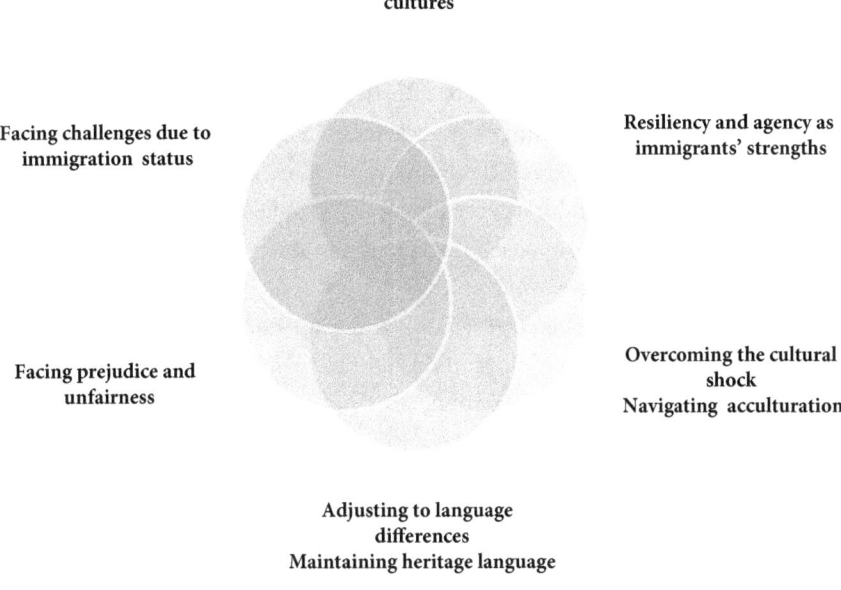

Figure 4.2 Topical areas explored through children's books about immigration.

Exploring the Experiences of Child Immigrants in the Classroom

Consideration and conscious attention to social justice realities have been a struggling issue for decades despite the efforts and work of multicultural and diversity educators. At the time of writing, recently published children's book titles noticeably have become a bridge, presenting themes and episodes reflective of a demand for more intense scrutiny of social justice issues. Brought to readers through children's literature, they are titles more directly addressing the challenges and injustices linked to human diversity. They are conveying with clarity some of the difficult topics such as exclusionary practices and challenging prejudice.

Growing up in our times has made us all more aware about the need for building a sense of social justice. Social justice begins from early childhood and happens as children have opportunities to learn and consider experiences continuing to demand attention and action. Critically and consciously reading immigration stories, one finds ways to bring into the classroom some of these topics that, mostly, were kept unaddressed. Carefully and purposely selected, they provide a source to explore with children realities continuing to happen in society with many in their own communities. Children are members of society and need to learn about circumstances continuing to call for change and justice. This, we must keep in mind as we prepare and provide children with opportunities to guide their awareness and invite their agency. Essential to sharing topics of immigration is: keeping in mind the appropriateness of a topic; the children's backgrounds and prior knowledge; and all the possible ways in which they connect with children's experiences.

In our experience, more realistic children's literature, openly addressing topics about immigration and children, is helping today to build interest for learning and delving into some of those issues of immigration many consider controversial. Stories like Danticat's *Mama's nightingale: A story of immigration and separation* (2015) and le Guen's *The refuge* (2020) shake up our conscience with their skillful use of a narrative and illustrations and uncover the difficult experiences of immigration that children continue to face. Powerful images in wordless books as Watanabe's *Migrants* (2020) convey today the multifaceted experience of immigration. The emotionality shared through the illustrations allows us to recognize that the need for honest understanding and responsive action for children cannot wait. They are stories helping us to learn about actions still needed to address and support their well-being (Comber 2014; Vasquez, Janks, and Comber 2019). They also denounce the fact that society needs to remember that children have rights to develop and become, a right that cannot be denied.

Reading Consciously and with Intentionality

Ahead in this chapter, we continue to read into the world of children growing up as immigrants. These stories allow us to connect with the realities of immigration and of children. The call is for intentionally examining, with a critical mind, what the printed words and images reveal to us. Purposely reading the stories to uncover the realities of immigration for children causes us to place our eyes on the constructs and ideas that define and identify them as immigrants. It also leads us to consider experiences that deny children what is socially just and owed to them. The call for critically examining what the narratives uncover loudly resounds for everyone, but especially for educators who pursue fairness for the children they teach (Matteson and Boyd 2017). As experiences are discussed, we invite you to consider,

- *what these imply for a child's well-being*
- *what they represent in terms of their rights as children*
- *what the stories allow us to learn about the lives of immigrant children in our own communities.*

Growing Up and Blending Cultures Together

Immigration is an experience of many cultural dimensions. It is especially for children as they embark on a developmental journey across cultures, their own and that of the places they live. When we read *I love Saturdays and domingos* (Ada 2004), with a group of college students, their reactions led to a lively discussion. Many shared their own experiences growing up as immigrants, some talked about those of peers and their families coming from so many different places. The conversation led us to highlight the unique way children have to navigate through cultures and adapting just like the young girl in Ada's story. Like so many other immigrant children, the young girl in the story represents the growing number of immigrant children born in the countries where one of their parents is an immigrant, bringing two cultures together. The character in this story represents one of the realities of immigration for children, crossing cultural borders and blending cultures as they grow up and develop. They cross and blend cultures and languages with ease as they adapt to their realities living as immigrants in a context that is both culturally and linguistically different.

Growing up in settings prompting them to become bicultural is perhaps one of the experiences and challenges facing children of immigrants. Researchers consider that a bicultural person is one who feels comfortable and appropriately responds to living and interacting in two different cultures (Schwartz and Unger 2010; Safa, White, and Knight 2020). It is, too, one where their resilient capacity to overcome challenges defines their incredible ability to grow up strong. Their ability to adjust and blend linguistic and cultural differences tells us about the remarkable resilient response of a child, capable of managing differences and emerging with the abilities to function across diversity lines. Early childhood years are a time when children more readily learn languages. This developmental fact contributes to their adjusting to life in new environments. In fact, scholars have posited that the ability to become bicultural can be considered as a protective factor, providing the individual with ways to manage, navigate, and ameliorate the impact of stressors emerging from crossing cultures (Bacallao and Smokoswki 2005; Safa, White, and Knight 2020).

Learning another Language, an Emotional Experience

Several children's book authors have addressed the issue of language. In some stories they have portrayed how the child's ability to acquire a new language bridges their adjustment, easing their stress and making them feel more emotionally comfortable. One of these is Aliki's *Marianthe's story: Painted words/Spoken words* (1998), where readers meet the young girl recently arrived from another country and who speaks a different language. The story, written in two parts, allows readers to learn about the girl's trying experience while she acquires the language of the place where she now lives. Resolving to paint to share her feelings and experiences, Aliki reveals to us how the young girl begins to break the language barrier in *Painted words*, the first section of the story. Her clever decision brings to attention the need for communication to express her feelings and share her own experiences. It highlights the vital role of language that gives children a voice of their own.

The fear of losing one's heritage language is one of the stressors facing immigrants as they adjust to another culture (Toppelberg and Collins 2010). Still demanding understanding and support, it particularly brings attention to recognizing that children have a right to maintain their first language while acquiring a new one. Some children's books have brought the language challenge to attention, unpacking its emotional impact on children. In *My two blankets* (2014), author Irena Kobald uses blankets as a metaphor to describe the powerful role language plays for an individual. In this case, it is a young girl, forced by conflict to escape her homeland, coming to live in a place where as she says, "Nobody spoke like I did" (n.p.). Through her own words, we learn she felt her language was like a blanket that made her feel safe. A powerful statement, it underlines the role of language and how it provides a sense of safety for their speakers. The mother tongue, where our heritage is captured, continues to be a powerful factor in defining and contributing to an individual's own sense of identity (Moll et al. 1992; Esteban and Moll 2014). Entering other cultural and linguistically diverse environs, language remains as one of the elements continuing to link you to your roots. It is also what provides people with a sense of identity, conveying who they are. Through the story, Kobald

---

Thinking and Reflecting ... Language, My Voice

One of the first challenges for immigrants is finding themselves in places where the language spoken is different from their own. This is a huge challenge. Consider what you would do to convey to children that their language and their voice is welcomed. What would be your message to children who may find themselves learning a new language?

shows us how relationships and finding one self to be welcomed can ease the struggle and lead to feeling comfortable in acquiring another language. Using the metaphor of a blanket to represent language, we experience together with the young refugee how her relationship with a young girl, who offers her friendship, leads to finding herself now having not one but another blanket. She now finds her new blanket as she learns the language of the place where she now lives.

It's a Challenge! Consciously Understanding the Language Challenge for Children

On many occassions, learning another language becomes a struggle for children, especially when they cannot understand why they need to learn a new one. Sometimes, it is due to their own fears of losing who they are. In Levine's story, *I hate English* (1989), we see how the main character, is reluctant to learn another language, revealing her uneasiness now that she is in a different country. We see how her response changes as she realizes that she can keep her own language while acquiring a new one. Her teacher, who wisely understands the child's concern, is the key to her change and helps her understand that acquiring a new language enhances her experience. Levine's story powerfully shows how the intervention of an understanding and conscientious educator, who understands the struggle of the young Chinese girl, sympathetically responds, dispelling her fears.

Growing up between languages, immigrant children find themselves living and crossing invisible linguistic boundaries. These are the boundaries that delimit their family and home realities where their heritage language continues tying them to their culture. Stepping into their communities and schools, they again cross into another linguistic reality where they eventually become speakers of the language spoken by the mainstream group of the places where they now live. Pat Mora takes us to palpably experience these invisible linguistic boundaries in *The rainbow tulip* (1999), where we meet Estelita, a young immigrant Mexican girl. While she and her brothers speak English, at home, it is Spanish that her parents speak. Two different worlds, linguistically and culturally are being crossed all the time. Even her name reveals how she crosses that invisible boundary: at home her parents call her Estelita, while at school she is Stella. Mora allows us to go even deeper into the implications of language differences. Through the story, we learn about Estelita's social and emotional struggle that reveals to us how the young girl wishes her parents would learn English to avoid being different. "I wish my mother would learn

English" (n.p.), we hear her say. The dichotomy of two languages and two worlds are clearly reflective of the struggle of many young immigrants who, similarly, may find themselves crossing boundaries invisible to others but clearly present to them.

Resilient and Resourceful

Captured through children's stories of immigration, the topics addressed describe the different challenges immigrant children continue to face. Clearly conveyed, through the storylines we see two salient traits. It is their resiliency and agency that emerge as central traits describing how they navigate cultural and societal challenges. It also showcases how children of immigrants, arrived from other countries or born in the nation they live, emerge strongly to defy constraints to their own development and well-being. We recognize the resilient character of immigrant children while reading *I was dreaming to come to America* (Lawlor 1995), a book taking us back to learn about the many young children who came as immigrants during the early part of the twentieth century. Their resilient voices talk about their aspirations where we have a glimpse into what has continued to define young immigrants. We also see their determined and resilient spirit in the characters from stories like *La frontera/El viaje con papá/My journey with Papa* (Mills and Alva 2018), where we hear children's voices from real stories still repeating themselves in present time.

Resiliency continues to be conveyed every time we read, learn, and interact with immigrant children. Considered as the human capacity to face and experience challenges and yet to be able to strongly emerge from these (Sorrels 2015; UNICEF 2017), resiliency fittingly defines young immigrants. Evidenced in many of the stories of immigration, this is a quality identified by researchers who highlight their resiliency as a factor describing children (OECD 2018; Gatt et al. 2020).

Biculturalism and Children's Agency

Children's bicultural capacity, in many ways, also propels their sense of agency. This capacity, even during their early childhood years, becomes instrumental for parents and adults in the family, particularly for those struggling with cultural differences and with languages different from those of the receiving culture. Children's assistance becomes a fundamental asset for the family as they help parents, relatives, and others to navigate life experiences in the cultures of the countries where they now live. The child's bicultural ability enhances his/her role played as a family member where helping becomes more "a norm" (Katz 2014, 2) and role expectation for children. Conversations with many adults who came as children or who were born in the places where their families settled reveal an array of memories about the many times they helped their families. Able to speak the language of their host culture and familiarized with the culture of their community, many assumed important roles helping their families.

Children's agency is showcased in many different ways. Sometimes their agentic power is evidenced through specific tasks carried out to support their families; other times it can be observed as emotional interventions. We find examples about children's agency in many stories. Some of those, specific to immigration, are discussed in this section.

The challenge of language diversity is one faced by many immigrants as they cross not only geographical but also cultural borders. In Stanek's book, *I speak English for my Mom* (1989), we meet Lupe, a young immigrant girl, who becomes her mother's interpreter. Her ability to speak both English and Spanish is shown as an element that empowered her to help and support her mother who struggles not being able to speak the language of the place where they now live. Her actions serve as encouragement for her mother, whom we learn is motivated to build her language proficiency

In Ada's story, *I love Saturdays and domingos*, we see how the young girl enjoys her two grandmothers, each one from a different culture and language. This time, we learn how the young girl's agency contributes to building relationships with her parent's families. Her disposition and feelings toward her grandmothers show how she manages to connect both families. This becomes evident as we see how she enjoys spending time with both grandmothers, crossing language and cultural borders and learning what they each share.

When we meet Francisco, the young boy who accompanies his grandfather to find work in Bunting's *A day's work* (1994), we come across another example of children's agency. Aware that his grandfather does not speak English, the young boy is determined to serve as his interpreter. His story echoes the role that thousands of children continue to play today. In an interview with an educator who arrived as a toddler to the United States, she revealed how for years, she used to accompany her father and translate whenever he had any appointments (Robles-Melendez and Driscoll 2020), a practice that is not uncommon especially when the child is the only one who speaks the language. Language brokering, where the child serves as an agent to translate and communicate

(Tse 1995; Bauer 2015), remains as one of the many roles displaying immigrant children's agency.

Navigating Realities with Resilient Determination

Through the years, we have learned and felt great admiration for the many accomplishments of immigrant families and children. They are a living example of their determination to succeed despite the challenges. Beyond the nature of their arrival into other lands, their saga begins with their decisions to leave, embarking on a journey of changes, challenges, and adjustments, as they pursue and become part of a new reality. Resiliency is perhaps what best describes the multiple stories continuously being learned about immigrant children in places near and far and in our classrooms and communities. Whether shown by their capacity to face challenges emerging from different cultural frameworks, or from prejudice and misleading realities, accounts about children's experiences remain as lessons to everyone, describing their tenacity to face changes and even adversity (Garza, Reyes and Trueba 2004).

Real Stories Share about Children's Resiliency

Amid the disparate realities that many may encounter, the resilient disposition is revealed in multiple stories about young child immigrants, some autobiographical and others based on real lived experiences of children. The experience of leaving and crossing borders, the difficulties faced, and their open determination demand attention and considerations to ensure their well-being. The experiences in these stories allow us to learn about the realities of those who came across borders during their childhood. Their accounts provide an important lens into their personal experiences. They are a living document illustrating the immigration journey through their children's eyes.

Inspired by their own experiences as immigrant children, several authors have given voice to the events they lived in stories that bring us closer to understanding the drama and challenge of immigration for children. Some of those whose stories are discussed in this book are listed in Table 4.1. Among the stories authored by immigrants, we find *La mariposa* (Jiménez 1998), who tells us about the author's own trajectory growing up as an immigrant child and coming to live in the United States. The story of Jiménez, who migrated with his family, reflects his experiences at school, in a classroom where the language was still unknown to him and where Author Muo Thin Van shares her experiences as

Table 4.1 Selected Children's Books about Immigration by Authors Who Arrived as Child Immigrants

Stories of immigration: Through the eyes of child immigrants		
Title	Author	Where they migrated from
La mariposa	Francisco Jimenez	Latin America
Wishes	Muo Thin Van	Asia
Hannah is my name	Belle Yang	From Korea to the US
La frontera. El viaje con papá-My journey with Papa	Alfredo Silva	Coming from Mexico into the US
The long road	Luis Garay	Coming from Nicaragua to Canada
Areli is a dreamer: A true story of Areli Morales, a DACA* recipient	Areli Morales	Arriving from Mexico as a child into the US

*Deferred action for childhood arrival (DACA) is the term used to describe immigrants who arrived undocumented in the US during their childhood. It protects eligible immigrants from deportation (Anti-Defamation League 2022)

a refugee in her book *Wishes* (2021). Through its pages, we relive her memories leaving Vietnam in a frail boat but strong with the hopeful aspirations of the families it carried. Images capture the sorrow and painful moments as they leave behind loved ones and the place they had called home. Visually conveying the danger and uncertainty of their voyage, this story echoes difficult moments continuing to happen today. These stories are also examples of the resilient and determined spirit of families, risking all for the sake of a future for their children. They are, as well, a testament to the resilient behaviors displayed by young immigrant children finding themselves in another land, culture, and many in a place where the language was different, too.

For Their Well-Being

> ... to ensure the child such protection and care as is necessary for his or her well-being
>
> —Convention on the Rights of the Child (1989)

Children's well-being and future are what drives the efforts of educators and society. Society must remember that they have a right to find the supports needed for their successful development. The United Nations declared in its CRC that society is responsible for making decisions that are in children's best interests and reminded us that they have a right to live in the "best way

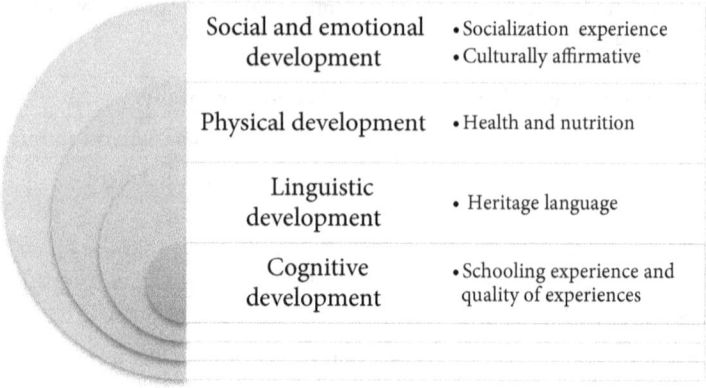

Figure 4.3 Children's Well-Being: A conglomerate of experiences to support their needs.

Thinking and Reflecting ... Meeting Children's Well-Being

Every day, we learn about children's needs, all necessary to ensure their well-being. A child's well-being is ensured when the needs across the developmental spectrum are culturally considered and responsibly met. Take a moment to reflect on the supports available in your community to address children's needs.

---

possible" (Principle #6). These two are vital considerations asserting the need for supporting and addressing their well-being. A child's well-being is constructed as we provide attention across developmental domains (Figure 4.3). Efforts to support and provide for their well-being are anchored in their rights as children and in the conscious determination to pave their childhood experience with what is fundamental to their success. There are no excuses for what children need and efforts toward reaching equity remain with society.

A Need to Know Their Experiences

Knowing their needs and especially their lived experiences (Rogoff, Dahl, and Callanan 2018) is vital if we are to responsibly provide what children need. Getting to know them and their realities is at the core of any efforts on their behalf. Reading about the experiences of immigrant children shared through the many stories gathered in children's literature, we see a reflection of the realities continuing to happen every day in our communities and across society. In the opening to this chapter, we learned about the sadness of the young girl who brought the book to share in her class. The feelings she shares about her own grandmother, whom she can no longer be with, reminds us about the magnitude of the experience of immigration and how it may influence a child's life (Garcia-Coll 2012; Crosnoe 2013; Adair 2015). Her grief may make some of us remember similar experiences. The book she brought to her classroom, *Nonni's moon*, uncovered her sentiments and revealed the young girl's feelings of sadness now that she was away from her grandmother. Reflecting on the vignette, we realize that it made us conscious about the many emotional episodes that children experience becoming and living as immigrants. How these experiences impact their own well-being continues a concern driving actions and calling for responsive attention.

Their Experiences Are a Call for Support and Attention

In every story we read, we find a reflection of life accounts happening all the time. In the powerful images of *Wishes* (2021), we are reminded about the continuing challenge of those pushed to leave and particularly about the circumstances defining their journey. Some take us to experience immigrant lives as they settle in the places they now call home. With young Hannah in *Hannah is my name* (Yang 2004), we look into the challenges of a child eagerly waiting for her parents to receive their official US residency papers or "green card," officially legalizing their life as immigrants. We also become mindful about their struggle trying to adjust to a new life reality and culture and how they manage to navigate among cultures.

Beyond the ongoing controversy about immigrants, we must bear in mind that immigration is a reality continuing to take shape as people, young and old, experience life in societies where they came to build new roots. How well do we know who immigrant children are and what they experience continue as questions challenging educators and advocates. Reading the stories that we selected gives us perspectives as we go beyond just reading the words and connecting the narrative with the context and reality of immigrant children (Freire 1985; Shor 1987). As we do, we find ways to guide our focus on the world of immigrant children that stories in children's books reveal.

> ### Thinking and Reflecting ... Reading the World
>
> For Freire, reading was a way not just to decode the words but to also learn and "read" about the realities in our world. Stories have the power to provide ways to become more conscious about the realities happening in society. We invite you to take a moment to consider stories that gave you new perspectives about children and their families. Share the name of one that has been instrumental in helping you learn about situations in the world.

Building Consciousness: Every Child Has Rights

When we read Nicola Davies' book *Every child a song* (2019), we clearly heard the call to remember the unique and special promise that we see in every child. Powerfully using song as a metaphor to represent children, she calls on everyone to consciously recognize the rights that every child has. In her words, she calls everyone to consider the needs of children and summons society to remember that "No song should be drowned out ... every song must be heard above the noise and chaos of the world" (n.p.) and that the future and well-being of a child is paramount. Davies' words resound especially as one considers the challenges continuing to face children and families of immigration.

For educators of children and advocates of children, one of the continuing premises still in need of emphasis is that every child has rights. This is at the center of any efforts to support and advocate for their well-being. This fact is also central in becoming conscious about the needs and efforts needed to support immigrant children. Understanding the significance of childhood is a fundamental step in recognizing that their rights as children transcend cultures and borders (United Nations 1989). Now, over thirty years since the landmark Convention of the Rights of the Child, today's events in many societies continue to overlook the fact that children have rights inalienable to them. Conscious efforts to understand children's needs begin when we are mindful about the aspirations and hopes children have. We are challenged to bring justice to society and honor the rights that children have (Jones and Walker 2011). "This is the century of children's rights" (Wall 2017, 4), declares author John Wall, challenging everyone to make sure that it becomes the defining trait of the times in which we live. Immigrant children are hopeful. They trust society that their rights will be recognized. Their innocent trust

> **Thinking and Reflecting** ... Rights of Every Child
>
> Every child has rights is the message from the United Nations' Convention on the Rights of the Child. Several children's books have addressed its meaning. One of these is Alain Serres' book *I have the right to be a child* (2012), where the title itself placed the emphasis on the fact that a child has the right precisely to be a child. Take a moment to consider the rights of children that society frequently ignores. What should be done to bring attention on them?

and faith in society must guide us to actions for their successful and equitable childhood. "There can be no keener revelation of a society's soul than the way in which it treats its children" was once said by freedom and human rights champion Nelson Mandela. His words continue to resonate today as we strive to ensure attention and respect for the right that children have to a successful development and life.

Building Our Consciousness Needs Intentionality

In a society that today continues to strive toward social justice, where the recent decade has brought forward the untold experiences of so many, the call for consciousness about the social inequities is heard loud and clear. Embodying the call from many that for years have demanded attention to the needs of children, the present decade is pressed to act with social justice. This is what we read about the world when we read the stories and headlines and when we listen to the demands from movements like Black Lives Matter and that of the immigrant "dreamers,"[1] voicing both the need for fairness and for socially just support. We are touched by the events and happenings and realize how our consciousness about existing inequities must be intentional.

Society itself is now calling for attention to what is justifiably owed to everyone. Becoming conscious about the stories taking shape and written by young immigrant children is today essential and necessary. It begins with intentional attention from everyone joining to end disparities experienced by children who are immigrants. It is especially relevant if we are to vanish the spectrum of inequities continuing to cloud the opportunities and experiences of children (Magnuson and Waldfogel 2005; Robles-Melendez and Driscoll 2020).

> ### Consciously Considering … Intentional Efforts Make Meaningful Experiences for a child
>
> Every time we read a story, our consciousness builds up about the ongoing experiences immigrant children face. Some are universally shared, as part of their development, and others are challenged because of their distinct heritage, while growing up in culturally different communities. We also learn about the impactful presence and actions from educators who understand and value each child and whose work opens doors to their success.
>
> Reading *Cleversticks* (Ashley 1992), we recognize the teacher's responsive way to the young Asian child who is challenged with tasks different from those in his culture. Intentionally wanting to make him feel successful and proud, she recognizes his skillful use of chopsticks, which also honored his culture. Gaining the attention and admiration of his peers, the message that he also mattered and was important clearly made the child feel he belonged. Finding those moments to make a child feel welcomed needs our determined and intentional action.

Demands for social justice resound across society and particularly in early childhood education where we are called to know children and their experiences to effectively provide for their individual developmental needs (NAEYC 2019). The request is also to understand and recognize their identity, culturally and individually. Efforts continue demanding attention to practices that acknowledge the unique heritage and culture of children and families. As society moves on, it is imperative to open our hearts to understand that children's diversity is to be appreciated, not to be eroded or denied.

In each of us lies the power to make a difference, reminded archbishop Desmond Tutu (UNICEF 1989) exhorting us to remember that children's rights must be protected. Addressing the needs of immigrant children in the United States, Takanishi (2004) reminded us that the challenges faced by many immigrant children "violated the American value of equality of opportunity" (p. 62) and called for levelling their opportunities for successful development. Similarly, there is an urgent call for attention to the needs of immigrant children in every part of the world. Their realities are multiple and, yet, they are the same. They are children waiting and expecting society to responsibly respond with support for them to develop. Stories have brought

> **Thinking and Reflecting ... Children Have a Right to Their Identity**
>
> The rights of a child are inalienable and, yet, they still need to be reaffirmed. According to the United Nations, Convention of the rights of the child, one of those fundamental rights is to recognize their identity (Right #9). Consider the right to an identity and share your thoughts about ways to support immigrant children's identity in your community and classrooms.

us to meet some of them, like Lubna, the young refugee girl in *Lubna and pebble* (Meddour 2019), living in a tent city. Her story is a reminder about the thousands of children who at the time that we write still wait to find a place to call home. With children waiting to find safety and peace, society continues to witness the forced migration of thousands of children. They are victims of multiple conflicts that threaten their equal opportunities and a childhood filled with promise. Equality, the core of social justice goals, is also what is at the heart of the Convention of the Rights of the Child as an aspiration for every child.

The Need Continues for More than Just Awareness

The number of immigrant children across the globe continues to increase, as circumstances attract or force families to leave their homelands. Many who were born to immigrant families are also counted and added to the mosaic of immigrant children throughout society. Their young faces, representing the dreams of their families, are hopeful with the illusion and innocence of childhood (Yohani and Larsen 2009). Their stories as immigrants are written every day. Young immigrant children are the seed of change and progress in every society (Peri 2013). Multiple situations, from a pandemic, climate, economic insecurity to violence and war conflict, are still challenging families. Becoming clearly mindful about who immigrant children are is critical, and demands everyone's attention. The calls for equity and social justice remind everyone that, as knowledge about children deepens, our ability to respond and provide for what holistically a child deserves and needs, increases (NAEYC 2019). It is reinforced with the determination to affirm what is rightfully owed

> ## Consciously considering .... *Children and Immigration: They Are a Global Reality*
>
> The faces of young children, depictive of a growing emerging ethnic presence, are today familiar to most. The growing number of children who are immigrants are an integral reality everywhere throughout the world (UNICEF 2021). Estimates in the early part of 2022 considered that among the world immigrants, children continue to be a significant part of those crossing borders for a multitude of reasons.
>
> The increased presence of immigrants in schools is today observed throughout the world. Their presence is a reflection of the increasing human migration taking place globally. Just in the United States, it is estimated that over 26 percent of students are of immigrant backgrounds (Migration Data Portal 2021). Reports revealed that in 2017, one in every four children in the United States was of immigrant backgrounds (Urban Institute 2019). No less different is the experience in other world regions where immigrant families with children continue to arrive. UNICEF (2021) reported that 30 percent of refugee children arriving in 2020 with their families into the European countries of Greece, Bulgaria, and Malta were aged between zero to four years, a reality revealing the emerging trend of an immigrant childhood growing up in this Western continent. Some hopeful for a better life and others challenged by difficult circumstances, migration of families and children continue to drive countless people to other places. According to UNICEF, the need for attention to their realities remains urgent. This is particularly relevant if we are to ensure that actions are taken based on what is in the best interests of children, the basic principle from the Convention for the Rights of the Child (UN 1989). Clearly, what is important is consideration for the well-being of children that they justly deserve. The call is for everyone to make children's needs and future a priority.

to every child. This is where the principle of "in the best interest" of the child, calls society to responsibly act on their behalf.

The Unfolding Story of Children of Immigration

Multiple stories continue to be written every day about immigration as children of immigrants grow and develop in communities and classrooms everywhere. Their stories continue to inspire authors of children's literature wanting to share and reveal their challenges, struggles, and successes. Through their stories, we are led to go beyond and "read the world and the word" (Seely Flint et al. 2013), just as Freire urged us to do so as to build our consciousness about the existing realities they live.

Through the encounters faced every day as they grow up, children are learning what it means to be an immigrant while they develop and come across new life experiences. Some of their experiences will affirm their cultural origins and their roots as they grow as part of the nations where they live. Other experiences may prove challenging for those who face ongoing discriminatory views and behaviors toward immigrants, sadly still upheld in many places throughout the globe. Even those born to immigrant families and are citizens of the nations where they were born and live will also experience what it means to be an immigrant child. For many, their life experiences, sadly, will not be void of insensitive comments and challenges. A reality continuing to plague society, discrimination spurred from prejudiced views, is not absent from the lives of immigrants (Suárez-Orozco and Suárez-Orozco 2002; Adair 2015).

A Look into the Immigrant Child's Experiences

Communities everywhere are experiencing a changing trend as immigration continues to expand its reach everywhere. In many places, the shifting demographic character is evident as a generation of immigrant families and children are now part of their communities (U.S. Census Bureau 2021; UNICEF 2021). Beyond the already established immigrant receiving communities, nowadays, many places are attracting and becoming areas where immigrant families are gradually establishing their homes.

Children's literature has a special way to bring us face to face with serious and difficult circumstances (Lukens 2007) just as immigration continues to be for society. Continuing to traverse through the avenue provided by children's literature, this time we look into some of the experiences of immigrant children finding themselves and adjusting to life in the places where they live. What are their experiences, how does it feel to be an immigrant, and what are their challenges as they grow up as immigrants? Many of these questions have served as thematic lines for authors addressing immigration from the perspective of childhood. They provide points to jumpstart conversations and to lead children in exploring and learning more about immigrants.

Immigration Stories Reveal Children's Diversity of Experiences

Reading the stories about immigrant children, we are reminded about the continuing presence and reality of immigrant children in neighborhoods and towns. Some born in faraway places and others born right here in our communities, they are the key to a society that continues to be enriched by the heritage and knowledge of immigrants. Just like the young characters in Sibley O'Brien's story, *I'm new here* (2015), who are facing their first day in a classroom where everything is new to them, thousands encounter life in places different from their experiences and ways. Some stories will bring us to face the challenges faced by families and children separated because of their immigration status just like the children we meet in *Waiting for papá/ Esperando a papá* (Colato Lainez 2004), a reminder about the issue of entry into a country continuing to impact the integrity of family. Other stories will lead us to understand the socio-emotional side of immigration through the eyes of children feeling the nostalgia for the places left just as the young girl we meet in *The color of home* (Hoffman 2002). Hoffman's story about the young Somalian refugee also prompts us to consider the emotional toll that immigration places on children. Through Hoffman's story as well as others, one learns about the empathy and compassionate response many children find from people in the communities they now call home.

The experience of immigration remains one denoted by its many and multiple facets. In each of them, we are called to reflect on their implications for children growing up as immigrants and about the response and role of society. Reading stories with the eye placed on building our consciousness allows us to perceive the challenges faced and appraise the still existing inequities demanding action (Takanishi 2004). Once again, we are reminded that as we read the word, we read

---

Thinking and Reflecting ... Talking about Children's Experiences

Experiences of immigrant children are sometimes topics difficult to approach for many. Children's stories provide a way to begin a conversation about difficult issues, such as immigration, not only with young students but also with adults and colleagues. Consider for a moment which story or stories you would choose to address the experience of immigration from the perspective of children. Why would you select it?

the world (Freire and Macedo 1987). When our eyes and mind are awakened to realities of unfairness and of challenges to children's rights, we open our hearts to welcome changes for the sake of what every child deserves.

An Experience of Many Dimensions

Coming to live in a place that is new to us is a journey of many dimensions. Not uncommon to most, we understand the challenges posed when you come to a neighborhood for the first time. An emotionally, physically, and culturally challenging experience for adults, it is even more so for a young child. The fact that a child is in its most vulnerable stage of development makes immigration an experience with many challenging implications (Crosnoe 2006; Garcia-Coll 2012). Even when immigration is planned and voluntary, transitions and the consequent changes will affect everyone. Implicit is the fact that for those who migrate, the experience from the places and culture where they come will remain. As they consciously and unconsciously negotiate with a new cultural reality, they continue to live in both, keeping the cultural frameworks they bring with them. These frameworks give them the strength to address and deal with the culture of the places where they now live (Abubakar et al. 2012).

Moving and migrating to a different place and location remains a highly complex and multidimensional experience. Awareness of the immigration experience for a child is central to understanding their implications more fully. Becoming an immigrant is, in itself, entering into a different reality that challenges individuals as they accommodate and adapt to new realities (Gallo and Dabkowski 2018). Physically or geographically, it implies a multiplicity of changes from climate to the overall landscape, including the layout of communities. Culturally and emotionally, it represents an encounter with new paradigms and expectations many times diverging from those one knows. This is experienced by second generation children of immigrants, as well, especially for those growing up in communities known to be home for an ethnic group.

Beyond the physical nature of relocating to another place, the social and emotional attachments that tie us to where we lived and to the special relationships one leaves behind, all add to the experience of immigrants. Many authors have gathered these in stories of immigration, taking us to explore the multiple dimensions traversed by immigrant children (Figure 4.4). In conversations with elementary age children who had immigrated, they shared that it was knowing that they could not be with a special relative or family member that was harder for them.

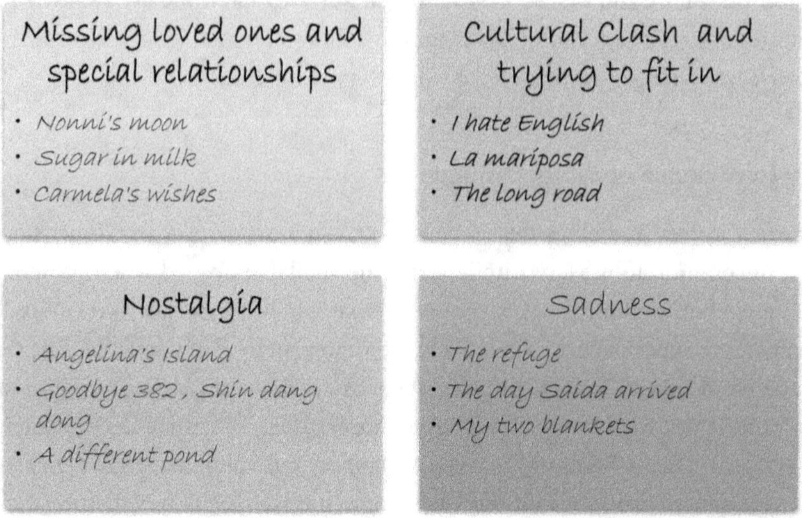

Missing loved ones and special relationships
- Nonni's moon
- Sugar in milk
- Carmela's wishes

Cultural clash and trying to fit in
- I hate English
- La mariposa
- The long road

Nostalgia
- Angelina's Island
- Goodbye 382, Shin dang dong
- A different pond

Sadness
- The refuge
- The day Saida arrived
- My two blankets

Figure 4.4 Some feelings and sentiments experienced by immigrant children: Selected Stories.

Immigration Brings a Stream of Emotional Experiences for Children

Many authors have allowed us to experience, and in some cases relive, through their narratives what children face as they start their new life in other places. Through their stories, we learn about the sentiments and distress experienced as a child tries to make sense about leaving and starting again in other places. Many authors of children's literature have purposely addressed the emotional challenges faced by children. Such is the case as we read the stories authored about immigration and children. Through them, we gain consciousness about the struggle that children experience. Unpacking these stories, reading the word to read the world (Freire and Macedo 1987), they take us to visualize the difficulties faced and how children navigate the challenges as they adapt and adjust to their new contexts.

Saying Goodbye

Leaving and saying goodbye is never an easy experience. Many of us may have struggled at some point trying to bring with us all those personal memories and recollections of our experiences and interactions. It is also for children who, just like adults, may feel they are leaving behind a part of themselves. Sometimes it may be just a toy or that special blanket that holds so many memories. Even when leaving is to seek new opportunities, one is challenged knowing that you cannot bring everything with you.

The need to remember and keep alive memories is a strong emotion shared as we follow a young girl trying to catch those special places full of happy memories. This is what we feel in Nuño's *The map of good memories* (2017), where we accompany a ten-year-old girl as she gathers all her special memories before leaving, this time, forced by war. With her, she carries belongings that are special memories—emotional, sentimental, all very personal belongings—something that no one will be able to take away from her. For her, just as for so many other children, they will be her "own place" as she rebuilds her life and relationships in a new place. Her story is a reminder about the circumstances at the moment that we write, driving families and children away from war. As the child revisits and remembers the special places she will leave behind, the emotional tone of the story conveys the harsh and dramatic episodes that are lived by thousands of children in many parts of the globe. The number of children in war zone areas amounts to thousands of millions (Liu 2017; UNICEF 2021). The 2022 war crisis in Ukraine added to the long list of factors pushing families away from their homelands. Half a million children were among the Ukrainians who escaped during the early days of the war (Moore 2022).

Many children remain in the dangerous areas where they live, while others have been able to resettle in places close and distant from the regions they know. For children who are making sense of the challenging reality of a forced migration, their needs demand conscious support and attention. It especially calls for consideration to the fact that they are children. In Chapter 6, we will address more in detail the experience of refugee children forced to leave their homelands.

Works from Francisco Jiménez immerse us in the emotional challenges experienced by Mexican immigrant children. His autobiographical work is collected through his poignant stories that transport us into the life of immigrants. In his book of stories, *The circuit (1997)*, Jiménez uncovers the varied feelings and emotions drawn from his own experience as an immigrant child. They are stories based on his own lived experiences as an immigrant arriving in California at age four with his family. His stories share the drama of children and their families who bravely make the decision to seek a better life. They also call attention to the multiple stories that are being written by children

> **Consciously Considering ... Difficult Experiences for Children**
>
> Today, countless immigrant children are in classrooms and communities everywhere. From West to East continents, immigrant children are integral to their societies, some more markedly than others, but with an undeniable presence. Their lived and living experiences are as diverse as their own cultures and roots. Many are also the different emotions and sentiments that come from immigration. In their young lives, many may have already witnessed first-hand the drama of immigration, while others, born to immigrant families, experience the conditions and responses from society toward immigrants. Feelings of excitement and anticipation together with those of loss, fear, and of anxiety are among those marking immigration and the many realities it brings to children. These are also indicators describing an experience deemed stressful and traumatic for some children (Sorrels 2015; von Werthern et al. 2018). Trauma maybe brought on by situations, experiences, context, relationships, and individual status, along with other factors. Cultural and racial diversity has been indicated by experts as one of the factors that may lead to difficult experiences (Sorrels 2015; Erdman and Colker 2020), adding to children's vulnerability.

who are becoming immigrants in society today. Through the narratives, as *La mariposa*, Jiménez also portrays the need for practices responsively anchored on the realities of the child, a fundamental principle in responding to children who need support as they navigate a different culture, language, and expectations (OECD 2015; NAEYC 2019).

My Name Is ... Feeling Proud about Who We Are

Have you ever thought about what your name means to you? What does it represent or who it honors? Our given names are one of the most individually meaningful traits that defines and gives an identity to people (Figure 4.5). They are, as well, what connect us to our family and heritage. Saying "I am ___" is not just a statement but an enunciation affirming our sense of pride about who we are. Yet, names are perhaps one of the first things many immigrants see being changed or modified as they experience life in a different culture. Some have considered that changing names is part of adopting the new

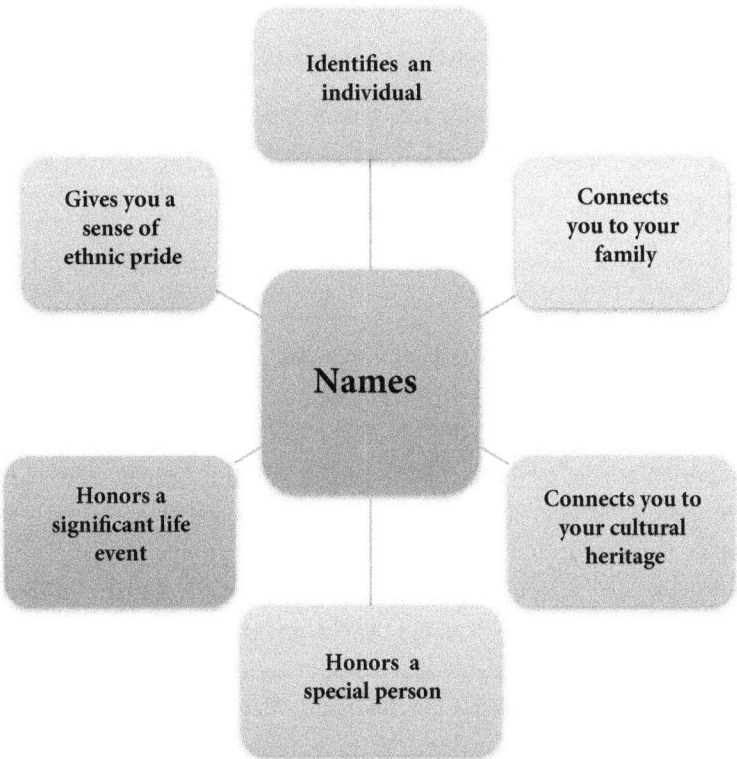

Figure 4.5 Names are more than just a name.

cultural norms, practices, and behaviors during acculturation. Some may be difficult to pronounce if they are in languages different from those one knows. Still, a person's name remains as that one descriptor giving us a sense about who we are.

In Jane Medina's *My name is Jorge on both sides of the river* (1997), the poetic narratives help us to experience the challenges faced by the boy who struggles to maintain his own identity as his name is changed from Jorge to "George." In the voice of the child, we recognize the emotional tussle as he tries to affirm who he is. Powerfully, we are reminded that a name is more than just a name. Embedded in a name is the very essence of the individual and his/her own cultural self (Robles-Meléndez and Beck 2019). Name changes are not unusual for immigrant children who often see their given names changed to suit the linguistic forms of their host country (Yang 2020). It is another event as part

> ## Thinking and Reflecting … Names!
>
> Names are one of the most distinctive ways to address an individual and are personally meaningful to people. Take a moment to consider the significance of your name to you. What do you know about its meaning or why it was given to you?

of the acculturation experience for immigrants finding themselves challenged to adjust to the expectations of the host culture where they now reside. This is, however, where we are reminded about the implications of such demands, as acculturation should never alienate or negate a child's heritage (Kurtz-Costes and Pungello 2000; Toppelberg and Collins 2010). Facing pressure, many end up accepting changes just to be accepted into their peer groups.

Embarrassed by their names being mispronounced and sometimes becoming victims of bullying, many will accept the changes all in an effort to fit into their new groups. While it may go unnoticed, responses and reactions to one's name is a difficult emotional experience for children particularly while they are forming their own social and emotional self. Various authors, as Helen Recorvits in *My name is Yoon* (2003) and Yangsook Choi in *The name jar* (2001), also explore children's struggle with their names. Thompkins-Bigelow also addressed the issue of names in her story *Your name is a song* (2020). In the story, the author celebrates the beauty of names from all different languages and reminds everyone to feel proud of one's name. Learning about their meaning and what they represent, or honor, is a way to welcome and show not only respect but also appreciation for children and their family heritage (Robles-Meléndez, Valdés, and Robles 2018).

Keeping Memories Alive of Special Relationships

The theme of relationships emerges clearly as a central experience that challenges children. In some of the stories, readers are reminded about the fragility of the emerging self as children separate from those with whom attachment has been developed (Miller, Hess, Bybee, and Goodkind 2018). Who has not felt the sadness of not being able to be close to a loved one? This is one of the emotional experiences many children encounter leaving or knowing that a loved one is far away. When we read *Nonni's moon* (Inverro 2018), we felt the longing that

Beanie, the young girl in the story felt for her grandmother as she was trying to make sense of her new life in a different country. We felt just like the children in the opening vignette to this chapter, saddened that someone they loved and felt that cared about them was so far away. Even though Beanie could still talk with her over the phone, the feelings of loss and separation were deep. This was the beginning of a new life journey for the character in the story. Her story is one very reflective of the experience of thousands of children across the world who become immigrants. Leaving behind families and friends all adds to the challenging emotions facing young immigrants. The characters from *Goodbye 382 Dang ding dong* (Park and Park 2002) and *Sugar in milk* (Umrigar 2020), both share their hesitation and emotionality as they begin a new life experience. The characters in both stories though reflecting different reasons for their migration clearly show us that the sentiments are shared by both.

Experiences Marking a Childhood

Getting to know how children experience immigration is an ongoing effort. Educators, developmentalists, and child advocates all continue to wonder about the realities experienced by children growing up as immigrants. Seeing immigration through children's eyes is a multidimensional effort, particularly because of the many diverse needs and realities defining immigrant children. Some of their experiences are difficult and point to topics many want to avoid. Regardless of the nature of their experiences, they still share experiences in common. Using the lens of what they more commonly share, in this chapter we look at some of those experiences in common, from their first impressions, reactions to the places where they come to live, friendships, language differences, to some of their family practices.

> ## Thinking and Reflecting ... Things We Miss and Remember
>
> Leaving your home and place that you knew is a huge transition for anyone. It is even more so during your childhood, especially when some of the things we love are left behind. If you were migrating, consider the things that you would find difficult to leave behind. What places would you miss? What people would you long to be with again?

First Impressions

When Maria Isabel arrived at her first-grade classroom, she found herself in a place where the language was not her own and where even her name was changed. This is what we read in Ada's (1995) story *My name is Maria Isabel*. Coming to live in a different place, just imagine the shock felt by the young nine-year-old child in Ada's story finding herself in a new place where her name, Maria Isabel, was no longer, and where she was now "Mary." Others will grieve having left their homelands, like the girl characters that we meet in *Sugar in milk* (Umrigar) and in *Goodbye, 382 Ding, Dong* (Park and Park 2015), who both lament and long for the places they used to call home. In both stories, the authors allow us to experience the feelings emerging from those first moments as one relocates in different settings. No different is the experience of children of immigrants born in the countries where their families settled as they move and encounter life in other communities.

Reading the story *The someone new* (Twisss 2018), we were reminded about the first impressions that people may have whenever a family moves into a community or those formed when a new kid is coming to our classroom. Some will welcome a new peer, while others will question why someone new is now in their classroom. Experiences of being welcomed are often paled by those from individuals who reject the presence of a new member.

Experiencing changes is a part of life. Their impact is greater during the early years. Changes, as we had previously mentioned, are always a stressful experience. They are even more so when they happen during the early childhood years. For young children, changes become milestone experiences. Coming to live in a new environment is one of those big changes as children transition into a new context. Those first impressions mark their lives. Developmentally, researchers posit that the age and developmental stage when experiences take place is an important point to consider given the impact these may have on a child's life (Ragavhan and Alexandrova 2015; Bajo Marcos, Serrano, and Fernández Garcia 2021). As children begin to process and make sense of a new place, their developmental stage and chronological age play a major role. Seeing a reality through the eyes of a preschooler versus a school-age child clearly will differ. Some people we interviewed who arrived as immigrants during their early childhood still recalled the sounds of the places where they resided. They shared that they were so different from those where they came from that they could still hear them. We also heard from some who also came as preschoolers how they still remembered being surprised by the size of the spaces where they lived. "It felt so small," one person shared remembering the apartment where they first lived, again, first impressions kept alive in his memories.

A Mixed Bag of Feelings, Not Always Welcoming

Coming to a new place is always an experience with multiple impressions for both those coming into a new place and those who already live there. Those first impressions stay forever and are markers of experiences for children of immigrants (Portes and Rivas 2011). People who spoke with us shared how those first experiences still remain alive, especially for the kindness and welcoming arms they found. Others, however, mentioned that their memories have not faded because of the many perplexing reactions and rejection they came to experience. Some of the reactions were very innocent, one person observed, that, over time, she came to realize were based on the many stereotyped ideas and fear of others that are still present in society.

Fear of the unknown is often what drives attitudes and responses of rejection toward those coming into a community. Some are likely to evade change and maintain things as they are. They are just like Jitterbug, the character in Twiss' story *The someone new* (2019), who "like it when things stayed the Same" (n.p.). Using animal characters, Twiss' storyline is reflective of the unfounded fear and rejection of immigrants experienced in many places. In this story, the author allows us to see experiences from the perspective of Jitterbug, one of the residents about the incoming arrival of "someone new." We learned that the "someone new" who is seeking a new home, was forced to leave after a storm that destroyed his home. The unwelcoming attitude of the fearful resident evokes that of many places where immigrants may find themselves being rejected. The plot guides readers to see that it is fear about the unknown and about change that drives the reaction of Jitterbug to reject the displaced visitor. Its plot and vivid illustrations bring readers to consider the experience of children and families, who similarly have felt the rejection and fearful attitudes.

Sentiments toward Immigrants

In *All are welcome* (Penfold 2018), children's diversity is celebrated and welcomed. Like other authors, Penfold's storyline is a reflection of the aspiration of a society still in search of tolerance and respect toward human diversity. The thematic line of stories celebrating diversity is also a reminder about the need for conscious consideration of efforts needed to counteract the oppositional views about immigrants. While kindness and welcoming practices continue to be experienced by many immigrants, still many are received with distrust and rejection. Sentiments opposing immigration and fear of immigrants are a continuing reality in society. Today, they are being felt every day and everywhere. From comments, gestures, and actions, to signs, and graffiti found in many places, opposition to immigrants remains as another challenge to tolerance and equity. The fact is, children are also witnessing them and becoming the victims of these, too.

Findings from a series of interviews conducted in the United States revealed that some people's concerns are rooted in their fear that immigration brings change, when the fact is that change is already defining the demographic character of places where they live (Rodriguez 2018). No different are the feelings in other places in the world where many continue to reject the idea of opening their doors to immigrants, even for those escaping from difficult and dangerous environments. Reports about boats of refugees that were denied from docking in some ports are but one of the many incidents revealing the groundless fear created about immigrants (Beitsch 2022). Unfortunately, many times sentiments of fear and concern about unknown threats are born out of longtime existing biases and stereotyped views about immigrants (Flores and Schacter 2018).

Emotions and Feelings

Feeling overwhelmed by a context and culture different from what is known is not uncommon. Similar to what people feel as they enter into new realities, for immigrants it is an experience deeply marked by sentiments, leaving long-lasting memories. What children experience calls for responsive and caring understanding that will help lessen the clash with different expectations and realities. The role of the adult is primordial, offering caring support and encouragement. That is precisely the response seen from the classroom teacher in the story *Cleversticks* (Ashley 1992), who finds a way to validate and affirm the young Asian child's sense of success and competence. Emotionally empowered, the child proudly displays his skillful way to use chopsticks. Beyond the encouragement gained from his demonstrated competence, one can see the emotional impact on the young child from the responsive actions of his teacher. Developmentally, teachers' actions play a meaningful role in promoting social development and scaffolding children's feelings of belonging in their settings (Copple and Bredekamp 2009). These interventions form part of the psychosocial anchors helping children to build their resilience as they adjust to life in new contexts (Masten and Narayan 2012).

Many accounts shared through immigration stories reveal the array of feelings and initial impressions experienced by children as they navigate life in different settings and cultures. Impressions from those first times have been the focus in numerous children's books where stories bring to life, moments reflective of real-life events for children. Their narratives highlight the clashing experiences as children moved to cultures and environments many times diametrically different from those of their own.

Nostalgia and Longing for What We Knew

Many stories allow readers to learn about the nostalgia and longing for places left behind. They share the feelings people have for a lifestyle and experiences they knew and that, in many ways, define who they are. In these stories we also find a special lens to learn about the struggles of immigration from the perspective of children as they enter and begin to negotiate life in a different context. Reading through their pages, we come to understand and gain an awareness of the major transition that moving and departing from what is known represents for a child. They are a reminder about the role and influential force of the contexts where one lives on our psychosocial being (Copple and Bredekamp 2009; Berk 2015). We are also who we are because of the relationships built in contexts and environments where we grow up and live. The cultural and social ecology of the places we call home play an undeniable role in shaping the individual and in bestowing a sense of safety and stability (Bronfenbrenner 1979; Escalera Reyes 2020).

Thinking and Reflecting ... Memories of the Places Where We Grow Up

The places where we are born and those where we grow up play a leading role in our personal, cultural, and identity development. Even though time may pass, memories of those locations are kept alive. We read in *Grandfather's journey* (1994) how author Allen Say reveals through the story character, the memories that years later still link the young man to his homeland. Children also bring many connections to the places to which they immigrate. If you were a child moving to another country, what memories would keep you tied to your place of birth? How can we honor those emotional connections in the classroom?

The feelings of loss and homesickness that children experience have been the subject in many children's stories. They bring forward the emotional impact on children as their social and cultural landscape changes. One of these stories is Park and Park's *Goodbye 382 Dan ding dong* (2002), where the narrative reveals the sentiments of a young Korean girl, who struggles trying to make sense of the place where her family has now migrated. She misses her home and place where she lived and tries to find ways to explain why they left. Her yearning is similar to that of many children who have moved in communities everywhere.

Relationships are integral to making children feel that they are important and that someone cares about them, all central to making them feel safe and that they belong. A significant protective factor, relationships are one of the forces that ease our adjustment to a new place. Missing the presence of those special people and of relationships children leave as they migrate are among the experiences most will face. The stress from the physical separation becomes an emotionally challenging experience for children especially as they try to feel they belong in a new place and reality. Inverro (2018) takes us to meet the child who misses her grandmother in *Nonnis' moon*, capturing the same sentiments that the young girl in the opening vignette to this chapter shares with her teacher and peers. Missing her grandmother, the young girl finds solace in knowing that both she and her *nonni*, grandmother, are still connected as they send messages "through the moon" (n.p.). The text reminds us about another story, *Sun kisses, moon hugs* (Shaefer Bernardo 2017). Though not specifically about immigrants, the author also shows us how to ease the sadness from being away from special people, using the magical connection of sharing love.

Umrigar's story *Sugar in milk* (2020) also takes us to meet another child, who is also saddened by being apart from her grandmother. A sense of loss emerges from the story where we see her struggle to adapt to a place she is now beginning to know. We feel along with young Angelina (*Angelina's island*, Winter 2007) who, similar to Jangmy in *Goodbye 382 Shin dang dong* (Park and Park 2007), was also making great efforts to accept where they now live. "My heart beats in two places" (Park and Park 2007, n.p.), Jangmy says, revealing she still misses her hometown where everything was known and familiar to her.

Changing Landscapes and Our Sense of Belonging

The places where we live and where we are born are more than just a place. They are part of the interconnected elements forming part of what gives us a sense of belonging. Belonging is a feeling essential for our well-being, one vital for children as they are growing up. The places where we live are part of the elements that contribute to our sense of belonging. Familiarity with the climate and the landscape of where we live all play a role in making us feel at home. It is not unusual to hear immigrants talk about how much they miss the colors of the flowers, the seasons, or the soothing sunsets of those places they once knew. These are all descriptors of the many different elements that help people to feel connected to the places where they live or came from. Studies conducted with immigrants from different countries have shown that emotional and physical bonds are built with the places where one lives giving people a sense of belonging (Herslund 2021). Researchers have also noted that our lived experiences form a "web of memories" (Peters, Stodolska, and Horolets 2016), which contribute to building connections with the places where one lives.

In *Tani's new home* (Adewumi 2020), we learn about the feelings experienced by an African child coming to live in North America and finding himself in a community different from his native Nigeria. Tani's initial reactions are a shock as he tries to build an understanding about what connects him to the place that surrounds him now. His experience is also reflective of the cultural shock similarly experienced by the young boy in *The long road* (Garay 1997). Another real-life story, Garay's story is based on the events leading a Central American young boy and his mother to North America. In the story, we learn about his first experiences finding himself in a place of cold and snowy weather. For the Central American child, the impressions from the cold weather are always remembered as we hear from the author and story protagonist.

Those physical bonds built with our environments, connecting and giving us a sense of belonging, are what are gathered through the experiences of another Central American child. Author Jorge Argüeta takes us to meet Xochitl, the young girl in *Xochitl and the flowers* (2008), who migrates with her family to the United States. Based on a true story, Xochitl misses the gardens and flowers from her hometown in El Salvador. "I miss the weekends when I sat in our garden with my mami and papi, arranging bouquets of flowers" (Argüeta 2008, n.p.), nostalgically she says to herself. Through the words and emotions of these characters, we learn how the changing environment and landscape could challenge a child. Emotionally tied to places and routines, it is difficult to adapt to places with a climate and geography different from that one knows.

What, Where, and Why: A Flurry of Questions!

Where are we now? Why are we here? Perhaps those are questions you have asked coming to a place unfamiliar to you. It is no different for children, who would probably try to find answers finding themselves in new environments. Leaving behind the place they know, as we mentioned earlier, is a critical experience for everyone. It is even more for children. A sense of belonging, a fundamental cornerstone for feelings of safety and security, is disrupted whenever one leaves familiar places and environments (Fullilove 1996; Kostelnik et al. 2012). Awareness about the social and emotional needs of children who are immigrants is essential and calls for empathy and mindful responses (Yohani and Larsen 2009; Garcia-Coll 2012; Robles-Melendez and Driscoll 2020).

Many story characters have led us to uncover the immigrant experience of children growing up in communities near and far away. Many will miss the feel of the emotional voice of children personified in characters like the young girl in Inserrro's *Nonni's moon* (2018). We learn how hard it is for children to live away from their loved ones, echoing the same sentiments that we hear from Angelina in *Angelina's island* (Winter 2007). Similar to the three characters in the story, *I'm new here* (Sibley 2015), countless immigrant children encounter a flurry of questions and experiences as they begin in a new place. Far from what they knew was home and many times in a culture and language unfamiliar to them, it is a dramatic and milestone marking experience for a child.

Author Sibley O'Brien takes us along with the story characters in *I'm new here*—Jin, Maria, and Fatimah—to witness a new reality and expectations they are yet to understand. Coming to their new classroom, this is where we hear Jin, a young boy from Asia say to himself, "Here I am confused," while Fatimah's cry reveals her feelings of loss and sadness. Their expressions clearly convey their feelings of frustration and anxiety as they try to make sense of where they are now. They are a reflection of what thousands of children continue to experience especially coming to school in a place still unfamiliar to them.

The Need to Belong

Do I belong? Feeling that you are part of a group is a major developmental milestone during the early childhood experience. Changes play an influential role in how a child builds his/her sense of emotional attachment and feelings of belonging (Kostelnik et al. 2015; Colorín Colorado 2018). Changing routines, leaving behind people and relationships special to us and saying goodbye to places known to us are all disruptive experiences that impact a child's feelings of stability. Finding oneself in a place where one has … no emotional or interpersonal connections challenges anyone especially when they are children. Immigration implies a major transition impacting those early steps leading to feelings of belonging and of being competent. Even if they are born in the countries where their parents migrated to, it will not be unusual for children to encounter the inquisitive eyes and questions of peers and adults wanting to know who they are (Toppelberg and Collins 2010; Adair 2015). Some will struggle with their feelings as they try to make sense of why they are in places unknown to them.

Coming into a different culture is an experience with many impressions and experiences that transform and impact our lives. This is what is evidenced by the characters in O'Brien's story. Many times, feelings of being "an outsider" are not uncommon as one encounters practices and behaviors different from those one knows. Those differences are what so often will make people feel, adapt, and adjust so as to fulfill the need to belong. The need to belong is considered "a fundamental human need" (Allen, De Leon, Gray, and 2021, n.p.). Simply said, we all have a need to feel that we belong, but especially children, whose need to belong is a factor that also influences their emerging sense of self and identity (Over 2016). Some of those aspects that typically are found to differ from culture to culture include language, dress codes, activities, social practices, among others. Efforts to make one feel that "you fit in" are what will make one want to change so as to be part of the group. The need to belong, is also what may explain children's behavior and responses. They want to feel that they are a part of the group, with whom they seek to build lasting relationships (Kostelnik et al. 2013; Over 2016). A major component supporting our well-being is the sense of belonging, essential of feelings of being accepted. Building and keeping bonds with peers has been posited as a leading factor in understanding a child's behavior (Over 2016; Souto-Manning, Malik, Martell, and Pión 2021). As an intrinsic social and emotional need, gaining a sense of belongingness into a group is also what challenges immigrant children as they navigate a new culture, negotiating and making sense of new social expectations. This is what takes place as children go through the acculturation experience while also learning their own heritage culture.

Experiencing Acculturation

Living and growing up in a different culture adds to the challenge and experiences of immigrant children. Unquestionably, age is a factor influencing their cultural learning experiences (Berry 2005; Pumariega, Rothe and Pumariega 2005). Wanting to belong, and trying to avoid feeling like a stranger, is what may drive children to reject some of their own cultural practices. In Wong's *Apple pie fourth of July* (2006), we learn about one of those instances. In her story, we meet a young Asian girl who wonders why her family cannot adjust to what is customary to celebrate a holiday where they live now. Wanting to belong is also addressed in Lin Grace's *The ugly vegetables (2001)*. The story takes us to meet the young girl who feels embarrassed when her mother plants vegetables instead of flowers in their flower bed. In her eagerness to feel that she belonged to the community where they lived, we learn of the struggle that many experience trying to fit in. We witness in Grace's story how the young girl could not realize that what her mother was planting was keeping the family tied to their heritage.

Language is one of the characteristics that typically identifies a person as being "different." Trying to avoid being the outsider is a motivator for many immigrants to learn the language of the places where they live. For children, acquisition is propelled through interactions and experiences at both school and community. Parents' support and encouragement also play a leading role in becoming proficient. Developmentally, a child will more readily become able to learn a language, and with supports, not only that of the mainstream community but also their heritage language, as well. Support from peers is known to provide encouragement and motivation for acquisition of a new language. In Kobald's story, *My two blankets* (2015), we see how Cartwheel, a young refugee girl, is encouraged by the friendship built with a child who breaks the language barrier and becomes her friend. Though she will still find refuge in her native language, her friendship motivates her to learn the language that her friend speaks.

Finding Meaning and Becoming in a Different Place

Moving and migrating is like being uprooted and put in a place where new roots are to grow. This is what we have heard from many who have experienced immigration. Some voluntarily leave with excitement and curiosity, while others forcibly leave finding themselves on the road to places unknown and sometimes not even heard of. One thing to keep in mind is the fact that for young children, immigration is not a voluntary decision but rather one that is made by their families (Guarnacia and Lopez 1998). Changing locations remains an experience continuing to be explored as scholars seek to understand its meaning and impact on children's wellbeing. The increasing number of immigrant children and families continues to demand closer attention to their experiences if we are to better respond and address their needs (Toppelberg and Collins 2010; Organization for Economic Co-operation and Development [OECD] 2015; UNICEF 2021).

Factors Influencing Children's Move to New Places

A spectrum of factors is known to influence a child's immigration experience. These are known to be varied and dependent on the individual experience and reasons that made their families leave their countries. Some factors are commonly known to be shared among the youngest immigrants. Age at time of immigration, language, and culture are among the factors known to influence immigrant children transitioning into a new place to live. The fact is that, even when immigration is a planned experience, young children will still face challenges particularly because, developmentally, they are still in a vulnerable social and emotional developmental growing time (Sheffield 2017).

Age is a factor that may influence how a child processes the experience of immigration. Indeed, for older preschoolers and primary-age children, the difference encountered when transitioning *into a different* location become more noticeable to them than what those changes are for a young infant. Trying to make sense about the place to which they have moved is especially compounded whenever children are confronted with fewer similarities to what is known to them. Language and cultural routines are two of those where differences are observed.

Challenges are known to exist for children, particularly, when the language, culture, and practices of their native environments are markedly dissimilar from those where they now live (Bhugra and Becker 2005). Together, they all add to the stressors children may face. Even the climate, if it is different, will impact their feelings of fitting in a new place just as we heard from *Angelina's story* in chapter 2, who missed the sunny days of her island (Winter 2007). The fact is that as they long for those special characteristics that defined their environments, their feelings and attachment to where they came from strengthen.

Reception from their newly adopted and host countries is also a factor to consider in how children respond and process their experience coming to live in another country. Feeling welcome is always a factor impacting everyone. Many children, sadly, face unwelcomed responses. These are experiences that remain in one's memory, something that we have heard from conversations

---

Consciously Considering ... Children Experiencing Immigration

Immigration experiences vary and begin from the moment children come into a different place. The immigration experience may become a difficult one with many traumatic and unexpected stressful circumstances, marking and challenging children and their families (Pumariega and Rothe 2010). How they perceive being received in a new setting, whether school or neighborhood, is a factor that influences their experience. Researchers (Portes and Rumbaut 2001; Sheffield 2017) have indicated that for many children their

> arrival into a new environment is denoted by feelings of being an outsider and not being welcomed. Others have also pointed out that those places known to be established immigrant receiving locations will differ in how they welcome immigrants when compared to those with little or no experience. The challenge is posed for educators and child advocates to find ways to ameliorate feelings of rejection when young immigrants come into a neighborhood and classroom.
>
> Yohani and Larsen (2009) call for integrating practices directed at giving hope to immigrant children. This brings attention to a need for settings where hope transpires as a welcoming tone. Needed are also activities guided to foster a hopeful outlook for young children that can promote their adjustment to their new settings. How can we each plant a seed of hope and awaken their sense of hopefulness is the challenge for everyone who cares and looks out for children's well-being. In her book, author Thompson (2008) says that "Hope is knowing that you are loved" (n.p.). Showing and letting children know that they are loved and that someone cares is precisely what we are challenged to bring into a reality. How can we make it into the marker of a child's experiences?

with students and adults who migrated to other countries. One of our students shared that, arriving with her family when she was eleven years old, she could still remember the smiling face of the person who received them.

The Longing for Places Left Behind

In previous chapters, we heard about the longing and sadness from children personified by some story characters who found themselves transplanted into new settings. Through their stories, they convey to us some of the episodes from many faceted experiences especially as they struggle to find meaning in the contexts where they live. Listening to the young girl from Jamaica in *Angelina's Island* (Winter 2007), we feel her nostalgia as she tries to understand where she is now. Her feelings are similar to those of the girl in Umrigar's *Sugar and milk* (2020), who now lives in what she feels is a "strange country" unfamiliar to her and where she feels alone. She misses her mother and even her pet cats all left behind in the Middle Eastern country from where she came. Umrigar's story leads us to consider the emotional emptiness that may describe the feelings of many children finding themselves in settings mostly unfamiliar to them. Faced already with the experience of immigration, the longing for what they had, its stability, and where they felt they belong follows children even in cases where moving was a planned and long expected event (Park and Katsifiacas 2019).

How it feels when you are the "new child" in the neighborhood is an experience that for many is a familiar one. The looks from people, neighbors, and the inquisitive questions and comments made are something we may forever remember. Those who came as immigrants during their childhood may well know how curiosity will lead peers and adults to wonder about "the new child" in the neighborhood or in the classroom. We probably would feel just like Jangmi, the Korean young girl whom we met in *Good Bye, 382 Shin Dan Dong* (Park and Park 2002), whose first reaction upon arriving with her family to live in Massachusetts was to say to herself, "I want to go home." She echoes the reaction of so many children who just like this character feel the same way.

Moving to another place implies change – that is, as discussed earlier, transitions that impact a child's socio-emotional and cultural well-being. Talking with adults who came during their childhood to live in the United States, we heard similar remarks as those from the two characters from the stories by Winter (2007) and Park and Park (2002). "It was so hard for me that I didn't want to leave my house" was what one of them shared with us, remembering those first weeks and months after their arrival. However, with time, children adapt and adjust to their new environments where they now live.

Facing the Challenge of Immigration Status

Immigration status continues to be a controversial and difficult issue in society. While laws ruling people's entry are to be considered, decisions about the legal

---

Thinking and Reflecting ... The "New Kid" in the Neighborhood

Every day an immigrant family moves somewhere in communities throughout the world. A big transition for anyone, for children, it is a major change especially as they become the new child that lives in the neighborhood. If you ever experienced being the new kid that moved to the neighborhood, share your memories of those days. What were the feelings as you came to live in a new home and community? What made you feel welcomed?

entry of individuals and families and their children remain a contentious issue throughout the world. Arguments have ensued as greater number of immigrants continue to move across borders throughout the world (UNICEF 2021). At the time of writing, immigration issues persist as an issue stirring debates in a society where the number of immigrants continues to rise. The fact is that reasons for unofficially crossing borders have not changed, especially as violence, conflict, economic hardships, and war experienced in the first decades of the century are still driving many who are seeking a future, especially for their children (Robles-Melendez and Driscoll 2020; Robertson 2021). Despite the challenges and difficulties many face as they set out on the road to safety, freedom and, a better future continue to guide their efforts. The constant reminder of what "having papers" means for those who daringly cross borders is experienced through the characters and storylines in the children's immigration literature.

Immigration Status as a Topic in Children's Literature

As a topic, immigration status has been addressed by a number of authors of children's literature, who have shared this controversial reality from the perspective of children. Some have actually addressed it from their very own lived experiences as immigrants entering unofficially into other countries. Such is the case of Francisco Jiménez whose stories like *The circuit: Stories from the life of a migrant child* (1997) and *La mariposa* (2000), provide a window into the experience of coming across borders and living as an undocumented family. Interest in the topic of unofficial or undocumented immigration has led authors to create an avenue leading the reader to follow and learn about the many life dimensions impacted by an immigrant's status.

Crossing Borders, with Hope

The long walks, the silent hopes, and the aspirations of a childhood crossing borders, counting on the kindness and empathetic humanity, is poignantly revealed through the images and narratives of a literature of immigration. These stories convey to us, readers, children, and adults alike the hopeful hearts of immigrants and especially of children. Author Margriet Ruurs' touching lines in *Stepping stones* (2016) make us feel the emotions of a girl and her family escaping from danger and the hopefulness that kept them moving. They are, as the girl declares, "A river of strangers in search of a place to be free, to live and laugh, to love again … A river of people in search of peace" (n.p.).

In *Marwan's journey* (de Arias 2018), we walk along with a young boy who confesses, "I walk … and I don't know when I will get there or where I am going" (n.p.). His statements are like an unending echo we hear from those who are forcibly leaving their homes. They echo the sentiments of Rama (*Stepping stones*, Ruurs 2016), the girl who sees herself and her family forced to abandon their home and saying "goodbye to the flowers in our yard, to our goat, to the soil we called home" (n.p.). Their stories bring alive those of people crossing and of immigrant caravans journeying through the world, like those in Central America and Mexico on their way to the United States, to those sailing perilously through the Mediterranean. These events mark immigration realities still in existence today (UNICEF 2021). Some are seeking asylum, while others are taking refuge unable to return to their own homelands. The narrative and stories about refugees and asylees are explored ahead in Chapter 5.

Stories Revealing the Challenges of Immigration Status

The diversity of themes of stories addressing immigration status, reveal as a whole the overarching impact that status has on an individual regardless of age. They make the reader conscious about the many implications that status brings into the life of families and children. In particular, some authors, writing from their own experience, allow us to delve into some of those implications still taking place. Many may question the reasons why immigration status bears such stigma and pain. In times such as these, the question becomes even more poignant given the multiple cases of families leaving their homelands. They all share one thing, a common goal to escape in search for a safe place to live.

> ## **Reflecting and Thinking** … Rights of Children Cannot Be Forgotten
>
> The *Convention on the Rights of the Child* is a milestone document for childhood. It has also served as the topic for several children's books. Today, it seems that some of those responsibilities are being overlooked. How would you bring attention to the rights that children have. How would you advocate for their rights?

Among those that stand out are stories where children are protagonists, participating in different life dimensions as undocumented immigrants. For instance, some of these include stories where children are participants in coming across borders, experience family separation due to deportation, and where they are a member of a family with undocumented status. For many of them, it is their hope for their children that drives their difficult trek in spite of danger, just as the father in *Facing fear* (Williams 2021) reveals to his son: "We wanted a life where you would be safe, with enough food, no guns shooting" (n.p.). Their story is reflective of what has driven countless families to also cross borders seeking safety and a better life for their children. This is what we hear in *Dreamers* where Morales (2018) shares her hopes and wishes for her infant child. Through the narratives and actions of the characters, we also learn about the psychosocial challenges imposed on children and the courageous way in which they and their parents defy their own circumstances. It is imperative to remember the impact that the uncertainty of their immigration status has on children's relationships, education, and health (Takanishi 2004; Suárez-Orozco and Hernández 2012; Menjívar and Gómez Cervantes 2016).

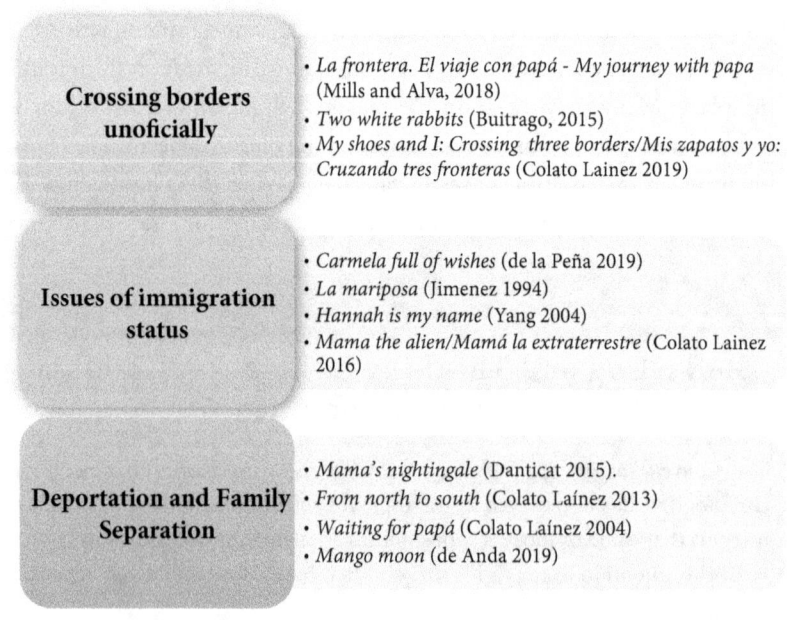

Figure 4.6 Key issues about immigration status: Selected children's books.

Family Separation, a Continuing Reality

"I wish Papá would be here with me" (Colato Laínez 2013; n.p.), we hear the eight-year-old boy say in the story *Waiting for papá/Esperando por papá*. The story opens a door into a reality impacting families who find themselves separated. Family separation, sadly, is another face of the story of immigration. Through time, decisions to migrate for many families have also brought the reality of separation. The reasons vary, with some motivated by a need for improving life's opportunities for the family. In other cases, separation occurs due to the nature of their immigration status (Figure 4.7).

A difficult decision, many times one of the family members would leave seeking opportunities for the family left behind. Repeated throughout the

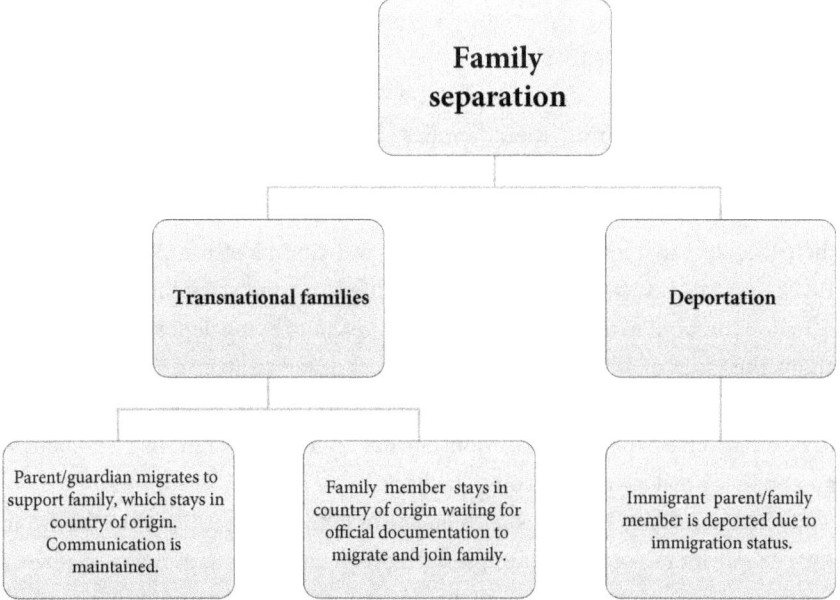

Figure 4.7 Circumstances leading to family separation.

world, it is an unending story leading to what has been called transnational families, where a parent or responsible adult migrates to another country and where family relationships are kept through their communications, whether electronically or in writing. We learn about the need to leave in Aliki's *Marianthe's story* (1998), where conditions in their "poor village" motivate her father to migrate just like others in their village. His letters are what keep the family together until they are finally able to leave "to the land far away, where Papa was waiting" (n.p.). As authors, we have heard that expression so many times from students and children who shared their long-awaited reunion with a parent or family member.

Similar to what is portrayed in Aliki's story, the need for a better life has been the driving force for immigrants through centuries, a reason still leading individuals to leave their families. Other reasons also contribute to the realities of separation, with many due to legal reasons that sometimes lead to deportation of a family member. Such is the case of the mother in From North to south (Colato Lainez, 2013).

Deportation, an Unending Family Dividing Issue

Countless children have experienced the challenges posed by the nature of their immigration status. The unofficial or undocumented entry into a country remains as a haunting experience for many, particularly given the fear of deportation. This sensitive issue has been at the center of heated discussions that continue to this date. Deportation continues as one of the reasons separating children from their families. In the United States, thousands of families continue to be separated from a parent or family member because of their immigration status. In many ways, the status of their families has impacted their life. Researchers (Dreby 2012; Zayas and Cook Heffron 2016; American Psychological Association 2019) have pointed out the stressful nature of the situation for families and children, who live in fear of being deported. Awareness about the issue of their status leads many children to live in fear of losing a parent or family member. The trauma of being forcibly separated remains today to be an adverse experience for thousands of children and families who lament and hope for that special person to be back.

Recent years have brought the challenge of family separation to the forefront, with people more aware about its presence, yet it continues as a source of adverse experiences for children because of the stressful nature of losing a parent or adult. The topic has also been addressed by various authors whose narratives provide windows into this dramatic experience for children. They have also presented separation from various perspectives, giving us an opportunity to sample some of the possible scenarios happening in real life. Their reading lends itself to present and reflect on the various social justice issues posed. It also allows us to ponder, from a child's rights perspective, how separation due to undocumented entry also impacts children and places family stability at risk.

When we meet Carmela in *Carmela's wishes* (de la Peña 2018), who celebrates her birthday, we learn how the happy and smiling young child wishes for her father to return. A cheerful young girl, we feel her sadness that she quietly keeps to herself as she is "imagining her dad getting his papers fixed so he could finally be home" (n.p.). With Carmela, we meet a story character that represents thousands of children also waiting for a parent to be back to make their families whole again. *No tiene papeles* (he doesn't have papers) is a statement heard many times in the United States and a reason why many children end up without a parent and sometimes the cause for a family member or relative to be away.

Author Colato Laínez addresses family separation in *From to north to south* (2013). Through his story, we follow what has become a routine for a young boy and his father, crossing the southern border into Mexico to visit the child's mom, who was deported. The images and text reveal to us the painful reality of separated families and of children, growing up knowing a parent or a family member is away. Enjoying their time together, the reader feels the emotion the child's mother displays as she tries to make the moments last. Danticat also lead us to experience separation, in this case, of a parent taken into custody and sent to an immigration detention center. In *Mama's nightingale: A story of immigration and separation* (Danticat 2015), we learn how the bedtime stories that her mother shares from the detention center keep the young girl hopeful and tied to her mother and culture. Similar to Colato Laínez, Danticat also describes another side of the story of separation, bringing readers to learn about the efforts to maintain a strong parent relationship despite facing their physical separation. One can sense the unbreakable bonds connecting mother and child.

We Need to Consider Children

Fear is perhaps what best describes the experience of children whose parents or a family member, because of their immigration status, are at risk of deportation. Living with the anxiety and concern of losing your parent, sadly, has become a common experience for many children, too many, in our opinion. Indisputably, laws are to be followed. Reading these stories, we read into a world's reality where immigration laws continue to separate children from their families (Pumariega and Rothe 2010). Too many are already experiencing what it means to be separated from a parent or a family member. The implications and consequences on their well-being are numerous and developmentally pose a challenge to their future. Once again, it comes to mind, the need for reminding society about what is in the best interest of the child. Reading about and revisiting the characters met and the events in stories, once more raises our attention to the impact of immigration on children and their well-being. Their fear and insecurity are an ongoing call for social justice we must hear and respond with their future in mind.

Reflecting and Beyond

1. Immigrant children are a growing presence in classrooms and communities everywhere. How is this reality reflected in your community and in the classroom?
2. Check your local library and investigate the children's books about immigration available. Are they reflective of different ethnic and cultural groups? What are some of the issues that the stories address?
3. Brainstorm and identify three key challenges immigrant children face as they come to live in a new community. Locate children's books that in your opinion address each of the challenges.
4. What are some of the emotional challenges that they may face? What efforts are available to support them? How can you assist them to overcome their experiences?

Note

1   "Dreamers" are those immigrants who came undocumented to the United States during their childhood and who grew up and call the United States home. The Deferred Action for Childhood Arrivals (DACA), an immigration policy, provides relief for the thousands of children who entered undocumented. Applications must be submitted and reviewed to officialize their status.

References

Abubakar, Amina, Fons van de Vijver, Lubna Mazrui, Josephine Arasa, and Margaret Murugugami. 2012. Ethnic identity, acculturation orientations, and psychological wellbeing among adolescents—of immigrant backgrounds in Kenya. In C. Garcia Coll (ed.). *The impact of immigration on children's development* (pp. 49–63). Basel, Switzerland: Karger.

Adair, Jennifer. 2015. The impact of immigration on the early schooling experiences of children from immigrant families. Reports. Migration Policy Institute. Washington, DC.

Allen, Kelly-Ann et al. 2021. "The need to belong: A deep dive into the origins, implications, and future of a foundational construct." *Educational Psychology Review*, 1–24: 31. doi:10.1007/s10648-021-09633-6.

Alejandro, Portes and Antonio Rivas. 2011. "The adaptation of migrant children." *Future Child* 21(1): 219–46. doi: 10.1353/foc.2011.0004. PMID: 21465862.

American Psychological Association [APA]. 2019. "Immigrant family separations must end, psychologist tells congressional panel." *Press Release*, February 7. https://www.apa.org/news/press/releases/2019/02/immigrant-family-separations.

Anti-Defamation League. 2022. *What is DACA and the dreamers?* https://www.adl.org/resources/tools-and-strategies/what-daca-and-who-are-dreamers.

Bacallao, Martica and Paul Smokowski. 2005. "Entre dos mundos" (between two worlds): Bicultural skills training with Latino immigrant families. *Journal of Primary Prevention* 26(6): 485–509.

Bajo Marcos, Eva, Immaculada Serrano and Maria Mercedes Fernandez. 2021. "The antecedents of well-being in migrant in first generation migrant children: A systematic review." *Applied Psychology. Health and Wellbeing* 13: 677–92. doi:10.1111/aphw.12282.

Bauer, Elaine. 2015. "Practising kinship care: Children as language brokers in migrant families." *Norwegian Centre for Child Research* 23(1): 22–36.

Beitsch, Rebecca. 2022. UN alarmed by increasing violence against refugee in Europe. *The Hill*. https://thehill.com/policy/international/595166-un-alarmed-by-increasing-violence-against-refugees-in-europe.

Benet-Martínez, Veronica, Jansin Leu, Fiona Lee, and Michael Morris. 2002. Negotiating biculturalism: Cultural frame switching in biculturals with oppositional versus compatible cultural dentities. *Journal of Cross-Cultural Psychology* 33: 492–516.

Berry, John. 2005. Acculturation: Living successfully in two cultures. International Journal of Intercultural relations, 29(6), 697–712.

Berk, Laura. 2015. *Child development*. Massachusetts: Pearson.

Bhugra, Dinesh and Mathew Becker. 2005. "Migration, cultural bereavement and cultural identity." *World psychiatry: Official journal of the World Psychiatric Association* 4(1): 18–24. https://www.ncbi.nlm.nih.gov/pmc/articles/PMC1414713/.

Bishop, Rudine. 1990. "Mirros, windows and sliding glass doors." *Perspectives* 6(3): ix–xi.

Bronfenbrenner, Uri. 1979. *The ecology of human development: Experiments by nature and by desugn*. MA: Harward University Press.

Colorín Colorado. 2018. How to provide social-emotional support for immigrant students. https://www.coloringcolorado.org/immigration/guide/student/.

Comber, Barbara. 2014. "Critical literacy and social justice." *Journal of Adolescent & Adult Literacy* 58(5): 362–7.

Copple, Carol and Susan Bredekamp. 2009. *Developmentally appropriate practice in early childhood programs serving children from birth to age 8* (3rd edition). Washington, DC: National Association for the Education of Young Children.

Crosnoe, Robert. 2006. "Health and the education of children from racial/ethnic minority and immigrant families." *Journal of Health and Social Behavior* 47(1): 77–93. doi: 10.1177/002214650604700106. PMID: 16583777.

Derman-Sparks, Louise and Julie Olsen. 2021. "Teaching about identity, racism, and fairness. Engaging young children in antibias education." *American Educator* 44(4): 35–40.

Dreby, J. 2012. "The burden of deportation on children in Mexican immigrant families." *Journal of Marriage and the Family* 74: 829–45.

Erdman, Sarah and Laura Colker. 2020. *Trauma and young children. Teaching strategies to support and empower*. Washington, DC: National Association for the Education of Young Children.

Escalera Reyes, Javier. 2020. "Place attachment, feeling of belonging and collective identity in socio-ecological systems: Study case of Pegalajar (Andalusia-Spain)." *Sustainability* 12: 3388. sustainability-12-03388.pdf.

Esteban-Guitart, Moisés and Luis Moll. 2014. Funds of identity: A new concept on the funds of knowledge approach. Culture and Psychology, 20(1): 31–48.

Fink, Lisa. 2016. "Windows, mirrors, and sliding doors." *NCTE Blog*. National Council for Teachers of English. https://ncte.org/blog/2016/02/windows-mirrors-sliding-doors/.

Flint, Seely, Teri Holbrook Amy, Laura May, Peggy Albers, and Caitlin McMunn Dooley. 2013. "Reading the world to read the word." *Language Arts* 90(6): 399–401.

Flores, René and Ariela Schachter. 2018. "Who are the 'Illegals'? The social construction of illegality in the United States." *American Sociological Review* 83(5): 839–68. doi: 10.1177/0003122418794635.

Freire, Paulo. 1985. "Reading the world and reading the word: An interview with Paulo Freire." *Language Arts* 62(1): 15–21.

Freire, Paulo and Donaldo Macedo. 1987. *Literacy: Reading the word and the world*. CT: Praeger.

Fullilove, M. T. 1996. Psychiatric implications of displacement: Contributions from the psychology of place. *American Journal of Psychiatry* 153(12): 1516–23.

Gallo, Sarah and Meghan Dabkowski. 2018. "The permanence of departure: Young Mexican immigrant students negotiations of imagined childhood *allá*." *Linguistics and Education* 45: 92–100.

Garcia-Coll. 2012. *The impact of immigration on children's development*. Basel: Karger.

Garza, Pedro, Encarnacion Reyes and Enrique Trueba. Resiliency and success: Migrant children in the Unitd States. London/NY. Routlege.

Gatt, Justine, Rebecca Alexander, Alan Emond, Kim Foster, Kritin Hadfield, Amanda Mason-Jones, Steve Reid, Linda Theron, Michael Ungar, Trecia Wouldes, and

Qiaobing Wu. 2020 Trauma, resilience, and mental health in migrant and non-migrant youth: An international cross-sectional study across six countries. *Frontiers in Psychiatry* 10: 997. doi: 10.3389/fpsyt.2019.00997.

González, Norma, Luis Moll and Cathi Amanti. 2005. *Funds of knowledge. Theorizing practices in households, classrooms and communities*. NY: Routledge.

Guarnaccia, Peter and S. Lopez. 1998. "The mental health and adjustment of immigrant and refugee children." *Child Adolescent Psychiatry Clinical N Am* 7(3): 537–53, viii–ix. PMID: 9894054.

Herslund, Lise. 2021. "Everyday life as a refugee in a rural setting—What determines a sense of belonging and what role can the local community play in generating it?" *Journal of Rural Studies* 82: 233–41.

Ikia, Yuko. 2015. "Using multicultural children's literature to teach diverse perspectives." *Kappa Delta Pi Record* 51(2): 81–6.

Jones, Phil and Gary Walker. 2011. *Children's rights in practice*. Los Angeles, CA: Sage.

Katz, Vikki. 2014. *Kids in the middle: How children of immigrants negotiate community interactions for their families*. NJ: Rutgers University.

Kostelnik, Marjorie, Kara Murphy Gregory, Anne Soderman, and Alice Whiren. 2012. *Guiding children's social development and learning* (7th edition). CA: Wadsworth Cengage.

Kurtz-Costes, Beth and Elizabeth Pungello. 2000. "Acculturation and immigrant children: Implications for educators." *Social Education* 64(2): 121–5.

Pumariega, Andres, Eugenio Rothe and Joanne Pumariega. 2005. Mental health of immigrants. Community Mental Health Journal, 41(5), 581–97.

Liu, Michele. 2017. "War and children." *The American Journal of Psychiatry Residents' Journal* 12(7): 3–5. https://ajp.psychiatryonline.org/doi/full/10.1176/appi.ajp-rj.2017.120702.

Lukens, Rebecca. 2007. *A critical handbook of children's literature* (8th edition). MA: Pearson.

Magnuson, Katherine and Jane Waldfogel. 2005. "Early childhood care and education: Effects on ethnic and racial gaps in school readiness." *The Future of Children* 15(1): 169–96.

Masten, Ann and Angela Narayan. 2012. "Child development in the context of disaster, war, and terrorism: Pathways of risk and resilience." *Annual Review of Psychology* 63: 227–57. doi: 10.1146/annurev-psych-120710-100356. Epub 2011 Sep 19. PMID: 21943168; PMCID: PMC5858878.

Matteson, Holly and Ashley Boyd. 2017. "Are we making 'PROGRESS'? A critical literacies framework to engage pre-service teachers for social justice." *Journal of Language and Literacy Education* 13(1): 28–54. https://files.eric.ed.gov/fulltext/EJ1141489.pdf.

McNair, Jonda and Patricia Edwards. 2021. "The lasting legacy of Rudine Sims Bishop. Mirrors, windows, and sliding glass doors and more." *Literacy Theory, Research, Methods and Practice* 70(1): 202–12.

Menjívar, and Gómez Cervantes. 2016. "The effects of parental undocumented status on families and children." *CYF News*. https://www.apa.org/pi/families/resources/newsletter/2016/11/undocumented-status.

Migration Data Portal. 2021. *Child and young migrants*. https://www.migrationdataportal.org/themes/child-and-young-migrants.

Migration Policy Council. 2020. *Children in U.S. immigrant families*. https://www.migrationpolicy.org/programs/data-hub/charts/children-immigrant-families.

Miller, Alexander, Julia Hess, Deborah Bybee, and Jessica Goodkind. 2018. "Understanding the mental health consequences of family separation for refugees: Implications for policy and practice." *American Journal of Orthopsychiatry* 88(1): 26–37. https://doi.org/10.1037/ort0000272.

Moll, Luis, Cathy Amanti, Deborah Neff, and Norma Gonzalez. 1992. Funds of knowledge for teaching: Using a qualitative approach to connect homes and classrooms. *Theory Into Practice* 31(2): 132–141. doi: 10.1080/00405849209543534.

Moore, Cortney. 2022. "Half a million children become refugees as Russia-Ukraine war destroys homes and services". *Fox News*, March 3. https://www.foxnews.com/lifestyle/unicef-gives-aid-russia-ukraine-refugees.

NAEYC. 2019. *Advancing equity in early childhood education. Position statement*. Washington, DC: NAEYC. https://www.naeyc.org/sites/default/files/globally-shared/downloads/PDFs/resources/position-statements/advancingequitypositionstatement.pdf.

Noll, E. 2003. Accuracy and authenticity in American Indian children's literature: The social responsibility of authors and illustrators. In D. Fox and K. Short (eds.). *Stories matter: The complexity of cultural authenticity in children's literature*, 29–43. IL: National Council of Teachers of English.

Organization for Economic Co-operation and Development [OECD]. 2015. *Helping immigrant students to succeed at school—and beyond*. OECD. https://www.oecd.org/education/Helping-immigrant-students-to-succeed-at-school-and-beyond.pdf.

OECD. 2018. "The resilience of students with an immigrant background." In The resilience of students with an immigrant background: Factors that shape well-being. Paris: OECD Publishing.

Over, Harriet. 2016. "The origins of belonging: Social motivation in infants and young children." *Philosophical transactions of the Royal Society of London. Series B, Biological sciences* 371(1686).

Park, Maki, and Caitlin Katsifiacas. 2019. *Mitigating the effects of trauma among young children of immigrants and refugees: The role of early childhood programs*. Policy Brief. Migration Policy Institute. Washington, DC.

Peters, Karin, Monica Stodolska, and Anna Horolets. 2016. "The role of natural environments in developing a sense of belonging: A comparative study of immigrants in the U.S., Poland, the Netherlands and Germany." *Urban Forestry & Urban Greening* 17(1): 63–70.

Peri, Giovanni. 2013. "The economic benefits of immigration." *Berkeley Review of Latin American Studies, fall*: 14–19. https://clas.berkeley.edu/migration-economic-benefits-immigration.

Portes, Alejandro and Ruben Rumbaut. 2001. The story of the immigrant second generation. CA: University of Californai Press.

Pumariega, Andrés and Eugenio Rothe. 2010. "Leaving no children or families outside. The challenges of immigration." *American Journal of Orthopsychiatry* 80(4): 505–15.

Raghavan, Ramesh and Anna Alexandrova. 2015. Toward a theory of child well-being. *Social Indicators Research* 121: 887–902. 10.1007/s11205-014-0665-z.

Robertson, Lori. 2021. The facts on the increase in illegal immigration. *Fact Check*. https://www.factcheck.org/2021/03/the-facts-on-the-increase-in-illegal-immigration/.

Robles-Melendez, Wilma and Vesna Beck. 2019. *Teaching young children in multicultural classrooms. Issues, strategies, and perspectives* (5th edition). CA: Cengage.

Robles-Melendez, Wilma and Wayne Driscoll. 2020. *Issues and challenges of immigration in early childhood in the USA*. London, UK: Bloomsbury.

Robles-Melendez, Wilma, Mabel Valdes, and Eric Robles. 2018. Supporting children's identity. Paper presented at the Annual Conference the National Association for the Education of Young Children. Washington, DC.

Rodríguez, Ana. 2018. What are we so afraid of when it comes to immigration? *The Catalyst. The Bush Center*. https://www.bushcenter.org/catalyst/immigration/what-are-we-so-afraid-of.html.

Rogoff, Barbara, Audum Dahl, and Maureen Callanan. 2018. "The importance of understanding children's lived experience." *Developmental Review* 50, Part A: 5–15.

Safa, M. Dalal, Rebecca White, and George Knight. 2020. "Family contextual influences on bicultural competence development among U.S. Mexican-origin youths." *Developmental Psychology* 56(8): 1596–609. doi:10.1037/dev0001022.

Schwartz, Seth and Jennifer Unger. 2010. "Biculturalism and context: What is Biculturalism, and when is it adaptive? Commentary on Mistry and Wu." *Human Development* 53: 26–32. doi: 10.1159/000268137.

Sheffield, Tali. 2017. Understanding the challenges faced by immigrant children. *Blog*, May 17, 2017. https://www.psy-ed.com/wpblog/challenges-faced-by-immigrant-children/.

Shor, Ira. (Editor). 1987. *Freire for the classroom: A sourcebook for liberatory teaching*. NH: Heinemann.

Sorrels, Barbara. 2015. *Reaching and teaching children exposed to trauma*. Lewisville, North Carolina: Gryphon House.

Souto-Manning, Mariana, Karina Malik, Jessica Martell, and Patricia Pión. 2021. "Troubling belonging: The racialized exclusion of young immigrants and migrants of color." *International Journal of Early Childhood* 53(1): 101–18. https://www.ncbi.nlm.nih.gov/pmc/articles/PMC7985751/.

Suárez-Orozco, Carola and Marcelo Suarez-Orozco. 2002. *Children of immigration*. MA: Harvard University Press.

Suárez-Orozco, Carola and María Hernández. 2012. Immigrant family separations: The experience of separated unaccompanied, and reunited youth and families. In C. Garcia Coll (ed.) *The impact of immigration on children's development* (Vol. 24; pp. 123–48). Basel: Karger.

Takanishi, Ruby. 2004. "Leveling the playing field: Supporting immigrant children from birth to eight." *Future of Children* 14(2): 61–79.

Toppelberg, Claudio and Brian A. Collins. 2010. "Language, culture, and adaptation in immigrant children." *Child and Adolescent Psychiatric Clinics of North America* 19(4): 697–717. doi: 10.1016/j.chc.2010.07.003.

Tse, Lucy. 1995. *When students translate for parents: Effects of language brokering. California Association for Bilingual Education.* https://files.eric.ed.gov/fulltext/ED402733.pdf.

UNICEF. 1989. *For every child. The UN Convention on the rights of the child in words and pictures*. New York: Fogelman Books.

UNICEF. 2017. *Resilient migration. Tools for the emotional rescue of migrant children and adolescents*. UNICEF Mexico.

UNICEF. 2021. *Child migration*. UNICEF. https://data.unicef.org/topic/child-migration-and-displacement/migration/

UNICEF. 2021. *Latest statistics and graphics of refugee and migrant children*. https://www.unicef.org/eca/emergencies/latest-statistics-and-graphics-refugee-and-migrant-children.

United Nations. 1989/2021. Convention on the Rights of the Child. https://www.ohchr.org/en/professionalinterest/pages/crc.aspx.

Urban Institute. 2019. *Part of Us: A data-driven look at children of immigrants*. https://apps.urban.org/features/children-of-immigrants/.

U.S. Census Bureau. 2021. *Characteristics of U.S. population by generational status: 2013*. https://www.census.gov/library/publications/2016/demo/p23-214.html.

Wall, John. 2017. *Children's rights. Today's global challenge*. Lanham, MD: Rowman and Littlefield.

Vaghri, Ziba, Zoe Tessier, and Christian Whalen. 2019. "Refugee and asylum-seeking children: Interrupted child development and unfulfilled children's rights." *Children* 6(11). doi: 10.3390/children6110120.

Vasquez, Vivian, Hilary Janks, and Barbara Comber. 2019. "Critical literacy as a way of being and doing." *Language Arts* 96(5): 300–11.

von Werthern, Martha, Katy Robjant, Zoe Chui, Rachael Schon, Livia Ottisova, Claire Mason, and Cornelius Katona. 2018. "The impact of immigration detention on mental health: A systematic review." *BMC Psychiatry* 6;18(1): 382. doi: 10.1186/s12888-018-1945-y.

Yang, Michelle. 2020. "Honoring ethnic names is an important way to celebrate diversity of families in America." *Parents*. https://www.parents.com/baby-names/ideas/origin/honoring-ethnic-names-is-an-important-way-to-celebrate-diversity-of-families-in-america/.

Yohani, Sophie and Denise Larsen. 2009. "Hope lives in the heart: Refugee and immigrant children's perceptions of hope and hope-engendering sources during early years of adjustment." *Canadian Journal of Counselling* 43(4): 246–64. EJ858079.pdf (ed.gov).

Yokota, Junko. 2009. Learning through literature that offers diverse perspectives: Multicultural and international literature. In D. Wooten and B. Cullinan (eds.), *Children's literature in the reading program: an invitation to read* (3rd edition). (pp. 66–73). Newark, NJ: International Reading Association.

Zayas, Luis and Laurie Cook Heffron. 2016. "Disrupting young lives: How detention and deportation affect US-born children of immigrants. Research on the impact of parental detention and deportation on U.S-born children." *CYF News*, November. https://www.apa.org/pi/families/resources/newsletter/2016/11/detention-deportation.

Children's Books Cited

Ada, Alma Flor. 1995. *My name is Maria Isabel*. NY: Simon & Schuster.

Ada, Alma Flor. 2004. *I love Saturdays and domingos*. NY: Atheneum.

Aliki. 1998. *Marianthe's story: Painted words/Spoken words*. NY: Greenwillow Books.

Argueta, Jorge. 2008. *Xochitl and the flowers/Xochitl, la niña de las flores*. San Francisco: Children's Book Press.

Ashley, Bernard. 1995. *Cleversticks*. New York: Dragonfly Books.

Colato Lainez, Rene. *From north to south/Del norte al sur*. CA: Children's Books Press.

de Arias, Patricia. 2018. *Marwan's journey*. New York: Michael Neugebauer Publishing.

Danticat, Edwidge. 2013. *Mama's nightingale. A story of immigration and separation*. NY: Dial Books.

Davies, Nicola. 2019. *Every child a song*.

Inverrro, Julia. 2018. *Nonni's moon*. Jamaica Plain, Massachusetts: Three Beans Press.

Jiménez, Francisco. 1997. *The circuit*. Tucson: Arizona University Press.

Khalil, Aya. 2020. *The Arabic quilt. An immigrant story*. Maine: Tillbury.

Kobald, Irena. 2014. *My two blankets*. NY: Houghton Mifflin.

Levine, Ellen. 1989. *I hate English*. NY: Scholastic.

Medina, Jane. 1999. *My name is Jorge on both sides of the river*. PA: Wordsong.

Mills, Deborah and Alfredo Alva. 2018. *La frontera. El viaje con papá/My journey con papá*. Massachussetts: Barefoot books.

Mora, Pam. 1999. *The rainbow tulip*. NY: Puffin Books.

Nuño, Fran. 2017. *The map of good memories*. Madrid: Cuentos de Luz.

Park, Frances and Ginger Park. 2002. *Goodbye 382 Dan ding dong*. Washington, DC: National Geographic Kids.

Penfold, Alexandra. 2018. *All are welcome*. NY: Alfred Knopf Books for Young Readers.

Sibley O'Brien, Anne. 2015. *I'm new here*. NY: Charlesbridge.

Serres, Alain. 2012. *I have the right to be a child*. United Kingdom: Amnesty International.

Stanek, Muriel. 1989. *I speak English for my mom*. NY: Albert Whitman.

Thompson, Lauren. 2008. *Hope is an open heart*. NY: Scholastic.

Twiss, Jill. 2019. *The someone new*. NY: HarperCollins.

Umrigar, Thrity. 2020. *Sugar in milk*. Philadelphia: Running Press Kids.

Winter, Jeannete. 2007. *Angelina's island*. NY: Farrar, Strauss and Giroux.

Yaccarino, Dan. 2014. *All the way to America: The story of a big Italian family and a little shovel*. NY: Dragonfly.

5

An Unending Saga: Forced to Leave Home: Children and Families as Refugees

This chapter aims to:

- Discuss the reasons forcing children and their families to leave their homelands
- Identify some of the implications of forced migration on children's well-being
- Define who are refugees and asylees
- Explore some of the experiences of child refugees and asylees through the lens of children's literature

Key words:

- Refugees
- Asylees
- Rights of refugees
- Emotions and feelings
- Children's wellbeing
- Children's rights

In Our Hearts

It was during a teacher meeting in the primary school that we read a story that brought tears to many and memories of their childhood to some. They were talking about the recent incidents that forced millions to leave their countries. Concerned about children in their classrooms, they were trying to find ways to respond to any of their questions as these would emerge, to address their fears. But specially to address their fears that some had already expressed. Images on the media and comments from people were making children aware that something was happening.

One of the first-grade teachers in the team had brought a story to share. "I have something to share that I just reread," she said opening a book, The map of good memories *(Nuño 2016), and reading the story about a ten-year-old girl that war was forcing to leave the place she has always called home. Everyone felt glued to the story, as the young girl created her own map of special places. Places like her school and the park, where memories were built and that as a line in the story read, "that made her feel happy." "You see, this is what we need, to look at what is special for children," suggested one of the teachers, adding, "We need to share more about what we can take with us and stays in our hearts. How about having children create their own happy moments' maps?" They all seem to agree that it was a good idea to bring their attention to the special happy moments we always carry in our hearts, no matter who we are or where we go.*

Those Forced Goodbyes

How do you say goodbye when your heart is staying in the places that you call home, in the places where you learned your first words, where you shared those special times with your families and friends? How do you say it when you are forced to leave? Sadly, this difficult reality has been an ongoing experience for generations of children and families. Beyond geographical lines and cultures, the forcible exodus of people remains to this day as a challenging reminder of families and children with no other option but to involuntarily migrate. The young girl in the vignette that opens this chapter represents so many that like her today, right now, may be saying goodbye to their lives while wanting to find again a place where they can feel safe.

Society continues to be a place where the future is born every day, born as children are born. They are trusting, vulnerable, and counting on people to support them. Yet, for many, their future is in jeopardy with ongoing and

---

Think and Reflect ... Forced Goodbyes

The last few decades have told endless stories of people forced to abandon their homes seeking a safe place to live. Take a moment to consider the actions needed to responsively address the needs of children who have been pushed to leave. What would you propose?

difficult conflicts, a myriad of socially unfair conditions, all compounding the uncertainty experienced by those who are forced to leave their homelands. Their voices and their pleas have moved many children's literature authors who have brought to life their stories.

Opening New Windows

Many authors of children's books have opened a special window, on one hand historical, for it reflects the concerns and experiences of a time, that leads us to meet and learn about the protagonists and events from the past and of today. They have also opened a social justice window allowing readers and listeners to open their eyes to continuing unfairness, denying people of their rights, especially those of families and children (Figure 5.1).

Of particular interest are those stories presenting the experience from the perspective of children, which gave focus to this book. They have given us a special window, widely opening doors into the dramatic reality seen from the point of view of the child. Drawing from current realities with some inspired by real-life experiences, stories about child refugees and asylum seekers reveal the emotional and painful events continuing to happen, many being seen and witnessed so close to us. With the media turning us all into witnesses, author Nicola Davies (2016) revealed that it was the immigrant refugee crisis what inspired her to write the poem that became the story *The day war came* (2018). Her story, like many others, transports us right into experiencing the

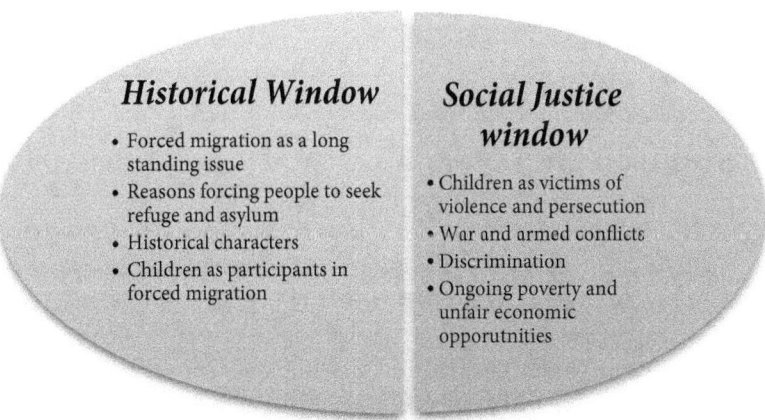

Figure 5.1 Children's literature as windows into the experience of forced migration.

despair, surprise, and pain of children trapped in difficult situations and forced to migrate. Some will leave with their families, others, like the girl in Davies' book, alone, after conflict took everything from her. The story does not end when we end reading the book. Beyond the story, one must remember that this is not just fiction; rather, it is a currently happening experience. Similar to Davies' story, others, which are discussed in this chapter, are also making us aware that every day, children, some unaccompanied, and others with families, are continuously finding themselves leaving their homelands. For educators of children, awareness about what many children are experiencing is demanding our attention to lead actions for their support, whether in the classroom or in efforts in our communities.

It Continues to Happen ...

Conflict and violence have made their presence clearly felt in recent decades and even more clearly now in the first decades of the twenty-first century. As educators, we have witnessed the wave of people pushed and forced to leave for multiple reasons seeking refuge or petitioning for asylum in other lands. For children, it is a childhood robbed, and for society it is a cloud that takes hopes away while the call to respond to the needs of children continues to be heard. One of the authors remembered comments from a colleague, who, as a child, came with her family as asylum seekers. For her, as she said, "El día que la puerta de mi casa se cerró, dejé de ser una niña de ocho años y me volví mayor [The day the door to my house was closed, I stopped being an eight-year-old girl and grew older]" (personal communication). In her words, we continue to read and feel the emotional scale of those forced goodbyes for children and for families. These

---

Thinking and Reflecting ... A Message to Society about Children

In multiple places throughout the world children are also saying goodbyes to their homes. Many of these are being lost to unprecedented violence and conflict, and natural disasters. With their goodbyes is also the precious time of their childhood years. If you had an opportunity to send a message to the world community on behalf of children continuing to be forced to seek refuge and asylum, what would you say to them?

are goodbyes that change lives and claim from everyone sincere and conscious understanding. They are a call for action, urging society to prevent children from being denied of their childhood.

They Have Rights

Every child has the inherent right to life.
—Article 6, Convention on the Rights of the Child (UN 1989)

Images from the news media reports unveil the trauma of children's experiences rooted in violence, conflict, and injustices. They are too often what is showcased in the news, a constant reminder about a childhood experiencing dramatic and traumatic circumstances. The implications and concern are multiple. Seen through the lens of children's rights, one must first remember that all children have rights and that these remain and ought to be considered, always, in times of peace and in times of conflict. They are, as well, rights that belong to every child, no matter who they are or where they are. Regardless of the circumstances faced, their rights belong to them and "**cannot be taken away from children**" (UNICEF n.d., emphasis added).

In the spirit of the Convention of the Rights of the Child, UNICEF's efforts are directed to safeguard and protect children, particularly in times when they are most vulnerable (Lake 2016). The voice of children demands to be heard and conscientiously answered with actions for their well-being. In powerful and profoundly emotional ways, children's books about refugees speak to us through their imagery and dialogue of a childhood still facing unimaginable challenges. The dangerous and difficult challenges children may face are many and continuing to happen. Responsibly responding to children during times of challenge is one of the rights due to children. Their hopes are in the actions of humanity. The overall aspiration that drives the Convention on the Rights of the Child is precisely a child's well-being, recognizing their right to thrive and enjoy their childhood. Serres (2009), in his book about children's rights, emphasizes their right to be protected by adults "and sheltered from disasters … or because of other sad things" (n.p.). Conscientiously reading, in stories of immigration, we can hear the voices of children. They make us realize that efforts to support children still need to be more diligently considered. Just as the child refugee character in Maclear's *Story boat* (2020), says, *"And grow, and wait, and wait, and wait adding words to this story"* (n.p.), clearly telling society that actions are needed. Meanwhile, we must remember, that childhood cannot wait.

Happening Now

The dramatic and striking images in *The day war came* (Davies 2018) sadly came alive while we were writing this book. The calmness of life was shattered for Ukrainians, who found themselves in the middle of bombardments. The fear and disbelief of the young girl in Davies' story revealed emotions that, we are sad to say, are now being experienced by children. They brought to mind the experiences of children awakened and forced to seek safety, lives disrupted, a childhood changed. They are the lives of children living in places where incivility, conflicts, and violence threaten their lives. They remind us of children in Afghanistan dreaming of peace, of the Rohingya children in Asia escaping persecution, of children trekking through Central America and Mexico seeking security and safety, of African children seeking a better life, and more recently, of Ukrainian children displaced and sent across European borders.

Looking through the illustrations in Davies' story, we read the harrowing experiences and are shaken even more when we are learning that consideration for children and their rights is absent. We are struck by the illustration of the missing chair that frustrates the young girl's desire to be at school. But we are also shown how compassionate hearts are also present, leading us to think that so many more are needed. Davies' story, along with those of other authors, is a reminder that protecting children and respecting the rights of a child is important, even more so given when the threat from war and conflict, urges consideration to their welfare and future. At stake is the safety and well-being of child refugees and asylum seekers. Urgently needed are actions based on what is in the best interest of the child. Needed, as well, is attention to the right they have to survival and to live without fear and free of discrimination.

Let Us Not Forget …. Children Living in War and Armed Conflict Areas

Millions of children, according to UNICEF are escaping from dangerous and unfair conditions in an unending flow. In the meantime, thousands of children still in places of conflict are growing up in environments where the uncertainty of the moment gives shape to the experience of their childhood. In some of these areas, more than one generation of children have spent their entire childhood living under the threat of attacks. The fact is that after decades of declining violence, a surge in conflicts has emerged during this century (World Bank Group 2018). Estimates from UNICEF (2022) point out that in 2022 over 400 million children were living in places of war and conflicts (Figure 5.2).

These cannot be forgotten. Unable to leave for multiple reasons, they are children with the same rights as others and for whom society must also respond with concern for their well-being. In active war zones like Ukraine, efforts are being made to safeguard children from the threatening attacks. Some of those efforts include creating safe spaces, a UNICEF initiative, that turned the subways in the city of Kharkiv into places for children to meet and engage in child-oriented activities (UNICEF 2022b).

Numerous authors of children's books have opened the door for us to learn about children's lives in conflict zones. The message received is one of resilience and perseverance, firmly anchored in their hopes for peaceful times. When we meet Sami in Heide and Heide (1992) *Sami and the time of the troubles*, the

World Region	Country
Africa	Syria- ongoing civil war Somalia- ongoing drought Nigeria- Boko Haram attacks on schools for girls
Asia	Myanmar – Crisis of the Rohingya families and children persecuted and forced to flee the country
Middle East	Iraq; Afghanistan, Pakistan, Yemen- ongoing civil wars and internal persecution due to religious and political differences
Europe	Russian attack on Ukraine
Central America South America	Various countries (Nicaragua, Venezuela, Mexico, Guatemala and other countries in the region). Internal violence; issues of poverty and discrimination

Figure 5.2 A sample of active zones of war and conflicts in 2022.

Source: United Nations. 2021a. *Children and armed conflict. Report of the Secretary General.* https://www.un.org/ga/search/view_doc.asp?symbol=S/2021/437&Lang=E&Area=UNDOC

images made us feel the uneasiness of the place where the ten-year-old boy and his family live. From the start, it is heartbreaking to learn how this child has adjusted to living all his life as he declares in "the time of the troubles." Emotionally, his comments about his life's routines unveil his strong resilience and capacity to overcome the traumatic reality. In him, we can see the lives of children who have never known what peace is like, reminding us of those still being born and living in places where fear and uncertainty reign. Although, the setting of the story is not revealed, which seems to reflect events in the Middle East during the 1990s, when the story was published, it represents the experience of millions of other children and families. In 2022, millions continued living in places of armed conflict with new areas surging with violence and fighting events.

They Are Hopeful

Hopefulness is also what characterizes children living in conflict zones. Dreams and hope for peace continue to guide their day to day lives. Emerging from the real-life example of Malala Yousufzai, a Nobel Peace Prize winner, her story is an affirmation about the determined attitude of children and young people who dare to defy injustice. In her autobiographical picture book, *Malala and her magic pencil* (Yousufzai 2019), Malala's wishes are a testimonial of her own aspirations. In each of her statements, we find the spirit of hope and of peace for a childhood growing up in places where they are being robbed of the opportunity to be children. Her story is of courage, which, despite the attacks that placed her life in danger, inspires promise and action as she invites children to also allow their voices to be heard. Living now in Europe, Malala continues her work, defending and advocating for the rights of children and of education for girls, who, as she experienced, are being denied of what is inherently theirs.

Lessons of extraordinary resilience are learned every time we hear the voices of children who live in war and conflict areas. Children continue to be hopeful for things to change, for peace to come. This is something that is woven through their stories today just as those from the past. Captured by the author Ana Eulate (2012) is their enduring hope, which we hear in the voice of the Afghan child saying, "I am a little girl who doesn't stop dreaming ..." (*The sky of Afghanistan*, n.p.). The serene and subtle colors of the illustrations transmit the powerful dream for peaceful times. Her dream of kites flying for peace in a country with decades immersed in conflicts, gathers the dreams of children living everywhere in places where they yearn for the calmness of peace.

> **Thinking and Reflecting ... Envisioning Peace**
>
> The dream for peace continues to be shared by children who live in places where conflict defines their environments. In *The sky of Afghanistan*, the young girl dreams of a time "where the sound of war has truly gone forever" (n.p.). Reflecting on her statement and considering all the places where conflict continues, how would you imagine a time of peace for children? What images would describe peace?

Unceasing Challenges

In Chapter 1, we pointed out the multiple conflicting and dangerous circumstances continuing to threaten living conditions for people in numerous places throughout the world. These are increasingly being experienced everywhere. Added to these are the existing social and ideological violence and extreme poverty, depriving families and children from fair opportunities to sustain their lives and future. These pressing realities have not subsided but rather emerged even more markedly since 2020, the year when the world was besieged by the pandemic. Reports from the United Nations Refugee Agency (2021) revealed that by mid 2021, globally, 84 million had been forced to leave their countries. Numbers continue to increase with new conflicts and emergencies being declared, forcibly leading more to leave their homes. As a result, millions of children have seen their lives changed. According to the United Nations (2021b), unprecedented numbers of children "more than ever before" are living as migrants and refugees. Many are still seeking to find a home they can call their own, while thousands are growing up in refugee camps or in transitory places. Their stories and voices are reflected in characters like Lubna (Meddour 2019) and Cartwheel (Kobald 2014) hoping to find home again.

People Need to Know: Telling Their Stories

Many of the reasons forcing families to leave what they have called home are based on the urgency to find a safer place. Conditions threatening life and its well-being are such that no other option exists but to leave. Repeated throughout the many stories of people driven out of their homelands is the statement *we need to leave*. The urgency can be heard again and again in the narratives about people turned into refugees and asylum seekers, where the faces and voices of children are marked by their surprise, faced with the imminence of departure. "I never thought such a thing would happen to me" (Kumar 2019, 8) is what we hear from a Rohingya child in the story *I am a refugee*, echoing the thoughts of so many other child refugees. Happening throughout society, so many unexpected and unavoidable journeys are revealed through stories addressing forced migration. They help us to capture and become consciously aware about conditions many too difficult to conceive. Authors like Francesca Sanna in *The journey* (2016) and Muo Thi Van (2020) in *Wishes*, among others, write from the children's perspective allowing readers to experience moments and journeys spurred by forced goodbyes. Through their storylines, with settings in geographically different places, we are transported to experience the shocking reality of children uprooted from their homelands. Their harrowing experiences continue to alert everyone to the need for concerted efforts to safeguard children's well-being and future. Let's remember that "childhood is entitled to special care and assistance" (Preamble, Convention of the Rights of the Child 1989).

No Options but to Leave: Reasons Pushing People to Leave

"Understand that all children are precious" (n.p.), UNICEF reminds us in the book *For every child* (1989), where the rights of the child emphasize the need to act with attention to the best interest of children. This is a reminder to every one of the shared responsibility society has for every child. Recent times have seen numerous cases that continue to bring attention to the plight of children driven away from their homelands. In each one, their story and the concern for their well-being continues to add up to the many others already known. These difficult events have been portrayed in children's literature where clearly reflected is the concern for their safety and future. Revealed through the narratives there is a call for attention to the needs of children and to their rights for a successful childhood. Violence and armed conflict have sadly continued for years to happen in many places in the world, with thousands of families and children forced away from their countries to save their lives. Stories like Milway's *The banana leaf ball* (2016) and Williams' *Brothers in hope: The story of the lost boys of Sudan* (2013) bring to us the experiences of children who became refugees, victims of internal armed conflicts that robbed them of their homes and families. During the summer of 2014, when the world shockingly learned about the hundreds of children who, alone, crossed the US borders, was a moment that led society to become even more aware about a childhood forced to seek safety faced with danger and unjust circumstances. Unrelentingly, groups of Latin American families with their children continue trekking through Central America and Mexico. More recently, since 2020, they have been joined by people from different regions of the world. Among them, were thousands of Haitians, victims of the 2021 earthquake that worsened their living conditions after the previous seismic activity in 2010. Some crossing in frail boats and others coming across the US borders, their journeys evidence the difficult challenges driving them to seek asylum.

Stories That Document and Reveal a Need to Leave

Many authors have brought to us stories revealing the motivations leading children to leave, some with their families, and others unaccompanied. Of particularly dramatic effect is the wordless story *Migrants* (Watanabe 2020), through whose images one captures the constant danger that the immigrant caravan faces. Powerful imagery, it tells a story that reminds us of and connects with those of people who set out to find a safe place. Garay's account in *The long road* (1997), based on his own experiences, brings to the reader the difficult political conditions that led the child and his mother to leave Nicaragua and seek asylum.

Some stories have allowed us to experience the realities of children seeking asylum, particularly of unaccompanied children. One of these is Argueta's poetry in *Somos como las nubes/ We are like the clouds* (2018), which took us along to experience together the path followed by children who are coming alone, firmly embraced in their hopes to reach a safer place. The graphic illustrations in Argueta's book grab the readers' attention, conveying the arduous journey of children traveling alone through the difficult terrain in their quest to find safety. Duncan Tonatiuth also brings to us the perils of children traveling alone in his story *Pancho Rabbit and Coyote: A migrant tale* (2014). Seeking to find his father, the young boy leaves home heading to the border. The emotionally charged story is revealed through the tone of the narrative and images. Meeting Pancho, we are led to learn of the experiences of children whose parents continue to migrate to support their families. These and other stories today, remind us of the ongoing migration of unaccompanied children who alone continue to traverse the borders. In Buitrago's *Two white rabbits* (2015) our attention is drawn to the plight of parents who, despite the risks, do everything possible for their children. This is another story also taking readers along the pathway of migrants journeying through Central America and Mexico. This time, the author allows readers, young and old, to experience the uncertain path of a father and his young daughter. One is struck by the innocence of the young girl who, as the child that she is, plays while the reality of their journey continues to unfold.

The faces of children grab our attention as they continue to write their own stories about their exodus and journey across the hemisphere. Their harrowing journeys, now publicly displayed through the media, cause concern and motivate authors of children's books who revealing their experiences, are making people aware about the realities of young immigrants

Images of children turned into forced migrants touch and capture our conscience. Their presence is made clear as protagonists in stories similar to those in *La frontera: My journey with papá* (Mills and Alva 2018) and in Garay's *The long road*. They uncovered the journey of children who repeatedly came alone, crossing through Central America and Mexico. Consciously considering their narratives, these are stories telling about bigger challenges facing families and children. Entrenched in unfairness, fear, and inaction from agencies to address their rightful needs, several authors have openly shared the difficult reality of unfulfilled hopes and aspirations of families. The outcome is seen as these experiences are stamped on the spirit of children.

The Specter of War

In recent times, and just as we were writing, the specter of war conflict raised its head pushing millions to seek refuge away from their homelands. To the long standing conflict in the Middle East, the unprovoked invasion of Ukraine during the winter of 2022 came as another experience denying millions of their peace and safety. Once again, scores of children had to flee their homes. Many of them left with their families while others ended arriving at other borders unaccompanied or separated from their families. Their reality increasingly underlined the need for attention to children trapped in the middle of war conflicts. The recent case of Ukrainian children captured the attention of everyone and, once again, brought to light the plight of child refugees and asylees (UNHCR 2021). Repeating itself, events during the early part of the century unveiled the story of thousands being forced to find other lands where they can survive. Fear and the sadness of dreams lost could be read on the faces of people and children seeking ways to escape to safety.

> **Consciously Considering ... Children's Needs Today and Beyond Conflicts That Displaced Them**
>
> *War* is a word that evokes fear. In winter 2022 society saw the fear reflected on the faces of children from Ukraine. Reports from UNICEF (Hamilton 2022) described that every fifty-five minutes a Ukrainian child was becoming a refugee. Their case added to the already existing numbers of children who have been displaced by conflict in every corner of the world. To all of them, society needs to remember that we must pledge our efforts for they are a generation taking shape in front of us. The need is to erase the fear that took them away from their homes and rebuild their trust in humanity. The charge is for everyone as we are reminded by the Convention of the Rights of the Child (UN 1989), where the best interests of children (Article 3) and the inherent right to be safe (Article 6) are declared.
>
> Responses are needed and they are continuing to demand attention and especially action throughout the world. Their cases remind everyone to understand that children's welfare is a shared responsibility in society. Thinking about what is in the best interest for children, society must understand that the fate and future of thousands of children who suddenly became refugees must be prioritized. Critically and consciously considered, the plight of children displaced by conflict calls for attention not only to their immediate needs, which are fundamental to their survival, but for their future. Inherent to their well-being is consideration for their developmental needs. This is where action is vital to ensure that they will be able to overcome challenges, not only those immediate but those to come, to make them feel safe and at home again, wherever they are. The challenge is for everyone.

Children's Literature about Refugees and Asylum Seekers

Through centuries, children and their families have been the victims of conflicts. Recent years have shown us that they continue being victimized as new struggles emerge. Children's literature authors continue bringing to life many of the episodes forcing people to escape, leaving behind their homes as they courageously hope to begin again in other places. Their work contributes to raising awareness about the plight of children and families trapped in difficult circumstances. Through the literature on refugees, we learn about the aspirations of people in the stories that are written about an experience happening every day. Their narratives allow readers to learn and delve into some of the insights of the experience of children and families. Feelings of despair, questions unanswered, and the difficult moments when home is left behind are among the emotional experiences facing children as they leave their homes. One cannot forget that at the time we were writing, these images were real for children in places where armed conflict and violence took hold of their cities and lives.

Stories as Windows, Doors, and Avenues

Literature about refugees and asylum seekers embodies the experiences and emotions of people left with no options but to leave their homelands. These stories are windows into a reality still happening in society, and clearly open doors (Sims Bishop 1990; Botelho and Rudman 2009) to enter into a world of difficult circumstances, allowing us to learn about the lived experiences and challenges of children and families forced away from their homes. Together, they provide avenues into the challenges posed by conflict, violence, and injustices. Vicariously, they bring to readers, opportunities to uncover and understand the strong sentiments of difficult moments continuing to be experienced in society.

Children's resiliency
- Resilient and showing strength despite challenging and difficult realities.

Hopefulness
- Staying hopeful despite challenges.

Family connectedness
- Showing concern about family members during difficult moments.

Relationships
- Establishing relationships of trust and friendship with peers and adults.
- Affective relationships with pets.

Childhood Innocence
- Use of imagination and engaging in play activities despite challenging realities.

Cultural encounters
- Life in refugee camps
- Adjusting to schools and affirming their culture

Figure 5.3 Some of the thematic strands in children's literature about refugees from the perspective of children.

An Unending Saga   173

Children's books addressing stories about refugees provide a variety of themes. Intentionally selected, those included in this chapter are stories that are presented from the perspective of children. They were chosen to provide a voice for children, allowing us to learn from their views about the experience of refugees and asylum seekers. Thematically, they provide windows into some of the main aspects that define the experience of children whether they are refugees or asylum seekers (Figure 5.4).

Vicariously, through children's literature about immigration, we have been able to take the perspective of children as they experience difficult circumstances that displaced and forced them to leave. Some examples of titles providing windows into issues of conflict forcing people to seek refuge and asylum are listed in Figure 5.4, many of which are also discussed throughout this chapter. They are also stories appropriate to be shared with young children to explore challenges from a social justice and anti-bias perspective. Bringing them into the classroom, we must reiterate, provide ways for addressing issues happening in society which leads to building concepts supporting the child's sense of tolerance, justice, and fairness (Colby and Lyon 2004).

In every story about forced migration, we find an open avenue to navigate the complex experiences of children and families. Through the story narratives, some fictional and others based on actual events, we find episodes reflecting lived experiences of children and families, who similarly today are facing the challenge of finding a safe place to live.

Refugees	Asylum seekers
• *Where will I live?* (McCarney) • *Lubna and pebble* (Meddour) • *The journey* (Sanna) • *My two blankets* (Kobald) • *The banana leaf ball* (Milway)*	• *La frontera* (Mills and Alva)* • *Two white rabbits* (Buitrago) • *The long road* (Garay)* • *Somos como las nubes/We are like the clouds* (Argüeta)

Figure 5.4 Selected titles serving as windows into stories about refugees and asylum seekers.

*Based on author's experiences

Seeing Conflict through Children's Eyes

These children may be refugees, internally displaced or migrants, but first and foremost, they are children: no matter where they come from, whoever they are, and without exception.

—Uprooted (UNICEF 2016, n.p.)

Capturing the impact and painful realities of conflict for children, stories powerfully tell the experience of those times and moments. Many authors have particularly focused these conflicts through the eyes of children. On that moment when war and conflict happen, life is transformed in inexplicable ways. Those are moments marking a child's life with events that cannot be explained. The powerful narrative in Nicola Davies' *The day war came* (2018) unveils from its beginning the difficult path of children caught and wisked away from what they knew. Similar to the experience of so many children, one feels the appalling moment of fear when life is disrupted. Through its compelling images, Davies takes us to feel the trauma experienced by the young girl, reminiscent of the thousands today also seeking an opportunity to be a child again. Right from its first pages, Davies confronts us with the innocence of the child. The naiveté of the young girl in her story, who sees her day at home and school as just another day, emotionally impacts the reader, recognizing the spirit of childhood that is abruptly shaken. One cannot help but feel just like the child as she is taken by surprise in the moment when "war came" (n.p.). There is a need for everyone to understand how a typical day for children becomes a time when everything is taken away. Their innocence is shattered as their world disappears under the thunderous noise and rubble-laden neighborhood. Unaware about threatening realities, one cannot avoid but feel the despair of finding yourself in an unreal reality just as the young girl in the story.

Consciously Considering ... Waiting to Be Safe

Stories about children forced to say goodbye are endless. The oral accounts heard reveal the challenges paired with the fear and emotionality of those moments. Reminiscing some of her own experiences as an asylum seeker, one of our colleagues* shared some of her memories from the time when escaping was the only way to be safe. Here is what she wrote about that time during her childhood when her family made the decision to leave.

> *My family still remembers the night they arrived at what has been now our home for many years. We wanted so much to leave from where we had all lived our entire life. It was a dangerous time, and we could hardly even talk always fearful someone would hear us. My mother knew that one day we would have to leave but she kept her smile even in those times when we could not even leave our house. I was only six but still remember that day when my parents said goodbye to our home. We left in the middle of the night with the promise to someday return. Behind stayed our grandparents, who gave us their blessing, with a hug that I can still feel. My heart wanted anxiously to be where we could laugh again, where we could shed away our fears. Such a long wait! They said that it was a long journey, but for me it was the beginning of a new life. A different place, a language strangely sounding to me, buildings, and places unknown to me, but finally we were all safe again!*
>
> *Name kept anonymous to respect her privacy.

Storying the Plight and Realities of Children

Forced migration remained at a high point during the first decades of the century. Millions of children across the world have been led away from their homelands for multiple reasons. Technology has led everyone to learn about their journeys and realities. It has brought faces and stories to an episode of immigration continuing to appeal for understanding and support from humanity. Emerging from their harrowing realities are multiple stories telling about the existing experience and their impact on children's well-being.

Many authors have conveyed the experience of refugees using the perspective of children. Their stories have contributed to accentuating their presence and participation. In each of their narratives, readers have come to experience the deeply emotional episodes experienced by children. A sense of despair, a need for emotional connection, a need to remain who they are, and the need for remembering the happy place they called home are but a few of the experiences shared through stories about refugees.

Selecting stories addressing children in forced migration revealed the growing interest on this topic. Evidently, events from recent years with armed conflicts and natural disasters such as those in the Middle East, Africa, and Asia have brought attention to the fate of children. An increasing number of children's literature titles addressing refugees and asylum seekers provide a broader perspective telling stories with children as the protagonists. In many ways, there is a wider spectrum of topics defining the experience of migration.

Emotional Ties, Unbreakable Ties

The place where we live and were born always remains as the special setting where we feel we are at home. Forced to leave everything behind, is sadly happening too often in current times, displacing children and families from places they will always call home. In their minds and spirit, those places never leave them. Emotional connections with places of birth remain strong and fill many with ideas of hopeful returns.

Learning about the impact of forced departures on people brings attention to the emotional sentiments that tie us to the places left behind. Images and storylines from children's literature open windows to the intense emotions felt for their homelands, emotions that remain forever. One cannot forget the emotional expression of grandma in *Grandmother's records* (Velazquez 2001), who, listening to a musical piece, is transported to her place of birth. These feelings are connections and unbreakable ties remaining despite distance and time. Emotionally, we are connected to the places where we live and grow up. Interactions, relationships, and familiarity with a location are all factors influencing and leading people to develop what has been called place attachment. Emerging during the early years and increasingly building as we mature, place attachment emotionally, affectively, and culturally links us to where we are born and grow up (Hidalgo and Hernandez 2001). Feelings developed for a place are part of the composite of emotional connections that make us who we are and that build our identity. Like an intricately built puzzle, experiences and relationships give meaning to the places from where we came (Lewicka 2011). Those memories affirm us and help us keep our cultural roots.

Reading *The sky of Afghanistan* (Eulate 2012), we were made aware about those emotional ties to one's homeland. They seem to tighten up even more in moments when circumstances are the harshest and riled with danger. Revealed through its images is the deep affection of the young girl telling the story, anxiously aiming for peace, erasing the contrasting reality of conflict and danger surrounding people in her country. Her dreams for peace among the struggling times of ongoing conflict, send a message of hope that is repeated throughout the pages. It is an ambivalent reality, where her imagined world takes her away from the hard experience of life in her homeland (Bocagni and Kivisto 2019), echoing dreams and aspirations for peaceful times.

"Can we go home now, Papa?", was the question that the young boy asked his father in the children's book *Gleam and glow* (Bunting 2001). In the story, war had forced them to leave when it became dangerous to stay at home. Still, the boy's longing to return never faded. Where we come from invisibly seems to keep us tied to it. Witnessing recent acts of war and conflicts, we have repeatedly heard people affirming their desire to return. It has also been what some of our students, who came as refugees shared. "Even if I am old, but will return" was what one student expressed.

An Urgency to Leave

As a recurring reality, in every story about refugees and asylum seekers that was reviewed, the pressing reality of danger and of exhausted options but to leave was clearly evident. Each of the narratives denounced the dangerous challenge experienced by those becoming their victims, forcing some to seek refuge and others asylum (Figure 5.5). Seeking peace and safety, refugees and asylum

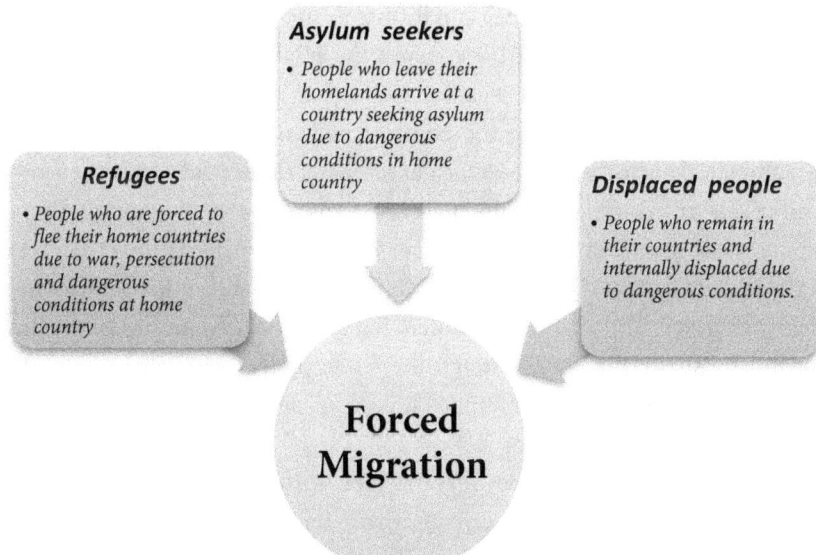

Figure 5.5 Typology of people impacted by forced migration.

Source: J. Smith. 2022. *The different types of displaced people*. Borgen Project; United Nations. 2022. *What is a refugee?* United Nations. 2022. *Who are displaced people?*

seekers are a reminder of injustice and of violent armed conflict continuing to emerge in recent decades.

Gathered from the children's books about refugees that were reviewed was the urgent nature of departures. Compounded through the stories was an array of profoundly emotional experiences, of surprise, shock, loss, denial, and of hope, outlining those moments when the child characters found out about their forced departures. While each story that we examined presented different settings, times, and geographies, in common, they all presented the traumatic reality of finding themselves with no options but to escape and leave their homelands.

Author Sandra le Guen stresses the painful reality that war conflict brings, pushing families to leave, leading readers to understand that they "had no choice" (2020, n.p.). There are no options, is the silent cry that we hear through the statements and illustrations, that forced the family to the difficult decision of leaving their home. This is what is echoed throughout the children's literature about refugees, exposing to readers, both children and adults, the heartbreak of people victimized by conflict and calamitous disasters. "We came to this country to be safe" (Kobald 2014, n.p.), says Cartwheel, the young refugee girl in Kobald's story. Through her words, the message of hope is clear. Clearly, one can perceive that they are guided by their hope and confidence in the kindness of people who will recognize that their goodbyes came from the need the find a place where they can be safe again.

Ruurs' *Stepping stones* (2016) conveys the plight of refugees through its artistic images and the emotional narrative that denounces the devastating reality of conflict. Told from the point of view of a young child, we learn how the family is forced to leave just as so many others did. With the family joining the "rivers of people," the image takes us to see the flowing rhythm of people walking to find safety and peace. We hear with clarity how their fears begin to fade as they "walk in hope" (n.p.), coming into other lands where there was peace. The journey is challenging as we hear from the child telling the story visually reflected through the stone figures walking in ways that uncover the difficult and sometimes unknown path taken as people escape into safety.

One of those powerful stories is Watanabe's wordless book, *Migrants* (2020). Speaking through its images, one perceives the moments when the group understands about the danger and imminence of the challenges that force them to leave. The dangerous journey is accentuated by the character following the group, always in the back, but signifying the inherent danger ahead.

The Force of Nature, Another Factor Forcing People to Leave

Nature and its many ways will always remind humanity about its power. Climate changes and the power of nature are another factor leaving thousands without a place to live. In recent decades, the intensity of natural disasters has devastated regions, displacing people who find themselves in uninhabitable conditions. Families and children over the last two decades have found themselves forced to seek places to live given the severity of the impact of weather and natural events. Implications for children's safety and well-being are multiple in different world regions. Johnston (2021) called the impact of climate on childhood to be "a children's rights crisis" (n.p.), with many children ending being displaced or forced to migrate to safer areas. This is a crisis, undoubtedly with devastating effects on the lives of children and their families. Hurricanes, typhoons, earthquakes, and other natural disasters have made their presence evident in many parts of the world. All over the globe, nature and climatic events are leaving a mark of desperation, displacing and forcing children and families to leave.

Earthquakes like those experienced in Haiti sent thousands away who became refugees. The impact of one of these on children is captured in Danticat's *Eight days* (2010), where the story portrays the resilient spirit of a child, trapped under the rubble and who is able to overcome the dangerous situation. Danticat's narrative allows us to appreciate the power of imagination that the child character has, using it to survive. In many ways, the young boy evokes the resiliency of his country, hopeful and continuing to maintain their strength despite the challenges. Set against the events during the 2010 earthquake, it reminds readers about the force of nature that painfully displaced thousands and forced others to seek refuge in other countries. Emerging clearly from the story is the resilience of children, seen through the character of the child who takes strength from his own imagination to overcome a tragic reality.

Many other episodes continue to reveal the power and unpredictable reality of weather and nature events. The aftermath of hurricanes and typhoons of recent decades have left indelible marks on children and families who suddenly find themselves displaced. A dramatic experience forcing many out of their homes, thousands of families and children may find themselves displaced in their own home countries or migrating across borders (Johnston 2021). Author Jonathan London's book *Hurricane!* (1998) immerses readers in the experience of a hurricane using as a setting the island of Puerto Rico that in 2017 was struck by a powerful hurricane that left thousands homeless and displaced. Informational children's books provide a good way for children to understand the disruptive power of hurricanes. Two suggested ones are Gibbons' *Hurricanes!* (2019) and Simon's *Hurricane* (2007).

Children and Their Pets; They Are Important, too!

Watching the images of Ukrainian children and their families escaping across European borders, we saw how along with them were also hundreds of pets. Big and small, together with children, they were crossing into new destinations (Johnston 2022; The Strait Times 2022). Clutching to their pets, one could read in the faces of children and also on those of adults, the priceless companionship and sentiments shared. As children grow up, pets represent a relationship of affection, of emotional support, and of companionship (National Institutes for Health [NIH] 2018). Playing a significant role for children, pets promote and fulfil the need for building secure attachment connections, a major developmental milestone during childhood. There is increasing indications emerging from research that during difficult times, children become more attached to their pets and rely on their relationships (Purewal et al. 2017). For children, their support and trusting company of a pet is important. They are part of the world of affective relationships of a child, and their company helps them to lessen the impact of stressors.

The caring relationship of children and pets has long been a topic in children's literature. With interest in recent years on forced migration, a few new titles have added perspectives on pets and children during times of conflict. Three picture books particularly appropriate to share with young children, bring to us the dramatic experience of children and their pets escaping from conflict zones. Coincidentally, these stories were inspired by real experiences. A cat is the protagonist in Kuntz and Shrodes' story *Lost and found cat. The true story of Kunkush's incredible journey* (2017). The story, which became widely known, narrates the experience of a young girl and her family who took their cat with them as they escaped from Iraq, first by land and later crossing the Mediterranean. Lost during their arrival in European lands, the special bonds of the family with the cat led to their incessant search. Thanks to efforts of people who learned about the lost cat, he was finally reunited with the family. Kunkush's is an emotional story denoting the special affective relationships that pets have with children and their families. Kunkush's is also a story of compassionate response from all those who, learning about the lost cat and the refugee family still hoping for his return, made their reunion possible. It is in times of difficult situations that compassion and empathy emerge, alleviating the harshness of the realities experienced. The interesting and adventurous journey of this pet cat is also narrated in Marne Ventura's *Kunkush: The true story of a refugee cat* (2017), a book more appropriate for older children.

This time narrating the events of a pet dog, *Saving Stella* (Fakher 2020) allow us to learn about the difficult experience of leaving behind a pet, while her owner escapes from the civil war in Syria. Forced to leave a pet behind is a difficult experience and reveals the loss of a special relationship many children suffer as they leave home. Unable to bring his dog Stella, she is left under the care of friends, with firm plans to reunite again. The harrowing experience brings us closer to learn about the painful decision of leaving a pet, though entrusted to be cared for by a friend. Finally reunited with her owner, who did not hesitate to bring Stella back, the story reveals the caring sentiments and responsibility that guided the efforts to be together once again. The story also opens doors to learn about the traumatic impact that living in places of conflict represents for children and their families.

Author Eve Bunting also presents another experience of children and pets. Drawing from nonfiction sources and with the backdrop of the Bosnian-Serb conflict, this time, we learn how a gift of two fish brings the children in *Gleam and Glow* (2001) to focus attention on their new pets, while the war was coming closer to their home. Even as they were finally pushed to seek refuge, their concern was for their fish after learning they could not be carried. Leaving the fish in the pond in hopes that they would survive, years later as they return, a pond full of fish welcomed them—a sign of hope as the family initiated a new beginning. Messages of concern and responsibility permeate the story accentuating the meaningful role of a pet for a childhood facing difficult realities of life in conflict zones.

Keeping hope that all will be well again is what can be read in stories and images about children and their pets. The feelings and sentiments shown through stories are evidence of the emotional connectedness that children have with their pets (Figure 5.5). Clearly conveyed are the emotional bonds shared between the story characters and their pets. They needed each other, even more so in those surreal times of war and conflict, when departures are imminent, when just a few items can be carried along. In each of these stories, one can still appreciate the role played by pets in children's as well as in adults' emotional life. Bringing some solace, they also connect the child, as well as adults, to convey concern and feelings of responsiveness for the well-being of a pet. Their role is enhanced during times of despair when supportive emotional relationships are most needed (Purewal et al. 2017).

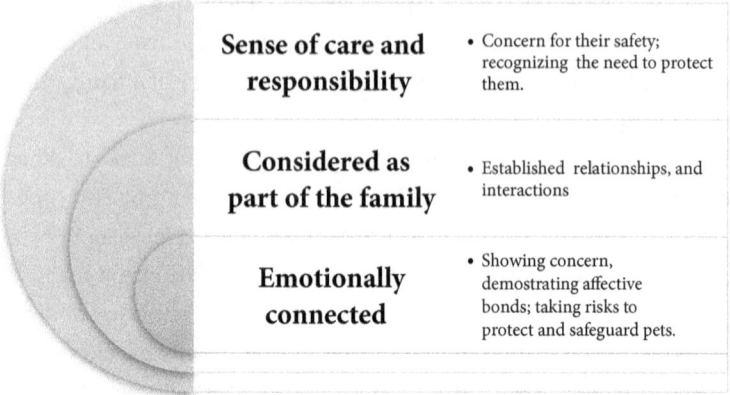

Figure 5.6 Emotional bonds of children and pets.

Finding a Safe Place

The search for a place to be safe and free from fear is what inspires children and families to leave their homes. We have witnessed it in the past and we are witnessing it today, "a river of people" (Ruurs 2016), continuing to leave in long and difficult journeys. They are seeking refuge or asylum and are moved by their hope for a place to be welcomed and safe. Wondering where their journeys are taking them is a question raised out of a concern for their well-being and future. This is another part of the story of refugees and asylum seekers that has been addressed by authors. Various authors have addressed their lives living in refugee camps after their forced journeys. In our experience, those reviewed provided views about life in the refugee camps while others focused on experiences particularly at school. Those of refugees' experiences at school are discussed in Chapter 6.

Some of the stories about life in the refugee camps were based on actual experiences, which opened a realistic window into the experiences of child refugees. Many, like those mentioned here, reflect the humanitarian work of agencies and of people who dedicate their efforts to support children during highly difficult moments. They also reveal to us the uncertainty of life that children experience waiting to find a place where they can start again. Despite the dramatic reality, one gathers from some of the stories how children engage in being children. Play and building relationships emerge as two of the childhood tasks addressed in those we reviewed and that are discussed in this section. They still keep the memories of happier times like the voice of the child in Kumar's *I am a refugee* (2019), who though in a safe place, reveals to us that "I still miss my family every day. I hope I can see them again" (12).

Among those stories of life in refugee camps, *Brothers in hope: The lost boys of Sudan* (Williams 2013) tells the events following a violent attack on a Sudanese village, leaving boys to wander until they were able to arrive at a refugee camp in Ethiopia. The true event that gave life to this storybook is a reminder about the horrors of war and its cruel consequences for children. Also, with a setting in Africa, this time in Burundi, another story narrating the lives of refugee children at a refugee camp is *The banana leaf ball* (Milway 2017). Here the author allows us to learn about the dramatic events that left a young boy to fend for himself after his village was attacked. Deriving partially, as the author points out, on actual events, it opens a window for readers to learn about the experiences of the boy while living in a refugee camp. The snapshot into his life at the camp highlights his adjustment to the setting and sheds light on the drama and trauma shared by the children housed at the camp.

Life at a camp, this time seen from the perspective of two girls, is also what the readers find in *Four feet, two sandals* (Williams and Mohammed 2007). Clearly evidenced in the story is how the two girls who meet after finding a sandal become friends. Valuing each other's company, their relationship grows, and their friendship strengthens. Among the reality of the camp, their friendship reveals how they are able to emotionally connect and share similar hopes to someday leave the camp. The need for relationships is also the message found in *Lubna and pebble* (Meddour 2019), this time about a young girl living in a refugee camp with her father. Evidenced through the narrative is how the young girl projects her need for someone to share her thoughts and resolves to turn a pebble into a trusted relationship. Her relationship with the "pebble" exposes the thirst for emotionally connecting with someone she could trust. The emotional needs of the girls in both of these two stories are very moving and remind us that children's needs remain and continue even more so when experiencing challenging moments and realities as those that refugees encounter.

Responding with Empathy: Helping Hands

Always look for the helpers for there are always people who will help (Rogers 2002) was a message left by Mr. Rogers, a TV host of a program for children, who shared his empathy and compassion and reminded us that there are always those who will answer to the needs of those in crisis. Compassionate responses have never been absent for millions of refugees and asylum seekers. Friendly and empathetic people continue to extend their hands to ameliorate the adversity experienced. Difficult and challenging times have also touched the hearts of many in society, especially seeing the presence of children. Recorded in many children's books are the unselfish actions of people who have answered to the needs of children refugees and their families. They speak about the empathy and understanding response of those who come to their aid. Some of those instances where caring, compassion, and empathy are displayed in stories about refugees can be found in Table 5.1.

Table 5.1 Selected Examples of Empathy and Compassionate Responses through Children's Books about Refugees and Asylum Seekers

Children's Book	Compassion and Empathetic Response
My two blankets (Kobald 2014)	Becoming a friend for Cartwheel, a refugee child
	Helping Cartwheel, to learn a new language
Lost and found cat. The true story of Kunkush's incredible journey (Kuntz and Shrodes 2017)	Efforts of people who helped to reunite the pet cat, Kunkush, with his family
My name is Sangoel (Williams and Mohammed 2009)	Sangoel and his family received help and assistance from Mrs. Johnson upon their arrival as refugees in America
The refuge (le Guen 2020)	The parent of the young girl recognizes the difficult experiences of a young refugee girl and encourages her daughter to play with the refugee girl. A relationship of friendship is built among the two girls.
Wishes (Van 2020)	Seeing the refugees who escaped on a boat, a vessel stops and picks them up, taking them to safety.
The day Saida arrived (Gómez Redondo 2020)	The determined efforts made by the child to help and become a friend to Saida, a refugee girl in her classroom.
Saving Stella (Fakher 2020)	Actions from people who located and rescued Stella making it possible for the dog to be reunited with her owner.
The cat man of Aleppo (Latham and Shamsi-Bhasa 2020)	The actions of Alaa toward the abandoned pet cats and other animals exemplify kindness toward pets still living in a war area.

Calling for Consideration: Children Facing Adversity

Many are the stories about refugees and asylum seekers, continuing to be written and told across today's world. Reflecting on the experiences shared through children's literature, the stories we hear and read in the media news come more clearly alive to us. In each of them, one feels the heartbreak and emotionally filled moments experienced by so many children. They are just as Maclear tells us through the storyline of *Storyboat* (2020), here and there, "and wait, and wait, and wait" (n.p.), to find a place they can call home once again. Images and the narratives presented through children's books we reviewed bring us closer to learn about children faced with unimaginable adversity who are robbed of their most precious life's moment as children. Many of these children have been and are now in our classrooms. Some of you who read this book may have been just like them, forced to leave the place you called home and becoming again in another land. Through the experiences of children, sometimes untold or quietly shared, we learn and are reminded about the difficult circumstances continuing to happen in society.

Where will I live? Who will I meet? Questions similar to those we read in McCartney's photographical essay about refugee children, *Where will I live?* (2017), are also heard from young refugees wondering about what may lie ahead for them. Talking about the challenges faced by refugee children and those seeking asylum is not always comfortable, especially when they are about children. Conscientiously considering children's reality, educators know that the adversity faced from their experiences is a traumatic marker in their young lives, one that cannot be ignored and demanding consideration (Muller et al. 2019; Erdman, Colker, and Winter 2020).

The drama of times of war becomes even more palpable when meeting, vicariously, the many characters in children's book stories. Their stories are ongoing and, in common, their narrative talks about the adverse times with traumatic realities and conditions shattering their childhood. Firmly considering the best interests of the child, actions are essential to address the needs of child refugees. UNICEF's six-point process outlines priority areas which would safeguard the future of refugee and migrant children (Figure 5.6). They provide us, as well, with an agenda to guide our efforts.

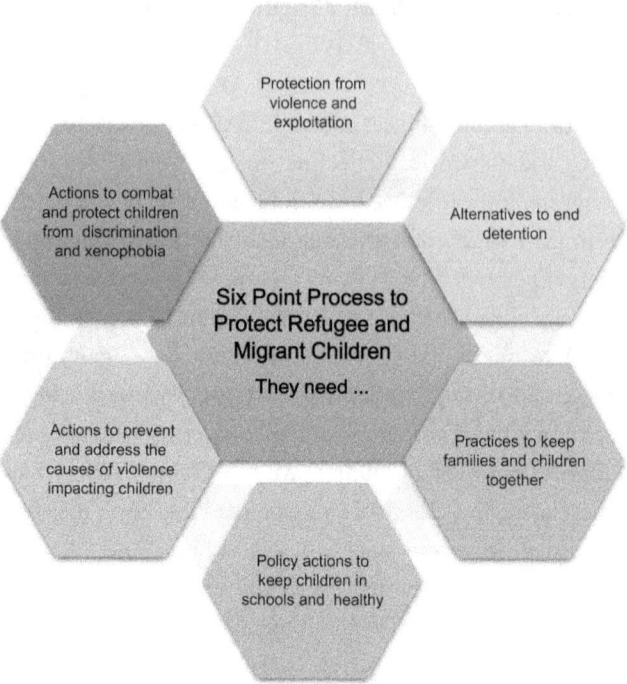

Figure 5.7 An agenda for children's protection: Six-point process to protect refugee and migrant children.

Source: UNICEF 2017. *A child is a child. Executive summary,* p. 4.

Happening Today: We Are Witnessing Their Realities

Peace is the only way to halt this tragedy.
—Filippo Grandi (UN High commissioner for refugees 2022)

During the time while writing this book, we became witnesses to children and families tearfully saying goodbyes in too many parts of the world. Too often, too many times, we have seen the faces of children forced to leave everything they know. Too early for them, we would agree, when learning that a child is living through these very difficult realities. Some were closer to us, happening right on shores not distant from us.

Winter 2022 brought to the world another chapter when peace was broken. This time, war came for the people of Ukraine, disrupting the lives of millions who suddenly found themselves trapped in a war zone. Their painful departures flashed on the news during those early months in 2022 when the world was shocked to see the attacks on Ukrainian cities (Aaro 2022). It is estimated that a million children were forced to leave just during the first two weeks of the conflict (Spike and Brito 2022). With their hands tightly holding a favorite toy, their expressions revealed without words a story being written with thousands of questions. Once again, society was watching how people were forced to leave their homes, their country. Adding to the many other ongoing situations forcing people away from their homelands, yet again attention was called to a continuing generation of people seeking refuge and asylum. The stories and experiences of children and their families continue motivating children's book authors, to capture these events, which have added to the existing literature on immigration.

With Hope for No More Forced Goodbyes

"We have to leave home ... maybe forever" (n.p.) is a statement that too many children have heard living and growing up in places where armed conflicts have altered their lives. It is, as well, what we read from the first pages in Parker Rubio's book *Far from home* (2019). Though a fictional story, it reflects the many unwanted realities still experienced by children and families. Through its pages, we follow the young child awakened one night to learn they had to leave, a story repeating itself over and over, so often now in society. We see in the story, the child holding his special toy, something that made us remember the multiple times that, during these recent decades, we have come across many similar images. On too many occasions, society has seen children with eyes that call for answers to the reasons they are taken away from what they know and where they feel at home. We hope that those images will never repeat themselves.

To Reflect and Do

1. If you are invited to talk about refugees, which story would you share to explain their realities? What are the reasons for your selection?
2. Topics about refugees and asylum seekers are difficult to share with children. However, they need to also learn about their experiences. What suggestions do you have to appropriately share stories about refugees with young children?
3. Choose any of the books mentioned in this chapter about refugees. Using the Freire's steps for conscious awareness, identify the main concerns facing children that the story presents. Propose actions to address the issues.

References

Aaro, David. "More than 1 million children fled Ukraine since start of invasion." *Fox News*, March 2022. https://www.foxnews.com/world/russia-ukraine-war-more-than-1-million-children-fled-ukraine-since-start-invasion.

Bishop, Rudine. 1990. Mirrors, windows and sliding glass doors. Perspectives, 6(3), ix–xi.

Boccagni, Paolo and Peter Kivisto. 2019. "Introduction: Ambivalence and the social processes of immigration." *International Journal of Comparative Sociology*. International Journal of Comparative Sociology 60(1–2): 3–13.

Botelho, M. and J. Rudman. 2009. *Critical multicultural analysis of children's literature: Windows, mirrors, and doors.* New York: Routledge.

Bryant, Brenda. 1990. "The richness of the child-pet relationship: A consideration of both benefits and costs of pets to children." *Anthrozoös* 3(4): 253–61, doi: 10.2752/089279390787057469.

Colvin, Susan and Anna Lyon. 2004. "Heightening awareness about the importance of using multicultural literature." *Multicultural Education* 11(3): 24–8. https://files.eric.ed.gov/fulltext/EJ783082.pdf.

Davies, Nicola. 2016. "The day the war came—a poem about child refugees." *The Guardian*, April 28. https://www.theguardian.com/childrens-books-site/2016/apr/28/the-day-the-war-came-poem-about-unaccompanied-child-refugees.

Erdman, Sarah, Laura Colker, and Elizabeth Winter. 2020. *Trauma and young children. Training strategies to support and empower. 2020.* Wahington, DC: NAEYC.

Hamilton, Heather. 2022. "Children of war. UNICEF says that Ukrainian children are refugees every 55 minutes." *Washington Examiner*, March 16. https://www.washingtonexaminer.com/news/children-of-war-unicef-says-55-ukrainian-children-are-refugees-every-single-minute.

Hidalgo, M. Carmen and Bernardo Hernandez. 2001. "Place attachment: Conceptual and empirical questions." *Journal of Environmental Psychology* 21: 273–81.

Johnston, Geoffrey. 2021. "Climate is also a children's rights crisis. Opinion." *The Recorder*, November 20. https://www.recorder.ca/opinion/columnists/climate-crisis-is-also-a-childrens-rights-crisis#:~:text=Children%20uprooted%20According%20to%20a%20report%20produced%20by,decisive%20action%20to%20get%20global%20warming%20under%20control.

Johnston, Geoffrey. 2022. "Ukrainian refugee children cling to pets." *Opinion, The Whig*, April 1. https://www.thewhig.com/opinion/columnists/ukrainian-refugee-children-cling-to-pets.

Lake, Anthony. 2016. Nearly 50 million children "uprooted" worldwide. UNICEF. http://press-releases/nearly.

Lewicka, Maria. 2011. "Place attachment: How far have we come in the last 40 years?" *Journal of Environmental Psychology* 31: 207–30.

Müller, Lauritz Rudolf Floribert et al. 2019. "Mental health and associated stress factors in accompanied and unaccompanied refugee minors resettled in

Germany: A cross-sectional study." *Child and Adolescent Psychiatry and Mental Health* 13(8). doi:10.1186/s13034-019-0268-1.

National Institutes for Health [NIH]. 2018. The power of pets. *News in Health NIH*, February. https://newsinhealth.nih.gov/2018/02/power-pets.

Norton, Donna. 2013. *Multicultural children's literature. Through the eyes of many children* (4th edition). MA: Pearson.

Paul, Daylin and Jason Miks. 2022. *Childhood upended by war in Ukraine. One month on, displaced children and their families are in desperate need of safety, stability and protection.* UNICEF. https://www.unicef.org/stories/childhood-upended-war-ukraine.

Purewal, Rebecca, Robert Christley, Katarzyna Kordas, Carol Joinson, Kerstin Meints, Nancy Gee, and Carri Westgarth. 2017. "Companion animals and child/adolescent development: A systematic review of the evidence." *International Journal of Environmental Research and Public Health* 14(3): 234. doi:10.3390/ijerph14030234.

Rogers, Fred. 2002. *Mister Rogers' parenting book: Helping to understand your young child*. Philadelphia: Running Press.

Spike, Justin and Renata Brito. "1 million children leave behind lives, friends in Ukraine." *AP News*, March 9, 2022. https://apnews.com/article/russia-ukraine-business-europe-kharkiv-james-elder-1e6dad5edbd594d20334273d2f936f63.

The Strait Times. 2022. "In pictures: Ukrainians bring along pets as they flee amid Russian invasion." *The Strait Times*, March 4. https://www.straitstimes.com/multimedia/photos/in-pictures-ukrainians-bring-along-pets-as-they-flee-shelter-amid-russian-invasion.

United Nations. 2021a. *Children and armed conflict. Report of the Secretary General.* https://www.un.org/ga/search/view_doc.asp?symbol=S/2021/437&Lang=E&Area=UNDOC.

United Nations. 2021b. "More children than ever before live as migrants or refugees, outside their birth countries—UNICEF." *United Nations News*, August 27. https://news.un.org/en/story/2021/08/1098612.

UNHCR The UN Refugee Agency. 2021. "Forcibly displaced populations." *Midyear Trends.* report https://www.unhcr.org/mid-year-trends.

UNICEF. n.d. *The convention on the rights of the child: The children's version*. https://www.unicef.org/media/60981/file/convention-rights-child-text-child-friendly-version.pdf.

UNICEF. 2016. *Uprooted. The growing crisis for refugee and migrant children. Executive summary and key findings.* https://www.unicef.org/sites/default/files/2019-02/Uprooted_Executive_Summary_Sept_2016-ENG.pdf.

UNICEF. 2017. *A child is a child. Executive summary. Protecting children on the move from violence, abuse and exploitation.* NY: UNICEF.

UNICEF. 2022. *Children in war and conflict.* https://www.unicefusa.org/mission/emergencies/conflict#:~:text=Learn%20more%20about%20how%20UNICEF%20is%20meeting%20urgent,of%20the%20Congo%20%28DRC%29%2C%20Nigeria%20and%20South%20Sudan.

World Bank Group. 2018. *Pathways to peace. Inclusive approaches to preventing violent conflict. Executive summary.* World Bank. https://olc.worldbank.org/system/files/Pathways%20for%20Peace%20Executive%20Summary.pdf.

Children's Books Cited

Bunting, Eve. 1988. *How many days to America. A thanksgiving story.* New York: Clarion Books.
Bunting, Eve. 2001. *Gleam and glow.* CA: Voyager Books.
Danticat, Edwidge. 2010. *Eight days.* NY: Orchard Books.
Davies, Nicola. 2018. *The day war came.* New York: Candlewick.
De Arias, Patricia. *Marwan's journey.* Massachusetts: mineditions.
Eulate, Ana. 2012. *The sky of Afghanistan.* Madrid: Cuentos de Luz.
Heide, Florence and Judith Gilliland. 1992. *Sami and the time of the troubles.* NY: Clarion Books.
Kumar, Tyshya. 2019. *I am a refugee.* United Kingdom: SilverWoods Books.
Kunz, Doug. 2017. *Lost and found cat. The true story of Kunkush's incredible journey.* NY: Crown Books for Young Readers.
Le Guen, Sandra. 2020. *The refuge.* Seattle, Washington: Amazon Crossing Kids.
London, Jonathan. 1998. *Hurricane.* New York: HarperCollins.
Maclear, Kyo. 2020. *Storyboat.* Canada: Tundra.
Meddour, Wendy. 2019. *Lubna and pebble.* New York: Dial Books.
Milway, Katie. 2017. *The banana leaf ball.* Canada: Kids Can Press.
Parker Rubio, Sarah. 2019. *Far from home. A story of loss, refuge, and hope.* IL: Tyndale House.
Ruurs, Margriet. 2016. *Stepping stones.* Canada: Orca Book Publishers.
Serres, Alain. 2009. *I have the right to be a child.* Canada: Groundwood Books/Anansi Press.
Simon, Seymour. 2007. *Hurricanes.* Washington, DC: Smithsonian.
Tonatiuh, Duncan. 2014. *Pancho Rabbit and the Coyote: A migrant's tale.* New York: Abrams Books for young Readers.
Velazquez, Eric. 2001. *Grandma's records.* NY: Bloomsbury.
Văn, Muo Thi. 2020. *Wishes.* NY: Orchard Books.
Watanabe. 2020. *Migrants.* New Zealand: Gecko Press.
Williams, Mary. 2005. *Brothers in hope. The story of the lost boys of Sudan.* New York: Lee and Low Books.
Williams, Karen and Kadra Mohammed. 2007. *Four feet and two sandals.* Grand Rapids, Michigan: Eerdmans Books for Young Children.

6

At School! Immigrant Children Coming to School

This chapter aims to:

- Explore some of the schooling challenges faced by immigrant children.
- Discuss the linguistic challenge faced by immigrant children.
- Explore some of the experiences of immigrant children through the lens of stories

Key words:

- Socialization
- Ethnic identity
- Children's rights
- Emotions and feelings
- Children's well-being

Welcoming Children

They had just finished reading the story All are welcome (Penfold 2018), *which led the five-year- olds to talk about all the things in common they shared. One of the five-year-olds said how much he would like to meet more children, with others assenting. Listening to his comment, Ms. Elissa thought it was time to share some news with her class. "Children," she said, "I have some news. Tomorrow, two children will be joining our class. They come from a very faraway place." There were some cheers from the group, while others stared with surprised eyes. She followed her announcement with a question, asking, "How can we make them feel welcomed? Any ideas?" A couple of hands were quickly raised with suggestions. Some suggested writing "Welcome" in a big banner, with most liking the idea. Others proposed to write messages welcoming the two new classmates. As she* listens, Ms. Elissa thought about her own experience, coming many years earlier as an immigrant and about that very first time when she first came into a classroom in the place where she came to live. "Those are very good ideas," said their teacher. "I am sure that they will be happy to be here," she told them, inviting everyone to get started with the suggestions.

Going to School

Everywhere in the world, in some places more than others, immigrant children are joining classrooms in countries where they are coming to live. A first day at school is one to be always remembered, especially for young immigrant children beginning another special moment in their lives. A welcoming experience, just like what was being planned by children in the opening scenario, is what all children deserve. To welcome is to embrace the diversity of the child. Such is the message emanating from classrooms and schools where immigrant children's lived experiences and stories are consciously considered, valued and respected.

Places Where Children Become

New environments, new peers, and a myriad of experiences are what await immigrant children as they step into their new classroom. From that first time, feeling that they belong is what is hoped each child will find. Those positive feelings are a hallmark for a positive adaptation and successful adjustment as they navigate life in the setting of their classrooms (Genishi and Dyson 2009; Gagne, Shapka and Law 2012; Compton-Lilly et al. 2017). Spaces where children become, classrooms, continue to be places where immigrant children explore and make sense about their own selves in the context of new realities. No one doubts the role that classroom experiences have on immigrant children. Within the settings of schools and classrooms, they find some of the most influential experiences as they navigate the culture of the communities where they now live. Even if they are native born, immigrant children, as we have stated earlier, will be faced with an array of challenges. From their heritage to their language and ways of being, children of immigration find themselves learning about and becoming in context where they continue to form a sense about who they are. Every moment, new stories arise of young children coming face to face with the culture outside their homes. The anxious child that we meet in *My name is Sangoel* (Williams and Mohammed 2014) mindfully reminds us about the multiple experiences happening every day in classrooms everywhere. Who has not felt that same feeling not knowing what you would find in a new classroom?

The stories learned and taking shape are numerous, all telling us about the experiences, and challenges that immigrant children encounter. We delve into some of those through this chapter. Some reveal the welcoming hands and voices, while others tell us about the struggle children experience as they adapt and adjust to their new settings. Still, others will lead us to reflect on the social justice implications of the education experiences of young immigrant children.

A Milestone in a Child's Life

That very first day when a child goes to school is another of the milestones in a child's life. The anticipation and emotions of that very first time is an experience of a lifetime. The voices of children in playgrounds and classrooms define a time when children enter the culture of schools and education. Those are moments that will make one feel just like the girl coming to school in Woodson's *The day you begin* (2018). Eager but at the same time, with a sense of trepidation for what one may find stepping into a new classroom where you are new, where the language may not be your own, where "no one is quite like you" (Woodson, n.p.), you may wonder if you are welcomed.

That moment when we step into a classroom reminds us that going to school is another frontier, this time, one that for immigrant children also marks another border they cross (Figure 6.1), one with many personal and sociocultural implications. Socially and emotionally, experiences in the classroom play an influential role in how children construct their sense about themselves and about their identity. Relationships with peers and adults within the context of the classroom and school contribute to their development, providing repertoires

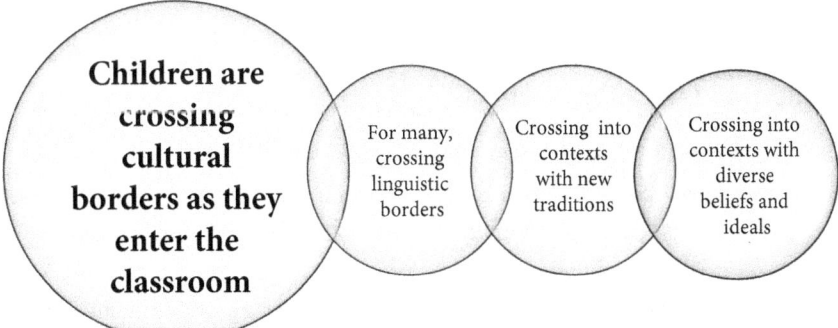

Figure 6.1 Classrooms, another border that children cross.

of experiences where immigrant children are led to negotiate their own ways and views with those of the settings where they now live.

Powerful Stories: Keeping Memories Alive

Going to school is an event to be always remembered, one where a child begins experiences in a context different from his or her familiar settings. There are so many emotions evoked when children start school. These are even more strongly felt for immigrant children. Like the teacher in the opening vignette, they are emotions kept forever alive in our memory. Those encounters, culturally clashing moments, remain with you, too. Everyone has a story about those first times at school. Reading those stories we find the power they have bringing those moments back to us. Their storylines, once again, open a window to a time where some will experience again an experience of growing up as immigrants, while others will be led to "be there" vicariously.

We remember our own students' reactions when we shared the *Name jar* (Choi 2001). After sharing and discussing its message with our students, we remember how for some, it evoked memories about their own names. Some of those who were immigrants, remembered how much they also wanted to change their names "to stop people's questions," remarked one student; others revealed they had actually changed their names to "make it easier to pronounce." We heard, too, from students who stood firm and kept their given names. Many other anecdotes from their classroom experiences were shared as we reflected about the story. Sharing storybooks have also led students to remember experiences of peers and neighbors. It has brought alive so many anecdotes from childhood experiences reaffirming the critical role of stories from children's literature. They are especially relevant to fulfil our desire to share life's events especially those of diversity through the special lens of children's stories (Dyson and Haas 1994).

Education Is a Child's Right

> ... recognize the right of the child to education, and with a view to achieving this right progressively and on the basis of equal opportunity ...
> —Article 28, Convention on the Rights of the Child (United Nations 1989)

A milestone transition, going to school is one of the memorable events during childhood. It is also a key experience preparing a child for life's successes. Because of its fundamental importance for a child, education is recognized as a right endowed for every child. The right to education is universal to all children and calls for equitable access to schools and classrooms. Because education is a factor contributing to the well-being of children, irrespective of the circumstances, it is critical to maintain their rightful access and participation in quality-rich experiences. Despite the universality of the children's right to education, for many child immigrants this is still a struggle to be overcome. Faced with limited or unequal experiences, children's right to education continues to demand attention from everyone.

Drawing from History, Stories to Remember

Educational rights have also been addressed in children's literature about immigration. In some stories, the lawful right to education has been the direct subject and focus of interest. They provide us with opportunities to value and appreciate the efforts made in the past and continuing today. Providing us a bridge into the past, through the pages of *Separate is not equal: Sylvia Mendez and her family's fight for desegregation* (Tonatiuh 2014), we learn about this true story, a blatant case of discrimination against immigrant children of Mexican descent. The powerful storyline allows us to witness the legal battle of parents in the Westminster school district in California during the 1940s who determinedly fought to stop the school from a segregation practice separating their children because of their ethnic origin (Madrid 2008). The imagery used to tell the story about this event, drawn from historical reality, leaves a vivid memory about the actions taken by the parents and make us aware about the incessant struggle for social justice for immigrant children. Under the pretext to provide special attention, the school placed the Mexican children in a separate facility called the "Mexican school." The decision led parents to fight for their children's rights. The parents' victory was a landmark in the struggle to ensure equal educational rights for immigrant children in the United States and a precursor to later milestone legal successes for children.

Another Historical Story of a Milestone Win to Be Remembered

A milestone in the legal battle for equal access to education, the case of the Lemon Grove schools, another story of discrimination against Hispanic children, recounts the events and actions of parents to stop their children from being separated from their peers. Based on the events that took place during the 1930s in a California school district, the Lemon Grove incident was a clear discriminatory experience against the education rights of the immigrant children attending their schools. Prompted by the decision made by the school board to separate the Mexican children from their white peers, the parents took the case to the courts, where their victory marked a precedent in the struggle against school segregation. Two authors (Hale 2019; Alvarez 2021), highlight this important story, each using a different format to tell their version of this story. Both accentuate the prejudice and excuses used to plan and carry out actions to exclude immigrant children from attending the same school as their white peers.

Christy Hale in *Todos Iguales/All Equal: Un Corrido De Lemon Grove/A Ballad of Lemon Grove (2019)* uses a Mexican musical genre, *corrido*, to tell the story. Her approach to present the story highlights the heritage of the children and families victimized by the discriminatory practices. Another version of this historical incident is presented in Brimmer's book, *Without Separation: Prejudice, segregation, and the case of Roberto Alvarez* (2021). The additional historical background information that Brimmer provides is helpful to further understand the significance of the Lemon Grove incident in the search for equitable experiences for children of immigration.

Stories about Immigrant Children at School

Many are the experiences collected through children's literature about children going to school. As a theme, it has allowed readers, a window and a wide avenue into the many different emotions and events in classrooms and schools. The power of stories has captured experiences and impressions of children, providing a wide view into those important times in schools and classrooms. Through many of these stories, we have a glimpse into many distinct aspects depicting the experiences of immigrant children. Reflecting on their storylines, we are led to explore a variety of events and experiences also defining important developmental milestones for young children. While they address and present a variety of issues and themes about immigrant children and their school experience, two fundamental areas that serve as the focus for those stories explored in this chapter are children's cultural encounters and feelings of welcome (Figure 6.2). With attention to issues of diversity and immigration, those discussed here are a sample of stories especially emerging in the recent decade.

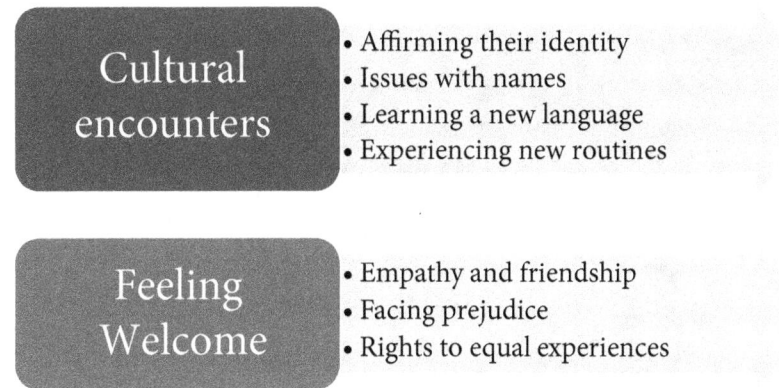

Figure 6.2 A focus on some of the immigrant children's experiences at school.

Growing Immigrant Diversity in the Classroom

Many stories remind us about the growing diversity of children in schools and communities. When reading Penfold's story *All are welcome*, the image of a classroom where children's faces reflect the world's diversity reminded us of today's classrooms. Welcoming all children, without making any distinctions just like the teacher in Penfold's story, recognizes and embraces their diversity that is already a predominant trait in many communities. It is precisely the growing diversity of ethnic groups, cultures, languages, and beliefs that altogether displays the impact of migration in communities everywhere. With an increase in immigration, the presence of immigrant children has contributed to the ongoing changing demographical nature of classrooms across many continents (Organization for Economic Cooperation and Development [OECD] 2015; Camarota, Griffith, and Zeigler 2017). In the United States, they already constitute over 24 percent of their school enrollment (Dinan 2017). It could be said that the clear evidence of an immigrant presence throughout communities has contributed and inspired interest in the experiences of child immigrants in children's literature.

"I am new here" seems to reflect what thousands of children continue to say every day entering classrooms in the places where they have come to live. Many classrooms probably are like that of Lola's, the young girl we meet in *Islandborn* (Diaz 2018), in a school "where everyone was from somewhere else" (n.p.). Children, just like Mariama, a child refugee in Cornelles' story *Mariama, different but just the same* (2015), eagerly wanting to learn, to play, and to affirm herself in a new community, remind us about the aspirations of young

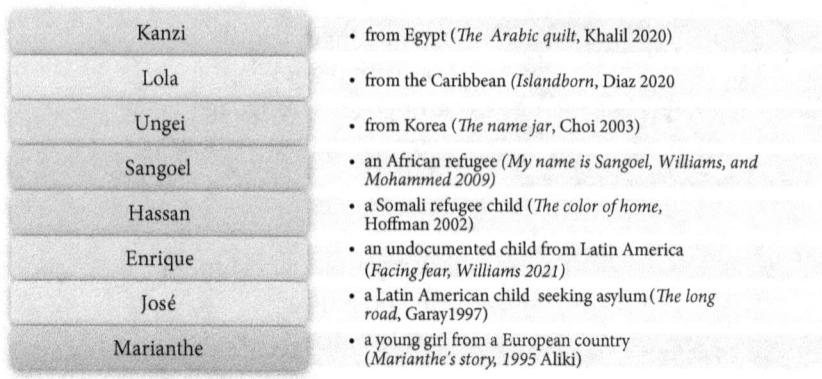

Figure 6.3 Meeting immigrant diversity through story characters: Selected story characters.

immigrant children coming into the classrooms. Perhaps they are children like young Kanzi, a girl who came from Egypt and who wanted so much to feel that she belonged (*The Arabic quilt*, Khalil 2020). Like these characters, thousands of children of immigration are joining and waiting to join classrooms everywhere where they will feel they belong (Figure 6.3).

A diversity of cultures and ethnicities, that is today what continues to define the demographic profile of classrooms as children and families continue arriving to communities near and far. There are multiple stories about the many experiences of children that will continue to be written as they come into the classrooms. Many more will be added to children's literature which already has reflected an increase in titles published narrating stories of immigrants. Those discussed in this chapter are just a selection of the many available in the literature on immigration.

Welcoming Experiences, Always Remembered

The dynamic realities of classrooms are experiences from childhood that we carry throughout our lives. Schooling is an experience always to be remembered by children, but even more when you are stepping into classrooms new to you, in a country that is also new to you. What you find in an environment when you first move in are impressions always remembered. Inevitably, one will compare what you find with what you knew. One colleague that we spoke with still remembers how she was struck by the school building that, as a second grader, she attended, after her family migrated to another country. Everything seemed so different, that was her first impression. She told us that it took a while for her to get used to going to school in an environment so different from what she knew. She missed the school where doors to classrooms were open and with windows you could see to the outside.

Feeling That You Are Welcome

A new experience always brings changes and for many, those first impressions clearly reveal they are in contexts different from those they knew. Many times, for peers in receiving classrooms, it is the first time they encounter diversity. It is not surprising to expect a variety of reactions to their new peers. Puzzled faces, questions, and sometimes rejection just as what Kanzi, the main character in *The Arabic quilt* experiences from a classmate who snubs and diminishes the importance of her peer's heritage language. We also remember what the girl in *One green apple* (Bunting 1992) says to herself as she travels with her new peers seeing "some that look at me coldly and smile cruel smiles" (n.p.).

Making children feel welcome into the classroom is an ongoing experience that calls for careful and mindful planning. For a child, that moment you enter a classroom is the start of many different experiences. It is just as Woodson (2018) powerfully states that "there will be times when you walk into a room and no one will be quite like you" (*The day you begin* n.p.). Diversity, which influences experiences in the classroom, continues to be a factor most immigrants share. The warmth of their welcome, the artifact brought to acknowledge their culture or place of birth, are details to be always remembered signifying that doors are open, and arms are, too, receiving them into the community of the classroom.

Welcoming Diversity, Consciously

From the very first moments, from preschool and beyond, classrooms are doors into sociocultural experiences embedded into the learning context of schools (Guerra et al. 2019). Finding themselves in the setting of the classroom, immigrant children will face a new cultural script including sometimes a different language, and an array of practices, expectations, and ways of doing things many times diverse from those they bring (Robles-Melendez and Driscoll 2020). These changes and new beginnings are exciting moments. They also imply, once again, emotionally loaded experiences calling for consideration. Consider the reactions of the young Muslim girl in *One green apple* (Bunting 1992), who on her second day at school goes on a field trip, a new experience, in a new place, and with peers she is yet to know, and with a language still to be learned. The multiple emotions experienced are obvious and a clear reminder of those children of immigrants encounter every time they begin a new experience.

Socially and emotionally, what children experience at school and in the community cannot be dismissed as simple events and changes. They demand mindful consideration given the impact they have on a child (OECD 2015; Kicks and Johnson 2018), especially during the years when their sense of self and identity is emerging and taking shape. Sensitive responses to a child's needs are what we find in Marianthe's classroom (Aliki 1998), a girl still learning the language of the place where she now lives. Aware that she enjoys drawing, her teacher allows her to use her drawings to voice her feelings and to share her stories, all while learning the language spoken where she now lives. Such responsive experiences convey to children a message of caring that welcomes them as who they are. Let us not forget that learning a language is a socio-emotional experience and the support received is one that will influence a child's efforts and memories (Lessow-Hurley 2013; Otto 2018).

A first day at school is always something to remember for many reasons. Those are memories, especially unforgettable when you went to a new school, and even more, especially if it was in a new location. What an experience! This must have been the thought that the children in Sibley O'Brien's story *I am new here* (2015) had after attending school for the first time in a country where they now live. They are three children coming to school for the first time, three children from different cultures, each joining a class where the language is different from their own, where the classroom culture also differs from their own. So many differences but so many things in common, all to be discovered and explored at school. This is what every day, everywhere immigrant children experience in the places where they now live.

Thinking and Reflecting ... Memories from Those First Days at School

A first day at school is always something to remember for many reasons. Those are memories especially unforgettable when you went to a new school and even more if it was in a new location. We invite you to reflect on the memories you have about attending school. What impressed you the most? What made that a moment to be remembered?

The classroom we visit in Sibley O'Brien's story is a reflection of environments where children are welcomed, where their own diversity is also welcomed.

In the Classroom: Responsive Attention to Immigrant Children Needs

The early childhood years are one of the most crucial moments in a child's development. Experiences and responsive attention in the classroom are one of the influential factors during those first years. A significantly meaningful time in their growth and development, for children, classrooms are an influential setting where a variety of cultural negotiations take place every day. Many more are the adjustments and negotiations that occur when children are immigrants (Suárez-Orozco and Suárez-Orozco 2001; Goodwin 2002). These adjustments and adaptations are even more complex when there are clear cultural differences between the culture of the child and that of the places where they come to live (García-Coll 2012). Many times, however, diversity is not openly acknowledged in the classroom. Those are classrooms that continue to place an emphasis on what is common to everyone. Following what seems like a more generic approach, which dismisses the diverse nature of individuals, deprives children of the opportunity to learn about their own diversity and to appreciate that of their peers.

In the Classroom: A Diversity of Cultures, Languages, and Practices

A culture that differs from that of the child, a language different from that they know, social expectations differing from those known, misinformed and stereotyped views, and even dissimilar classroom routines are but a few of the many cultural differences that immigrant children and their families may find during their school and classroom experience. Challenging as these are, still, most seem to agree that these can be successfully addressed when the classroom environment and the educator consciously welcomes children and their diversity into the classroom community (Takanishi 2004; Derman-Sparks and Edwards 2010; NAEYC 2020; Robles-Melendez and Driscoll 2020). The learning that ensues becomes mutual as both immigrant children and their peers will actively learn from each other. This is what is reflected in many children's book stories, a source itself for exploring and delving into the experiential repertoire of children of immigration (Szcesi et al. 2012; Norton 2013). There are many authors who have addressed cultural differences in the classroom context. Stories by Aliki

(*Marianthe's story: painted words and Spoken Memories*, 1998), Williams (*My name is Sangoel*, 2003) and Khalil (The *Arabic quilt*, 2020) all bring us examples on how cultures and diversity are intentionally and responsively addressed in the classroom. These are discussed in this section.

Responding with Welcoming Attention

Many stories already allow us to learn and vicariously experience some of the complex cultural differences children find in the classroom. Storylines in children's literature provide important avenues about cultural differences and how these are addressed when meeting some of the immigrant children's characters in Aliki's *Marianthe's story* and in *My name is Sangoel* (Williams and Mohammed 2003). Both stories provide insights into the experiences at school for children coming from very different cultural contexts and circumstances. The hesitancy that both Marianthe and Sangoel exhibit as they come to school, in a different country and where the language is different, reflects that of thousands of children, entering for the first time into classrooms where all is new and unfamiliar to them. Finding, as the characters in Aliki's and Williams and Mohammed's stories do, an environment where they feel welcome is a door that opens, socially and emotionally meaningful as a child begins a new journey. Reading through these two stories, clearly, the message in their classroom environments is one of understanding, sensitive to the individual experiences of children, who find themselves removed from what they knew and learning about a different reality.

Author Aya Khalil introduces us to Kanzi in *The Arabic quilt* (2020), who is faced with misinformed attitudes toward her culture. The unkind words from one of the classmates are, sadly, not an unusual experience. Responding with sensitivity, her teacher is aware about the need to address the challenge she faces. Seeing an opportunity for everyone to appreciate the young Egyptian girl's culture, she engages the class in a project that at the same time openly extends a welcome to both Kanzi and her mother.

Each of these stories reveals how children's individual needs are responsively met (Figure 6.4). In each of these examples, one also recognizes the empathic response displayed by both teachers and peers, toward these story characters.

Socioculturally, classrooms are an influential environment where children negotiate understandings, making sense about cultural practices and expectations that bridge their own with those of the society where they live. In the next sections of this chapter we will focus on some of the experiences, once again, through the window opened by stories of children and immigration.

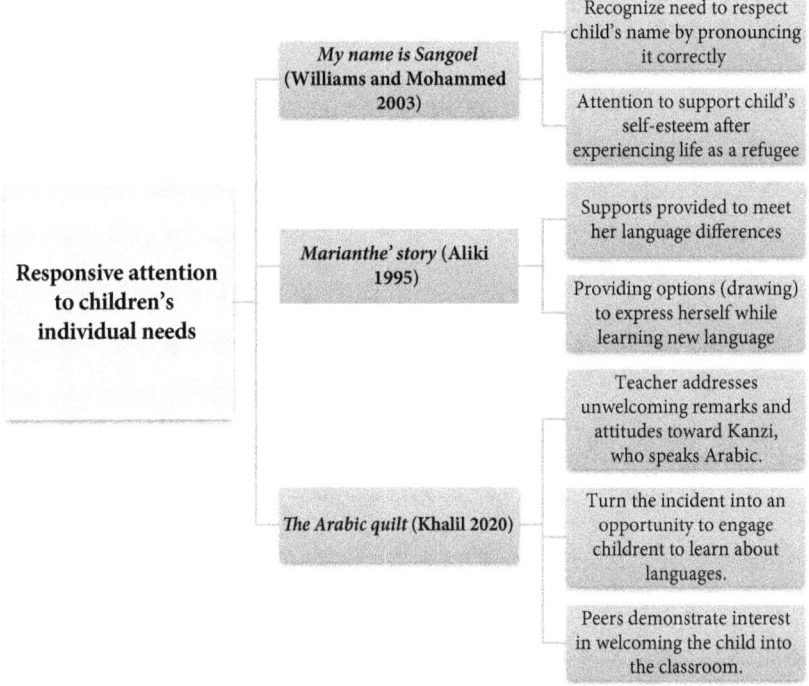

Figure 6.4 Stories about classroom responsiveness to immigrant children's needs.

… Walking in Their Shoes

Many stories continue to be written from children's experiences coming to classrooms in other countries. As early childhood educators, we may know many of them as we welcome and work with immigrant children in our schools and centers. Stepping into the classroom is the beginning of many important experiences for every child. They become even more so for immigrants especially as they come to face an unfamiliar cultural script in a context that often is also unfamiliar to them. Along the path of the school days, children's growth and development continue to unfold, which is now also influenced by the culture of the classroom and school. Many cultural and social negotiations await children from the first time they enter the classroom. These encounters are significant, marking their lived experience as they grow up and develop. Among the most relevant ones is building a sense that they, too, belong to the community of the classroom. This is what we experience reading O'Brien's story *I am new here* and in Diaz's *Islandborn*, where in each case, the teacher intentionally makes an effort to welcome and validate their diversity and culture.

Researchers tell about the vital role classrooms and school play in giving immigrant children that sense of being part of a community (Sonderberger, Barrett, and Creed 2004; Gagné, Shapka, and Law 2012). They also recognize the stressful moments children experience as they try to adapt and adjust to a new cultural context. Added to the stress are the times when they experience rejection and prejudiced actions in their classrooms and schools, just as we see in the images of Kerascoët story *I walk with Vanessa*, where the child is rejected and bullied by her peers. The wordless story makes clear the pain of what some may experience simply because of their diversity. These are experiences that even as minor as they may be, emotionally leave their mark on one's mind and soul (González, Stein, Kiag, and Kupito 2014). Early childhood educators agree that these cannot be ignored and demand attention as programs consider how to address and consciously respond to the experience and needs of immigrants in their classrooms (Villarreal and Rodriguez 2008; Liu 2021).

Encountering Cultures

Literature about diversity allows us to sample a myriad of cultural encounters and challenges. These stories are a wide avenue leading to a confluence of the realities of cultures coming to meet each other in the setting of the classroom. For immigrant children with diverse roots, they become a mirror where they may see themselves and relive experiences (Bishop 1990; Botelho and Rudman 2009). Some of these stories reveal cultural differences that may challenge young immigrants' sense of competence. We meet the young Asian boy in *Cleversticks* (Ashley 1992), who is challenged by tasks common to his peers but not favored in his culture. We also learn how proud René is about his name in *René has two last names* (Colato Laínez 2009) who decidedly shares why he carries two last names, not one. Similarly, we find Sangoel (*Sangoel is my name*, Williams and Mohammed 2009), who wants to keep his name pronounced correctly and creatively finds a way to ensure they learn it.

Together with Laila, the young girl in *Laila's lunchbox* (Faruqi 2015), we learn about daily efforts children make to maintain their heritage tradition in contexts where the culture is different. Addressing faith traditions, we walk together with Laila, who is determined to participate in her first Ramadan. Meanwhile, her classmates, unfamiliar with her traditions, wonder why she stays away from the lunchroom. Indeed, these are experiences many repeated with children who bring their traditions to the classroom. These are also moments prompting opportunities to explore and learn about the diversity of practices and traditions in society. These are relevant experiences and preparation for all children for success in an ever increasing culturally diverse society.

Making Us Become Conscious about Their Challenges

Stories allow us to walk together with children and experience the many episodes taking place in the classroom. Their narrative lines make their experience come alive to us. They provide visibility to the experiences of children with cultural and diverse roots and bring us closer to learning about the challenges they face. This is another first step leading us to become conscious about the issues of immigration. Social justice issues are afloat in stories about immigrant children and particularly throughout their classroom experiences. Many of those involve issues of cultural differences and of prejudice, with many stories allowing us to experience the challenge of discrimination and prejudice. One of those is the case of Vanessa, the young girl in Kerascoët's story *I walk with Vanessa* (2018), who, experiencing rejection from her own classroom peers, finds herself alone. Also revealing challenges faced because of cultural differences, is the struggle of a young Somali child refugee, Sangoel, who tries to find himself in the context of a new classroom. We are also made aware about the challenge of new realities experienced by children like Iliana (*The refuge* 2020), in a school and place all new to her while trying to make sense about her journey and herself. Reading and reflecting on these stories lead us to continue building greater awareness about the ongoing challenge facing children. The fact is, these challenges are simply prompted because of the children's own cultural diversity. Within the context of dynamic classroom interactions, both immigrant children and their peers, and adults are all encountering a different culture and respectively trying to understand and make sense of each other.

Living Experiences

Who am I and how do they see me, are but a few of the many questions and challenges posed which are negotiated at school during the early childhood years (Kostelnik et al. 2019). A crucial point is the fact that these cultural negotiations actively contribute to the child's formation of a sense of identity, which begins and is influenced by experiences during the early childhood years (Compton-Lilly et al. 2017). Among some of the most critical negotiations children face are those defining their own self through experiences and relationships giving a child a sense of identity (Corsaro 2018). Facing new cultural scripts, interactions in the classroom play a leading role in helping children to create new ways to respond in their social realities (Rogoff 2003). Walking together with immigrant children through their stories, we explore some of the experiences at schools. Experiencing their stories, we gain greater awareness about what they encounter, and learn about events challenging the child's own sense of self.

My Name Is…

> *Desde que vivo aquí, ya no sé ni cómo me llamo [Since I live here, I no longer know what my name is]*
>
> —Anonymous

Names are very personal and meaningful to individuals. A name is more than just a designation for a person; a name gives people a sense of identity. During our discussion about names in Chapter 4, we posed the challenge many faced when their names are in other languages. The issue has been addressed by many authors presenting it from the perspective of children, who today continue to find themselves challenged to keep their heritage names (Figure 6.5).

Stories about issues with heritage names in the classroom
- *Facing challenges with acceptance of heritage names*
  - *My name is Jorge on both sides of the river* (Medina, 1999)*
  - *My name is Maria Isabel* (Ada, 1993)*
  - *René has two last names/René tiene dos apellidos* (Colato Lainez, 2009). *
  - *Marisol Macdonald doesn't match* (Palacios, 2011)
  - *My name is Alma and how I got this name* (Martinez -Neal 2018)
- *Pronunciation of ethnic name*
  - *My name is Sangoel* (Williams and Mohammed, 2009)
  - *My name is Jorge on both sides of the river* (Medina, 1999)

Stories about immigrant children wanting to change their names
- *My name is Yoon* (Recorvitz, 2003)
- *The name jar* (Choi, 2003)
- *Always Anjali* (Sheh, 2018)

Figure 6.5 Selected stories addressing the topic about names.

*Bilingual

Your Name, Your Identity: Remember, It Is also a Child's Right

*... to respect the right of the child to **preserve his or her identity**, including nationality, **name** and family relations as recognized by law without unlawful interference.*
—Article 8, Convention on the Rights of the Child (emphasis added 1989)

Names, there is always more to what they represent. Recognizing its importance for children's well-being, names are also a component inherent to Article 8 of the CRC. Need for respectful and responsive attention to what a name symbolizes for a child is primordial. Implications are multiple given that your name represents you and demarcates your culture and identity. They are particularly meaningful for children as they are in the process of building a sense about their own identity. However, the practice of changing or "adapting" names of immigrants is a common one in many countries where names end up being changed to sound more like those in the host culture. In the United States, it is not uncommon to find names of immigrant children adapted or adjusted, some in such ways that completely changes and dismisses the essence of a child's given name (Hayleigh 2015). A call for consciously considering the implications of changing children's heritage names is critical. The issue is one of respect for the child and his culture according to educator Soto Pressley (cited in Colombo 2015), who talked about her experience when peers changed the name of a new young student from Jorge to George. She addressed the name issue in her classroom, and soon peers started to call him by his given name. Her experiences are a reminder about the need to honor family names and to consciously make children aware about their importance.

Many of us perhaps have experienced having your first name being changed to an "easier to pronounce" version of itself. It was through *My name is Maria Isabel* (Ada 1993) that we walked along with a young Hispanic girl whose name was being changed at school. Her story gave us insights into one of the ongoing cultural challenges confronting young immigrant children, where many are experiences with profound developmental implications. They raise attention to the numerous cultural adjustments that are made and taking place in the classroom during the early childhood years. Following Maria Isabel's story sheds light on what many children experience as they have their names changed.

In some cases, names have been completely changed into the language of the host culture. Such was the case of the young Mexican boy named Jorge that we meet in Medina's poems *My name is Jorge on both sides of the river* (1999). When for his teacher and peers, "Jorge" became "George," we witness his insistence in being "Jorge," keeping true to his own self and to his identity and heritage. Struggles with the influential cultural force of the classroom seemed inevitable for him. To his surprise, one day he finds himself responding to his name in English, when, "a girl called me 'George,' and I turned my head" (7). Surprised, he recognizes how despite his efforts to stay being "Jorge," he was beginning to internalize his other persona as "George." Medina's poems about this young boy give us a window into the struggles experienced by immigrant children striving to keep their identity while faced with the challenging acculturative influence of the classroom.

The importance of names and the pride one feels is also showcased in *My name is Sangoel* (Williams and Mohammed 2009). Wanting to make sure everyone would remember what his name was, Sangoel even prints it on his shirt. His actions remind us that names are more than just a name. They are a reflection and affirmation of our own self. Efforts to ensure they are appropriately pronounced are a respectful acknowledgment of the individual they stand for.

Trying to Fit In

When we read *The name jar* (Choi 2001), many will think about a time when they also wanted to change their names. For the young Korean girl, changing her name was the answer to avoid being different and to fit in. Like the challenges experienced by another Korean child in Recorvitz's *My name is Yoon* (2007) who also wants to change her name, in both stories the girls discover the meaningfulness of their names connecting each one to their heritage. Names, as pointed out earlier, carry so many meaningful memories. More important is how they also become such an inherent piece of the mosaic of our own identity. It is, as one of the authors of this book shared, a cultural and family foundational component giving you a sense of identity, a sense of unbreakable connection to your own history and heritage. Despite its vital role, the struggle and need to fit in will make some adapt or change their given names.

Who has not met someone who, trying to fit in, has wanted to change or even actually changed their names? When it comes to your given name, the issue is more than whether one likes your given name or not. Some children may actually find themselves pressured to do so, especially if they are from a different culture and want to avoid feeling as an outsider. One of our authors remembered what a colleague who immigrated from a European country shared about a time when he was asked to change his name "because it was too difficult." Still today, many continue to experience similar situations, sometimes having their names changed even without being asked to do so. Those are instances where one remembers the examples from characters like Jorge (*My name is Jorge on both sides of the river*), who struggle to keep his name from been anglicized, and of Sangoel (*My name is Sangoel*), who creatively found a way to maintain and affirm his given name.

The need to belong and the need to feel that you are part of a group are strong motivators driving us to make many adjustments. Those often include our own names and simply reflect an effort to see yourself fit into a new reality. Hesitancy to say their own names because "they sound different" and even feeling fearful of even saying them may lead immigrant children to change their own names. It all responds to the stress emerging from the acculturative experience of children trying to construct their sense about themselves taking place in the classroom as well as in their communities. This is an area where further research is still needed to more clearly understand children's experiences and feelings about their names (Drummond and Varvin 2020). In some cases, it is their parents who, also concerned about rejection and being looked at as a foreigner, may decide to use or adapt their children's names. One of the students we met shared how her family changed her name becoming *Blanche* instead of her given name, *Blanca*. She found out years later.

And Your Last Name Is …?

First names are not only what sometimes pose challenges for immigrants. Last names are another aspect also raising issues in the classroom. Pronunciation aside, practices about last names vary across cultures (Haynes 2015). Too many people probably have experienced being asked about their last names, sometimes with an inquisitive face especially when they are different from what is typically customary in some cultures. Because not every culture follows a universal practice when it comes to their surnames, diversity is what probably best describes the practice and traditional way to designate these. To those keeping true to their cultural traditions, a suggestion to "simplify" their surnames is likely something they heard more than once. There are cases, too, where some last names may be confused as first names. Such was the personal experience of one of the students of the authors whose child was being told at school to clarify what his last name was because "he had two names."

Those who follow the tradition of having two last names may find themselves reflected in *René has two last names* (Colato Laínez 2009). The author narrates the experience of a young Hispanic immigrant who, true to his tradition, insisted on keeping his two last names. Cleverly, he manages to share with his classmates the reason for carrying more than just one last name. The story becomes an affirmation of cultural heritage, one that continues calling for conscious understanding and for culturally respectful practices. Providing another opportunity to explore and learn about names, Colato Lainez's story presents another experience where immigrants find themselves being challenged. The challenge of adjustment and adapting to a new culture and the ensuing struggle to maintain one's heritage practices is documented through the story.

Colato Lainez's storyline is reflective of many of the author's own experiences. The experience is also descriptive of the many times where cultures clash. The practice of carrying two last names is traditionally followed in Hispanic/Latino cultures. It anchors people to their heritage and contributes to their cultural identity. It is a tradition for children to receive the last names of both of their parents. The first last name is that of the child's father, with the second one indicating the maternal last name. Limiting to only one surname is like taking away a part of who you are. Sensitivity to traditional practices is still a challenge. While many people may not have an understanding about the implications of changing names, these can be also construed as disrespectful actions. In the United States, many have opted to use hyphenation to keep their two surnames. This has created a whole generation with hyphenated last names.

I Speak ... Language Challenges

Do you speak ...? If you are a speaker of a language different from that of the place where you have come to live, you would know about the trepidation felt when entering a classroom where the language is unfamiliar to you. That dreaded feeling is one that continues to be experienced every time a child comes to a new classroom. The apprehension and feeling of being in a place where you do not belong is inevitable. It is as if your tongue is held back because the words, those they know, are yet unknown to you. That urge to communicate is one triggering a multitude of emotions especially when you are the child who just joined the

---

Thinking and Reflecting ... A Different Language

Those who are speakers of a language different from the place where you live or if you have traveled to a country where the language is unknown to you, you would know how it feels not knowing how to communicate. Considering those experiences, what made you feel that you were welcome? What relieved the stress of the moment?

class. In an already multilingual society, such emotions and experiences are repeated every day and are memories forever kept.

Educators agree that language learning is one of the commonly faced challenges experienced by immigrant children (Best Start Resource Centre 2010; Lynch and Hanson 2011; Maki, O'Toole, and Katsifiakas 2017). The nature of language itself makes it not only a learning challenge but one also of social and cultural implications (Otto 2018). During childhood, the need for communication and the urge to belong fosters and motivates children's language acquisition. For immigrant children, the journey of language acquisition becomes a dual one, where they are learning their heritage language and are challenged to learn a second one. Experience has shown that the determined support of educators enables them to engage in their dual language acquisition journey (Lessow-Hurley 2013; Robles and Beck 2019). The role of early childhood educators, their sense of caring, knowledge, and responsive attitudes, is fundamental in leading the child's learning success. Many examples are shared through some of the stories about immigration.

Consciously Considering ... Meeting the Needs of Young Immigrants Learning a Second Language

Every year, classrooms everywhere in the world receive thousands of children who are immigrants. In some countries, like in the case of the United States, one out of three children eight years and younger are from families where the language spoken is different from English (Park, O'Toole, and Katsifiakas 2017). This makes for a large number of children whose schooling experience will be faced with the challenge of acquiring a second language while they continue to learn their very own heritage language. While it is an additional developmental challenge, research has shown that children are ready to acquire a new language while continuing to build their primary language. But beyond the capacity they bring, the task itself is a monumental one dependent on the responsive and caring answer of teachers. Together with the supportive response already witnessed in classrooms, many agree that training is still needed to empower educators with the strategies and knowledge necessary to support learners of other languages (Lucas, Villegas, and Freedson-Gonzalez 2008). Despite the growing research revealing the need for effective preparation (Lucas and Villegas 2013; Heikkola, Alisaari, Vigren, and Commins 2022), this is still an area calling for action given the importance of language learning for the future success of a child. The question that remains is, are we ready to successfully support their linguistic needs?

In the Classroom: Supportive Responses

Once again, opening windows and sliding the doors through children's books, we learn about those classroom moments when children find themselves with the need for learning a different language. Perusing through many of the children's books about diversity and immigration, the illustrations powerfully reveal the shock, fear, and apprehension initially felt by the children's characters. They also bring to us the images of responsive and caring educators who bridge the challenge for children with their thoughtful approach (Figure 6.6).

Responsive attention to children's cultural and individual needs is central to fair practices and continues to demand attention for the sake of a child's successful experience and well-being. Attentive to the needs and challenges children may display, responsive educators are intentional and consciously respond through their actions. Many story characters bring to light responsive actions of educators as in Levine's story *I hate English* (1995), where her teacher recognizes the dilemma faced by Mei Mei, afraid of losing her own identity if she learned English. The understanding way in which her teacher reacts, helping her to learn that she will always be who she is even if she learns English, embodies her empathic responsiveness. It is also observed in the welcoming and inclusive way that the teacher in Diaz's *Islandborn* (2018) welcomes children's cultures leading them to show their pride in their ethnic origins.

There are many other stories also bringing to life examples of teacher responsiveness. One of those stories is *Marianthe's story: Painted words and spoken memories* (Aliki 1998). In this two-part story, Aliki introduces us to Marianthe and together with her, we learn about her experiences moving to a new country. As the title seems to reveal, this is also a story about her experiences as an

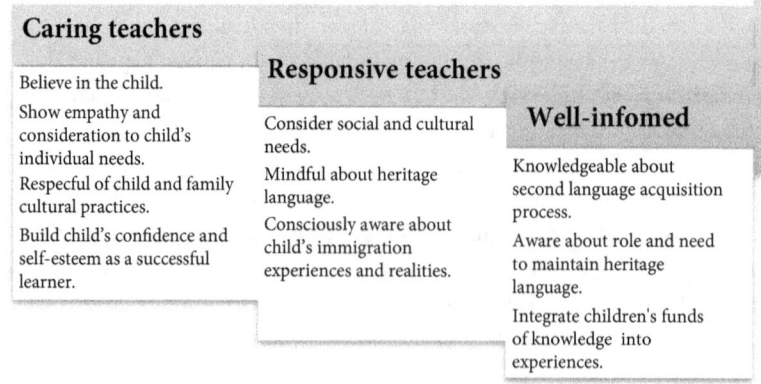

Figure 6.6 Teachers are Key in Supporting Language Acquisition of Young Immigrant Children.

immigrant in a new country and where the language is different from her own. Just from the first pages, her story is the story of thousands of children, happening every day. Accompanying Marianthe in her classroom journey, we learn about her teacher's responsiveness to the girl learning a new language. Obviously aware of her need to share and communicate about her experiences, her teacher encourages Marianthe to draw, giving her a voice to share her experiences with her classmates while her language learning progressed. Language learning is a progressive experience, and the story takes us along to hear how confidently she shared her memories, this time her spoken memories. The gradual transition from communication first through pictures and then conveyed as she spoke tells us about the impact of responsive actions of educators, who mindfully consider the need for supporting the social and emotional needs of children.

Responsive approaches are meaningful ways to connect with a child and they happen everywhere. In *One green apple* (Bunting 2006), we learn how a field trip to an apple orchard helps a young Muslim immigrant to find herself with things familiar to her. The story is a reminder that a variety of strategies are always key to supporting children's learning needs, particularly when considering those of children from diverse contexts facing cultural scripts and a language different from their own. Bunting's story also brings attention to the task faced by child immigrants trying to fit in and belong where they now live. Responsive actions from teachers continue to be central for successful adjustment to new environments. This has been the focus in many stories (Figure 6.7).

Selected Stories Opening Windows into Classroom Responsive Experiences
Cleversticks (Ashley 1995)
Marianthe's story: Painted words and spoken memories (Aliki 1998)
The Arabic quilt (Khalil, 2020)
Lailah's lunchbox (Faruqui 2015)
I am new here (Sibley O'Brien, 2015)
Someone new (Sibley O'Brien 2018)
All are welcome (Penfold 2018)
One green apple (Bunting 2006)
I hate English (Levine 1989)
The name jar (Choi 2003)

Figure 6.7 Ten Books Providing Windows into Responsive Experiences.

Friendship, Those Universal Experiences Happening in the Classroom

Who does not remember the friends made at school? Who has not wondered if you would make friends when coming to a new classroom? For many of us, those friends from our childhood years evolved into relationships held dear to date. Friends are part of the experiences we have in the classroom and the meaningful moments and learnings that come from those relationships. Many stories continue to be written about children's experiences coming into classrooms in other countries and meeting peers who become their friends. As early childhood educators, we know many of the stories of children building friendships. Witnessing how these relationships emerge brings us closer to understanding the vital influence of classroom experiences in adjusting and adapting to life in a different cultural setting. Friendship is an important factor contributing to children's successful adjustment in new settings. Bunting leads us to experience how friendship emerges as children interact with each other. In her story *One green apple* (1992), she presents some snapshots of those moments where the feelings of being different and isolated are overcome. leGuen (2020) in *The Refuge*, presents the powerful relationship that develops between the two classmates, Iliana, a young refugee, and Jeannette, who is intrigued by her new peer and becomes her friend. The welcoming attitude that converts into a friendship is also evidenced in *The day Saida arrived* where the young girl who welcomes Saida openly offers her friendship to the young refugee.

Developmentally, friendship is one of the supportive elements promoting children's well-being (Kostelnik et al. 2019). Friendship is known to be a powerful force and a meaningful factor helping children to feel they are a part of a group. These relationships are especially relevant when facing challenges, providing the support needed to confront and overcome difficult moments (Laursen, Bukoski, Aunola, and Nurmi 2007; Holder and Coleman 2015). Friends are also very significant, not only providing meaningful emotional support but also helping children to navigate the complexities of life in the classroom and in the community. These are mutually beneficial relationships helping peers to learn about diversity and experiences of immigrants. From language, types of play, to traditions, friends share and exchange ideas and ways of life that are mutually important for both.

Friendship plays a role in building a sense of perspective, which is promoted by the sharing of experiences that brings new viewpoints for both peers and immigrant children (Laursen et al. 2007). Beckwith's story *Playing war* (2005) is an example of perspectives gained through friendship. Though not set in the classroom, we meet a group of children who are getting ready to "play war" when they learn about the meaning of war from their friend, Sameer, a young boy from a Middle-Eastern country. Not wanting to play war, Sameer shares his own experience about the conflict that took his family and home. Sharing the reason why he came to live with his uncle, it is a moment when his friends discover his harrowing experience and learn what war really is. Conveyed through the illustrations and text, is their shock, learning how his friend lost everything he had. Their reaction to what they heard from their friend showed empathy and understanding after gaining a perspective about the difficult experience of war. With that knowledge, they discarded the idea to play war and instead focused on learning how to play the top that their friend Sameer shared with them.

For the Sake of Friendship

As a topic, friendship has been the focus of many stories of immigration, powerfully bringing attention to the role that relationships continue to have during those early years and beyond. One of those is author Gómez-Redondo, who led us to meet Saida in *The day Saida arrived* (2020), a young immigrant from Morocco. Saida's experiences in the classroom are narrated by the child who meets her and says to herself, "I knew I would always be her friend" (n.p.). Saida's smile is the engine that begins a friendship with the young girl who anxiously looks for ways to talk with her. Despite being speakers of two different languages, the story shows us the powerful energy of friendship that drives the two girls to overcome the challenge of communication. An example of the power of friendship, the storyline reveals the efforts that brought both to learn about each other. The story reminds us about similar efforts to befriend another child and overcoming language differences that we read in Kobald's *My two blankets* (2014) and in *The refuge* (le Guen 2020). Both stories are reminders of the driving force that friendship represents in the life of children. They both highlight the urge to establish relationships that overcome language differences. In *The refuge*, we also learn about the caring response of Jeannette toward her classmate, a young refugee, and how, again, she also overcomes language differences to become friends. The compassionate and determined caring attitudes of the child characters in these three picture books are clearly displayed as they take steps to build a friendship. Evidently, what also becomes obvious is how language and cultural differences are irrelevant when friendship connects individuals. Instead, these characters simply see the needs of the children and become friends. A message of valuing and appreciating people for who they are and of a disposition to help is communicated to the readers.

Immigration Status, an issue also Reflected in the Classroom

The case of undocumented children and families is addressed by various authors. As a topic and issue, immigration status is an ongoing experience that many children continue to face. Growing up in fear of deportation while others are unaware about the undocumented or unofficial immigration status of their families, their stories are also reflected in the classroom. Despite policies and practices that safeguard an immigrant's student immigration status, many may face challenging experiences (Connery 2018). Sadly, unkind comments and even threats, are known to happen, calling for intervention to deter their impact on the child. At present, the reality of their immigration status weighs heavily for many families and their children. Many times the fear of deportation of a family member becomes real just as we read in *Mango Moon* (De Anda 2019) and in Danticat's *Mama's nightingale* (2015). Many times, this is a guarded secret by adults, while in other cases everyone in the family is cognizant about their situation. Earlier we talked about the case of Hannah, the young girl in *Hannah is my name* (Yang 2004), whose family was eagerly waiting for their "green cards," to officialize their status. Meanwhile, with their parents working, Hannah and her family were careful not to be caught.

In Williams' *Facing fear* (2021), the issue of unofficial entry is directly addressed as readers learn about Enrique, the boy who suddenly discovers he and his parents were undocumented. Excited by a trip to play with his school team, he is puzzled by his father's denial to travel. It is then that he finds out about his family's undocumented entry, and after struggling with what he now knows, he courageously tells his coach that he cannot participate. The story ends with a demonstration of empathy for Enrique, who is surprised to learn that the team decided not to attend the game in solidarity with him and his family. Another story leading us to learn about issues relating to immigration status is *Hannah is my name* (Yang 2004). This time we follow young Hannah, who together with her family wait for her father to receive the card that will allow him to stay and legally work. Pressed to support his family and aware of the possible consequences if he is caught, her dad finds a job. Living with great tension, we witness the fear and anxiety felt by the young girl. The powerful images convey the challenging experience brought on by their immigration status not uncommon to so many families and their children who also come with the hope of finding a safe place and a future.

Areli is a dreamer (Morales 2021) allows us to learn about another side of the reality of immigration status, this time of a child who unofficially crossed the border to be with her family. Based on the experiences of the author, the story reveals the experience of thousands of children who have come, some together with their parents, others with adults to be reunited with parents already living in the country. Their classroom experience sometimes is not as pleasant as shown by that of the story character, where some peers may taunt children about their status and openly reject their presence. Areli, as the title reads, is also a reminder of the many called "dreamers," children like this character who arrived into the United States during their childhood. They, as the character says, "did not feel illegal [and] felt ... part of something really big" (Morales 2021, n.p.).

Classrooms as Socially Just Places for Immigrant Children

The classroom plays an important role in facilitating many social, cultural and developmental adjustments for children. These adjustments are experientially negotiated in the context of their classrooms. Classroom experiences during the early years remain foundational for every child. When stories have images and storylines, where children can see themselves and where they can understand the challenges faced, they become welcomed opportunities for young children to connect with events happening in society. Selected and shared with these goals in mind, stories do become a tool for addressing social justice issues in appropriate and developmentally conscious ways. Building a conscience and disposition toward addressing social justice begins in the early years through efforts and practices, allowing educators to engage children in learning about and exploring challenges in their community. A thousand and more stories continue to take shape every moment in classrooms everywhere. The hope is that these will also become stories grounded on social justice and conscious consideration of the needs of immigrant children.

Reflecting and Beyond

1. Reflect on the role of classroom experiences for young immigrant children and outline a plan to make them feel welcome. How would you convey the message? What story or stories would you share with them?
2. Choose one of the topics addressed about the classroom experiences of immigrant children and create your own bibliographical resource of picture books to share in the classroom with young children.
3. Considering some of the social justice challenges facing immigrant children addressed in this chapter, which two would you consider as most relevant? Explain the reasons for the selection and propose actions to address them.

References

Best Start Resource Centre. 2010. *Growing up in a new land: Strategies for service providers working with newcomers.* Toronto, Ontario, Canada: author newcomer_guide3 (beststart.org).

Bishop, Rudine. 1990. Mirrors, windows, and sliding glass doors. Perspective, 6(3), ix–xi.

Botelho, Maria Jose and Masha Rudman. 2009. Critical multicultural analysis of children's literature" Windows, mirrors and doors. NY. Routledge.

Camarota, Steven, Bryan Griffith, and Karen Zeigler. 2017. *Mapping the impact of immigration on public schools.* Center for Immigration Studies. https://cis.org/Report/Mapping-Impact-Immigration-Public-Schools.

Cervantes, Wendy, Rebecca Ulrich, and Hannah Matthews. 2018. *Our children's fear. Immigration policy's effect on young children.* Washington, DC: CLASP. https://www.clasp.org/sites/default/files/publications/2018/03/2018_ourchildrensfears.pdf.

Colombo, Hayleigh. 2015. "The first thing schools get wrong for English language learners is their names." *Chalkbeat*, July 27. https://in.chalkbeat.org/2015/7/27/21095300/the-first-thing-schools-often-get-wrong-for-english-language-learners-is-their-names#.VbgsR0Wi7_5.

Compton-Lilly, Catherine, Kristin Papoi, Patricia Venegas, Laura Hamman, and Briana Schwabenbauer. 2017. "Intersectional identity negotiation." *Journal of Literacy Research* 49(1): 115–40.

Connery, Chelsea. 2018. The impact of undocumented status on children's learning. Issue Brief. UCONN.

Corsaro, William. 2018. *The sociology of childhood* (5th edition). UK: Sage.

Derman-Sparks, Louise and Julie Olson Edwards. 2010. *Anti-bias education for young children and ourselves.* Washington, DC: NAEYC.

Dinan, Stephen. 2017. "Immigrant children's number growing up in US public schools." *Washington Times*, March 15. https://www.washingtontimes.com/news/2017/mar/15/immigrants-children-numbers-growing-us-public-scho/.

Drummond Johansen, Jennifer and Sverre Varvin. 2020. "Negotiating identity at the intersection of family legacy and present time life conditions: A qualitative exploration of central issues connected to identity and belonging in the lives of children of refugees." *Journal of Adolescence* 80: 1–9. https://doi.org/10.1016/j.adolescence.2020.01.016.

Genishi, Celia and Ann Dyson. 1994. *The need for story: Cultural diversity in the classroom*. Urbana, Illinois: National Council of Teachers of English.

Gagné, Monique, Jennifer Shapka, and Danielle Law. 2012. "The impact of social contexts in schools: Adolescents who are new to Canada and their sense of belonging." In C. Garcia Coll (ed.) *The impact of immigration on children's development* (pp. 17–34). Basel, Switzerland: Karger.

García Coll, Cynthia. 2012. "Introduction: The global, the local-Children and immigration around the world." In C. Garcia Coll (ed.) *The impact of immigration on children's development* (pp. vii–ix). Basel: Karger.

Genishi, Celia and Ann Dyson. 2009. *Children, language and literacy: Diverse learners in diverse times*. New York, NY: Teachers College Press.

González, Laura, Gabriela Stein, Lisa Kiang, and Alexandra Cupito. 2014. "The impact of discrimination and support on developmental competencies in Latino adolescents." *Journal of Latinx Psychology* 2: 79–91.

Goodwin, A. Lin. 2002. "Teacher preparation and the education of immigrant children." *Education and Urban Society* 34(2): 156–72.

Guerra, Rita, Ricardo Borges, Cecilia Aguiar, Margarida Carmona, Joana Alexandra, and Rui Costa-Lopes. 2019. "School achievement and well-being of immigrant children: The role of acculturation orientations and perceived discrimination." *Journal of School Psychology* 75: 104–18.

Haynes, Judie. 2015. "7 naming customs from around the world." *TESOL Blog*, August 15. http://blog.tesol.org/7-naming-customs-from-around-the-world/.

Heikkola, Leena Maria, Jenni Alisaari, Heli Vigren, and Nancy Commins. 2022. "Linguistically responsive teaching: A requirement for Finnish primary school teachers." *Linguistics and Education* 69. https://doi.org/10.1016/j.linged.2022.101038.

Holder, Mark and Ben Coleman. 2015. "Children's friendship and positive wellbeing." In M. Demir (eds.), *Friendship and happiness* (pp. 81–97). Dordrecht: Springer. https://doi.org/10.1007/978-94-017-9603-3_5.

Kicks, Anne and Ann Kimball Johnson. 2018. "For children, the immigrant experience begins in schools." *The Catalyst*, issue 09. https://www.bushcenter.org/catalyst/immigration/wicks-schools-and-immigrants.html.

Kostelnik, Marjorie, Ann Gregory, Alice Soderman, and Michelle Rupiper. 2019. *Guiding children's social development and learning* (9th edition). CA: Cengage.

Laursen, Brett, William Bukowski, Kaisa Aunola, and Jari-Erik Nurmi. 2007. "Friendship moderates prospective associations between social isolation and adjustment problems in young children." *Child Development* 78(4): 1395–404. doi:10.1111/j.1467-8624.2007.01072.x.

Lessow-Hurley, Judith. 2013. *The foundations of dual language instruction* (6th edition). Boston, MA: Pearson.

Liu, Hannah. 2021. "Back to school planning must consider immigrant children and families." *CLASP Blog*, August 31. https://www.clasp.org/print/5674.

Lucas, Tamara and Ana María Villegas. 2013. "Preparing linguistically responsive teachers: Laying the foundation in preservice teacher education". *Theory into Practice* 52(2): 98–109.

Lucas, Tamara, Ana María Villegas, and Margaret Freedson-Gonzalez. 2008. "Linguistically responsive teacher education: Preparing classroom teachers to teach English language learners." *Journal of Teacher Education* 59(4): 361–73. https://journals.sagepub.com/doi/pdf/10.1177/0022487108322110.

Lynch, Eleanor and Marci Hanson. 2011. *Developing cross-cultural competence: A guide for working with children and their families* (4th edition). MD: Paul Brookes.

Madrid, E. Michael. 2008. "The unheralded history of the Lemon Grove desegregation case." *Multicultural Education*, spring: 117–19. https://files.eric.ed.gov/fulltext/EJ793848.pdf.

National Association for the Education of Young Children [NAEYC]. 2020. *Developmentally Appropriate Practice. A Position Statement of the National Association for the Education of Young Children*. https://www.naeyc.org/resources/position-statements/dap/contents.

Norton, Donna. 2013. *Multicultural children's literature. Through the eyes of many children* (4th edition). Boston, MA: Pearson.

OECD. 2015. "*Helping immigrant students to succeed at school and beyond.*" https://www.oecd.org/education/Helping-immigrant-students-to-succeed-at-school-and-beyond.pdf.

Otto, Beverly. 2018. *Language development in early childhood education* (5th edition). Boston, MA: Pearson.

Park, Maki, Anna O'Toole, and Caitlin Katsiaficas. 2017. *Dual language learners: A national demographic and policy profile. Fact sheet*. Washington, DC: Migration Policy Institute.

Robles-Melendez, Wilma and Wayne Driscoll. 2020. *Issues and challenges of immigration in early childhood in the USA*. London: Bloomsbury.

Rogoff, Barbara. 2003. *The cultural nature of human development*. UK: Oxford Press.

Szcesi, Tunde, Maryann Manning, Gillian Potter, Vydia Thirumurthy, and Mariana Slakaja. 2012. "Teaching strategies: Children's literature to help young children construct understandings about diversity: Perspectives from four cultures." *Childhood Education* 86(2): 108–12.

Sonderberger, Robi, Paula Barrett, and Peter Creed. 2004. "Models of cultural adjustment for child and adolescent migrants to Australia: Internal process and situational factors." *Journal of Child and Family Studies* 13: 357–71.
Suárez-Orozco, Carola and Marcelo Suárez-Orozco. 2001. *Children of immigration*. Cambridge: Harvard University Press.
Takanishi, Ruby. 2004. "Leveling the playing field. Supporting immigrant children from birth to eight." *Future of Children* 14(2): 61–79.
United Nations. 1989. *Convention on the Rights of the Child*. United Nations.
Vygotsky, Lev. 1962. *Thought and language*. MA: MIT Press.
Villarreal, Abelardo and Rosana Rodríguez. 2008. "Equity, access and excellence in education for immigrant students." *IDRA Newsletter* XXXV(2): 2–6. ED505919.pdf.

Children's Books Cited

Aliki. 1998. *Marianthe' story. Painted words/Spoken words*. NY: Greenwillow Books.
Ashley, Bernard. 1992. *Cleversticks*. NY: Dragonfly.
Beckwith, Kathy. 2005. *Playing war*. Maine: Tillbury House.
Brimmer, Larry. 2021. *Without Separation: Prejudice, Segregation, and the Case of Roberto Alvarez*. NY: Astra Books/Calkins Creek.
Bunting, Eve. 1992. *One green apple*. NY: Clarion Books.
Choi, Yansook. 2001. *The name jar*. NY: Dragonfly.
Colato Laínez, René. 2009. *René has two last names/René tiene dos apellidos*. Houston: Piñata Books.
Danticat, (2015). *Mama's Nightingale: A Story of Immigration and Separation*. NY: Dial Books
De Anda, Diane. (2019). *Mango Moon*. NY: Albert Whitman.
Faruqi, Reem. 2015. *Laila's lunchbox*. Maine: Tilbury Publishers.
Gómez Redondo, Susana. 2020. *The day Saida arrived*. San Francisco: Blue Dots.
Hale, Christy. 2019. *Todos iguales / All equal: Un corrido de Lemon Grove/A ballad of Lemon Grove*. NY: Lee & Low Books.
Martinez-Neal, Juana. 2018. *Alma and how she got her name*. NY: Scholastic.
Medina, Jane. 1999. *My name is Jorge on both sides of the river*. Pennsylvania: Wordsong.
Morales, Areli. 2021. *Areli is a dreamer*. NY: Random House.
Palacios. 2011. *Marisol Macdonald doesn't match*. NY: Dragonfly.
Penfold, Alexandra. 2018. *All are welcome*. NY: Knopf Books for Young Readers.

Recorvitz, Helen. 2003. *My name is Yoon*. NY: Frances Foster Books. Farrar, Strauss and Giroux.
Root, Phyllis. 2003. *The name quilt*. NY: Farrar, Strauss and Giroux.
Sheh, Sheetal. 2018. *Always Anjali*. USA: Bharat Babies.
O'Brien, Sibley. 2015. *I am new here*. MA: Charlesbridge Books.
Tonatiuh, Duncan. 2014. *Separate is not equal: Silvia Mendez and her family's fight for desegregation*. Pennsylvania: Harry Abrams.
Woodson, Jacqueline. 2018. *The day you begin*. NY: Nancy Paulsen Books. Penguin Books.
Yang, Belle. 2004. *Hannah is my name*. NY: Candlewick.

7

Bringing Immigration Realities to the Classroom through Children's Literature

Literature expands children's understandings of themselves and the world.
—Galda, Liang and Cullinan (2017)

This chapter aims to:

- Discuss the role of the classroom in bringing attention to issues of immigration.
- Explore child-appropriate ways to select stories about immigration.
- Define the need for intentional practices.
- Identify strategies and activities appropriate to share books with young children.

Key words:

- Intentional practices
- strategies
- sharing books
- building consciousness
- critical literacy

A book to share

The news had been incessantly showing the harrowing episodes of people trying to escape from a war conflict zone. Some of the children in the primary school had already been talking about what they were watching in the local news broadcast. That was what prompted the meeting of the first-grade teachers. They were shocked, themselves, by the news and realized that the topic needed to be addressed in the classroom. How to do it was what they were discussing when one of the teachers decided to share an idea. "Well, why not use children's books to talk about what is happening?," she said as she pulled a book she had been holding in her lap. "Let me just share and tell me what you think," she said as she opened the book Marwan's journey (de Arias 2018). From the first pages, everyone in her team felt glued to the story. But it was probably a line that captured her colleagues. "Every night I pray that the night never, never goes dark again." "Yes, we need to share stories like this one," said one of the teachers, breaking the silence after listening to the words from the character, a child migrating alone, and hoping for a peaceful place to live. "They are so powerful and can't wait to see the comments that children would make," added another teacher. Everyone seemed to agree, nodding and getting ready to share other stories they loved, soon.

Teaching with Intentions: Building Conscious Awareness about Realities of Diversity

In today's world, it is more important than it ever was, to integrate experiences about diversity both in the classroom and at home. As we watched the horrors unfolding in Ukraine during the winter of 2022, we thought of the thousands of children being uprooted from their homes to countries and cultures many of which are unfamiliar to them. In our minds are also the faces of children from every part of the world. They are all children and in their hearts and mind they are hopeful for that place to call home. The journeys they start are long and will mark their lives. How long will it take for those children to learn the language of their new country and to get accustomed to the culture and way of life in their new home? Will they feel welcomed and that they, too, belong? What we know is that they are in our classrooms and that every day is another opportunity to meet their needs while we also learn from them about their diversity and living experiences.

Bringing Awareness about Diversity

In spite of the harsh realities that immigrant children face, they are experiencing first-hand people who are different from them, who speak differently, whose cultural practices differ from theirs, and who dress differently. Others, too, will be leaving their homelands, some voluntarily and some pushed because of multiple difficult realities. They will be following the wave of migration of the first decades of the century. Research shows that meeting people who are different is one way to diminish the effect of stereotypes (Derman-Sparks and Olsen Edwards 2010; Platts and Hoosier 2020) and to erase these from even emerging.

The reason is that when people meet others who are considered different, they learn more about them and while doing so, they realize that they have more in common than what is different. Welcoming everyone begins when we become conscientious about the shared humanity distinguishing every individual.

The Classroom Is the Place Where the Conversation Must Begin

This time, when immigration has become a focus of interest, continuously demanding attention in society, the need is evident to find ways to make us consciously aware of its multiple realities. Where we need to begin is in the classroom, where preparing our children for the future calls for learning and exploring the diversity and experiences defining ourselves and of people, children and families, in our communities and in the composite that we call society. Among those realities we must learn about are the diversity of cultures, languages, and experiences embodied by people who are immigrants. Today, with an intense global immigration wave (UN 2021), the call for building a conscience about immigrants and their multiple realities, their reasons to leave and their needs, concern everyone and everywhere.

Why Children's Books

Throughout the chapters in this book, we have explored children's stories, taking the time to unpack many of the dimensions of reality of a story readers may learn about. Simply said, stories have the magic to engage and attract even the most reticent person. We have it as a practice to share stories, and it has opened the door to address many topics that some would have avoided. Such was, once again, the response when we read the story *Room for everyone* (Khan 2021). The attractive illustrations in this picture book with its rhythmic and repetitive lines caught the attention of everyone. It opened the door to address diversity

> ## Thinking and Reflecting ... That Special Story
>
> *It was that story* ... that is what many may say when thinking about the influential role that stories have on us motivating, inspiring and leading us to learn more or even inspiring who we are today. Which one was it for you? Can you remember what it was that caught your interest and touched you?

facilitating a discussion on the cultures and experiences coming every day, and on the need for understanding why they come.

Children's literature has long been recognized as a tool for addressing issues of diversity, as immigration also is often difficult to discuss in the classroom (St. Amour 2003; Norton 2013). Addressing immigration both as an issue and as a societal reality is a challenge given the controversy that it evokes. However, as explored through the earlier chapters, here is where children's literature opens doors into the many and diverse stories of immigration. For some, it will be stories to mirror their own, others will find a window to look into, while for others, stories will be doors to enter into the diversity of experiences of immigrants. Through their storylines, we are ushered into dimensions of lived experiences opening minds to realities faced, and to actions still needed to address challenges and unfairness (Botelho and Rudman 2009; Lowe 2009; Short 2009).

Multidimensional Value of Stories

Children's literature allows us to meet and learn about people and their diverse realities. It is highly likely that everyone has met someone from other cultures and diverse realities while reading a story. It is, as well, that the story character inspired and motivated many to delve into the story and learn more about them and about themselves. The value and the role of stories are both multidimensional, highlighting their role and importance for children and also for adults. Some reasons supporting why we need to use children's stories are discussed below.

- **Stories Are of Interest and Appeal to Children**
  Stories have always had a place in children's education. They are, as well, an important experience in the socialization process during the early years. The interaction between child and story is undeniably a main infleunce, giving children opportunities to engage with issues and characters of significant impact. Many of us remember the deeds of characters that we admired and that influenced our own ways. The experiences and phrases in a story may still resonate as lessons that were learned vicariously and that remained with us. Such is the influential role that stories in children's books play in the shaping of our own social selves (Orgad et al. 2021).

- **Stories Are a Window, a Mirror, and an Avenue into Diversity**
  Children's books are also an avenue, wide and distinct where the broad diversity of realities can be found and followed vicariously bringing alive

experiences and circumstances to make us conscious about life's realities. With immigration as an influential factor in current times, the need is critical for learning about the experience of people from diverse realities and traits including ourselves (Bersh 2013). Books can act as mirrors, as windows, or sliding doors. This is what Sims-Bishop (1994) theorized demarcating the need for books where one could find our stories and also learn about those of peers and people from other cultures. Clearly, children's literature continues as an instrumental source expanding views and leading us to learn about our own triumphs and challenges but also about those of peers we know and of those yet to know. Books become mirrors because children see people who look like themselves and windows because they get to learn about people who are different from them (Epstein 2017; Potter 2019). In addition to seeing themselves in books, children can dream about who they can become and validate their thoughts.

- **Stories Introduce Children to Issues of Social Justice**
  Windows can also allow children to become aware about the experiences and realities of today. In this role, stories from children's literature bring children to learn about the commonalities shared with others. Through stories, children also discover and learn about their lives, of their peers, and of children in their communities and in distant places. Reading and listening to these stories is what triggers opportunities for children to become aware of injustices and difficulties calling for society's actions. Building consciousness through stories is a process that happens as we guide children in reflecting beyond considering what the words reveal.

- **Stories Play a Role in Supporting Children's Development**
  Literature for children has many roles and one we agree is that of building and awakening our sense about the world and its many realities. Stories not only serve as enjoyment but also have different roles supporting children's development. They particularly contribute to children's social, emotional, and cognitive development including as tools for promoting language and literacy development, highlighting the need for these to be shared as part of classroom experiences (Ezell and Justice 2005). They also have a pedagogical role fostering knowledge building. Conversations and discussions about characters, topics, and issues from stories lead to what Vygostky theorized as socially mediated learning where knowledge is socially constructed through interactions with teachers and peers (Smidt 2009).

We all have one special book that intrigued and opened our minds to learn more about realities and facts. They are what for some planted the seed that motivated them to learn more about themselves, and to take actions for others. As educators, we owe it to young readers to let them read books which portray some of society's realities. We had talked about many throughout the earlier chapters, children's books that open doors to children into the experiences of child characters who are immigrants. Together with these characters and stories, children are led to explore and learn about life's circumstances that for some are often different from their own while for other children they reflect their own lives.

Connecting Children to Stories

Oh, that story, it made me feel that it was me. More than once, after reading a story, we have heard that same comment from children and from adults. It is just that there is always a story that will speak to you and that will become a part of you. Why it happens is simply because stories have the power to connect you in ways unimaginable. They seem to speak to our inner self, raising interest and awakening in us memories of feelings, of concern and compassion, paired with a yearning to know more or simply to help. The fact is that anytime a story is read or shared with children, an opportunity for socially becoming involved emerges (Ezell and Justice 2005). Creating an environment where children are socially engaged invites comments and questions that further the discussion of topics and issues. Feeling connected to the story, is also why they are encouraged to share, to make connections, and to inquire.

In the classroom, connecting children with a story begins as these are chosen with the child in mind. How to engage children in making and feeling connected to a story starts when stories are carefully chosen. Stories to share with children

---

Thinking and Reflecting ... Books That Are Special to Us

There is always a book, a story, which touched you and became very meaningful. We invite you to take a moment to remember which was that story or children's book that was and still is special for you. Share the title and reflect on the reasons why it became meaningful for you.

should also have a purpose for bringing these to the classrooms. Knowing the reasons for selecting a story will guide the experience as these are shared. It will also make us aware and ready for those questions and comments that children may have. As first steps to ensure children feel connected to stories, particularly with difficult topics, begin by asking yourself: *How much do I know about the topic and issues? Is the topic or issue appropriate to share with children? What is my purpose for sharing this story? Am I prepared to answer their questions?* These are important questions to guide your decisions about stories to share with children on topics that address issues of diversity and social justice.

Knowing what your aims are for bringing a story into your classroom is essential. One crucial factor to consider is the age appropriateness of the topic and how it is presented in the storybook. Preeminent in any teaching endeavor with young children is to ensure that topics are consonant with children's development (NAEYC 2022). Because of the complex nature of these topics, it is relevant to consider the reasons and purpose for sharing them with children. Some key considerations are presented in Figure 7.1.

Children's Books Engage Children in Learning about Diversity and Social Justice

Despite the increasing societal diversity that immigration continues to instill, in many places, children may not have the experience of meeting face to face

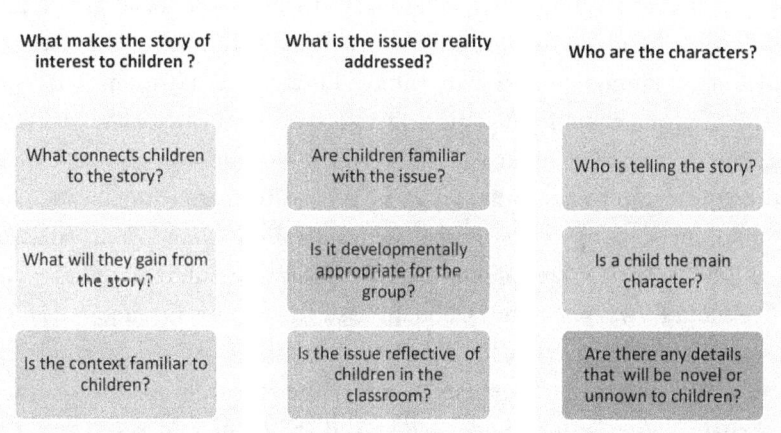

Figure 7.1 Connecting children to stories of immigration: Some points to consider.

those who are considered different, therefore, the need to learn about diversity vicariously. One of the best chances of getting this experience is through reading and sharing books and especially those from multicultural children's literature (St. Amour 2003; Norton 2013; Ikia 2015; Cummins 2016). Through carefully selected multicultural children's books one finds a window and a door into the worlds of people and also on the realities of ourselves.

Children's literature is known to be a resourceful and child-appropriate way to introduce children to topics of diversity and of social justice (Botelho and Rudman 2009; O'Neil 2010; Norton 2013). Because of its appeal, it facilitates discussion of controversial and difficult topics. As a strategy, stories engage children in exploring and raising attention to issues of inequalities in society. These are experiences integral to children's learning and to their readiness to become members of society. As children are engaged in the exploration and consideration of social justice issues, their consciousness begins to emerge about realities in their own communities and in society (O'Neil 2010; Reed, Saunders and Pfadenhauer-Simonds 2015). In this way, children begin to see themselves as participants in the discussion and consideration of issues calling for attention in society. As discussion and conversations take place about challenges and the issues presented in a story, opportunities arise for engaging children in considering the need for actions and solutions. These are also invitations promoting the sense of agency that children have.

Be Intentional!

One factor central to engaging children in discussion of social justice issues is to be intentional. A determined decision must be made when selecting stories about immigration to share with children in the classroom. There are a variety of stories about immigration, therefore teachers' careful and intentional selection is critically important. Being intentional means also to carefully and knowledgeably choose the topics or themes to share with considerations to children's developmental needs. Educators must know their goals and thoughtfully consider the appropriateness of issues for children.

We should always be mindful about the stories that we are choosing and the reasons for sharing them with children. Preparing ourselves by anticipating some of the children's comments is important to encourage the sharing of ideas that will further their understanding and build their interest (Giorgis and Glazer 2013). As always, it is relevant to take time to read and reflect on the messages in the story. Think about the nature of the topics addressed and about how these relate and responsibly present ideas. Consider the illustrations and what they convey and how children will interpret them. Even though they are in a children's book, some may be more complex for a child. Consult with your colleagues if you are doubtful about using a particular story. Remember to be thoughtful about the experiences of children, especially when some of the topics may be sensitive given their own lived experience.

Building Consciousness about Social Justice Issues

Learning is a social experience that is clearly influenced by interactions with peers and people we meet. We also learn and are influenced by those we meet as story characters. Their experiences and examples inspire and motivate our own sense of self in separate ways. We are moved as we meet the courageous child in *I walk with Vanessa* (Kerascoët 2018), who daringly decides to accompany the young girl, defying her classmates' rejection of young Vanessa, a child whose diversity is not welcomed. We are also encouraged when we read about the kindness of characters in *The suitcase* (Naylor-Ballesteros 2020), who after learning about the difficult experiences of the newcomer, extend their welcome. Such actions found in stories connect to our inner self and are what empower and influence our sense of consciousness about the realities lived in our own society. Those are the experiences, that though experienced vicariously, instill in a child a thirst for social justice and for compassionate actions. This awareness about what is fair and right for everyone is what is pursued in building consciousness, where one becomes mindfully aware that injustices are happening, and respond and react to counteract them. That is also how we build from early childhood a sense of civic responsibility of empathy (Robles-Melendez and Beck 2000; MacPhee and Whitecotton 2011).

> **Thinking and Reflecting ... Influential Story Characters**
>
> The power of stories is endless and especially for introducing readers to meet characters that leave impressions that impact us. We all have a character or more that is admired and that inspires us. Which one is yours? Tell us why and in what way it became a special character for you.

Reading and sharing stories have long been known to be a way to foster a critical literacy approach in the classroom (Short 2009; Giorgis and Glazer 2013; Norton 2013). Critical literacy engages children's understanding not just about what is read but guides children in opening doors into the multiple meanings embedded in a narrative about the realities not only of themselves but also of society. Many already consider reading beyond the text, with a critical lens as a fundamental experience in the continuing search for social justice (Gainer 2012; Janks 2013; Comber 2015). Building a conscience anchored on empathy and compassion for others is building a sense of perspective, a component essential to individual social and emotional development. Simply said, it is creating and fostering that sense of what connects us with others. It begins during childhood and during the early years, and is an experience relevant to their social and emotional development. Inviting children to view and examine narratives beyond the mere facts and to delve into the dimensionality of social realities promotes their awareness about existing perspectives and circumstances that people experience (Wolk 2003; Vazquez 2010).

Educator Paulo Freire's statement "to read the word and to read the world" is a statement challenging everyone to recognize the messages and realities present in what is read, waiting to be acted upon in our society. His vision of educational experiences that transform (Wallenstein 1987) continues to resonate today when we are more aware about the need for addressing the needs of those who are experiencing inequalities and unfairness. In the call for attention to the needs and realities of immigrants, his words resound as a reminder of the search for equity. That search begins in the classroom.

Consciousness about realities emerges as we create an environment where, first of all, we move beyond the practice of just centering on the basic linguistic aspects and invite children to critique what is read and experienced in stories (Wolk 2003; Vazquez 2010). It happens as we build a setting where questions such as *what else do we see* and the *whys* and *hows* are invited. It is, in essence, when children's ideas are welcomed as they question and analyze realities, uncovering what "looks different and not right," alerting the child to disparities and unequal circumstances. Promoting consideration about issues, as they examine, question, comment, and propose, leads children to also find out that they "have the capacity to transform the world" (Shor 1987, 105). Reading the word to read the world as Freire posed is, actually, building in the individual the capacity to be an engaged member of society responding to needs and realities calling for responsible attention and action (Robles-Melendez and Beck 2000; Wolk 2003).

A Freirean Approach to Intentionally Build Consciousness

According to Freire, building consciousness is centered on identifying problems and moving into a dialogue where existing challenges would be identified and recognized. Such a dialogue can happen in the classroom when, intentionally, we engage children into discussing issues and guiding them to uncover realities and concerns demanding attention in communities and society. Stories become prompts bringing children to meet characters and learn about experiences and circumstances calling for consideration and action. Building in children an awareness of social unfairness is central to developing individuals who are mindful about the need and rights of people. A similar goal is pursued in antibias education, where children are welcomed to delve into topics and issues which invite their comments and actions (Derman-Sparks and Edwards 2010).

Wallenstein's (1987) suggestions to bring a Freirean approach into the classroom propose a three-step problem-posing approach to engage learners in examining issues. They include the following steps:

1. Listening: to consider and find out about issues in their communities.
2. Dialogue: to uncover the issues and codify these based on their experiences.
3. Action: to propose solutions and actions to address the issue.

Wallenstein's process can be used in the discussion of stories of immigration, prompting children to examine realities and to engage in conversations to share feelings, experiences, and emotions. For Wallenstein, listening plays a key role in determining the issues that interest students and to hear their "hidden voices" (Wallenstein 1987, 35). Listening to their comments also brings attention to what children pose as concerns as they process realities. This is an opportunity to hear their "hidden voices" where their sentiments and feelings are revealed. Engaging students to propose actions and viable solutions further empower children and assert their own agency. Reed, Saunders, and Pfadenhauer Simmons (2015) in their experience implementing Wallenstein's process with primary-age children, indicated that when children's ideas and views are invited and shared, they contribute to erasing the "culture of silence about injustices" (1987, 56). Building an environment that welcomes ideas and comments is also how we support their emergent sense as members of a group.

Figure 7.2 presents an adaptation of the Freirean model with emphasis on listening and questioning to guide and invite children to consider and explore

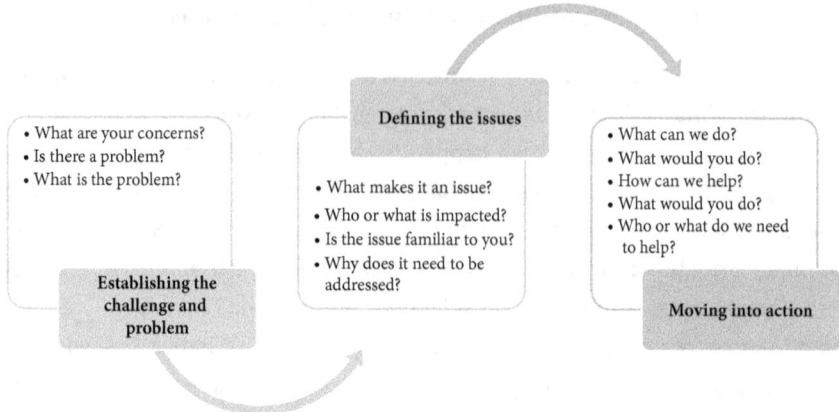

Listening and encouraging children's ideas

Figure 7.2 Applying a Freirean approach to engage children in critically reading stories of immigration.

Source: Adapted from Wallenstein (1987) and Reed et al. (2015).

issues in stories addressing diversity such as immigration. Stories of immigration serve as prompts to engage children in considering the experiences and the related challenges they pose. It also incites in children their empathy and agency, suggesting and recommending actions to address issues.

Planning to Share Stories about Immigration

Planning that is intentional and aiming at building conscious awareness is vital. Every effort in the classroom to address diversity and its many different experiences begins with planning. Teaching and engaging children in topics about immigrants call for intentional planning. It begins with a clear understanding on the reasons for integrating a topic into the curriculum. Because of the appeal that children's literature has, it is always relevant to consider the stories that you are planning to share. When teaching about immigration, there is a myriad of topics to select and bring into the classroom. Some points to consider as you begin planning are:

- *How will children connect with the story?*
- *How much do they know about the topic?*
- *What will catch their attention?*

- *How will they respond to the topic?*
- *What are some of the emotions that the story may evoke?*

Taking the time to reflect on the answers to these questions provides direction by centering the child in the planning process. It also prepares you by anticipating the possible experiences individually linking children and their responses to the topics that will be addressed.

Web of Possibilities

Bringing immigration as a topic into the classroom is an opportunity to explore multiple topics and a variety of issues. Its interdisciplinarity nature provides many opportunities to link with areas across the curriculum. Taking the time to read carefully each story and identifying its different themes helps in determining how to integrate them into the curriculum. Brainstorming and mapping possible topics and themes help in identifying areas to emphasize as part of curricular experiences. In a story, there are multiple dimensions to explore, and learning which ones they are informs our planning. One of our authors has as a practice to engage her students in creating webs of possibilities where they analyze possible topics and themes rendered in a story. It is a way to determine all the directions that a story can lead us to explore and how they can be integrated into the curriculum. An example is provided in Figure 7.3.

Don't Forget the Pictures!

Pictures and illustrations give life to stories in picture books. Together with the text, they are a voice that speaks with images. A picture is many times what entices and engages children and remains as the connecting point to the events and message in a story. Kiefer (1994) considers that often pictures are not given all the consideration needed as part of a story and suggests taking the time to see how they add to the narrative. We agree with her comments particularly because of their visually impressive way in conveying the emotions and realism of experiences told in stories. Powerfully illustrated is what perhaps describes most of the children's books about immigration. Pictures like the ones in *The day war came* (Davies 2018), *La frontera. El viaje con papá/My journey with papa* (Mills and Silva 2018), or those in *The banana leaf ball* (Milway 2017), just to name a few, add realism and depth to the emotional and difficult topics that are addressed. They call attention to the experiences of immigrants and

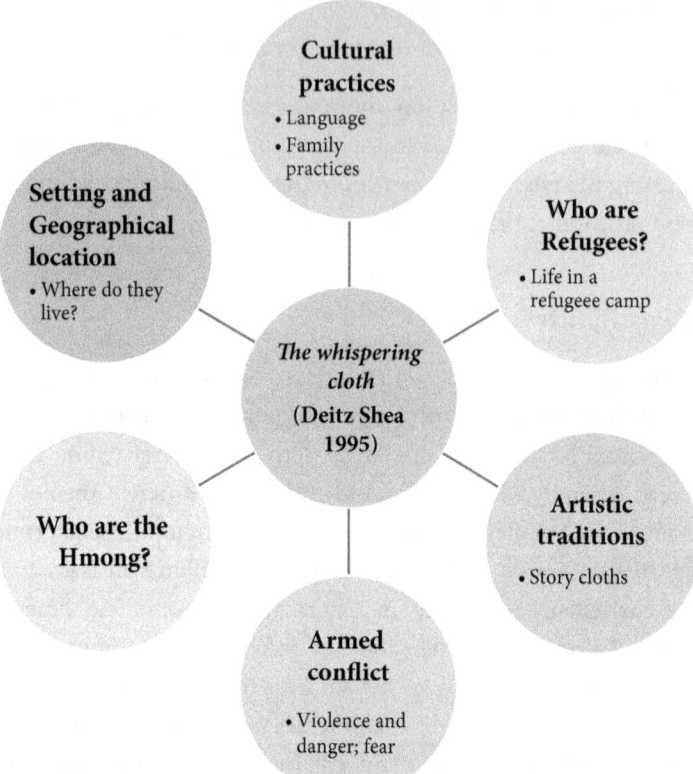

Figure 7.3 Mapping possible themes and topics from a storybook.

allow readers to experience the events and emotionality of the story. In those examined and discussed in this book, we found numerous ways in which pictures continued to tell the story depicting the actions of characters, some of which are described in Figure 7.4.

In your planning, you are urged to make the most of the illustrations by taking the time to carefully "read" them. Take note of what is revealed and reflected and consider what may be familiar or unfamiliar to children. Think about what you know or need to learn more about. As you visually read the illustrations, consider the representations that they provide and how these connect with the story. If some of what is presented in an illustration or picture is unfamiliar to you, take the time to find out what they are. Remember, you want to be ready to answer any questions from children who are curious and will likely ask what they are. Consider the overall tone that the illustrations give to the story and what they convey to children.

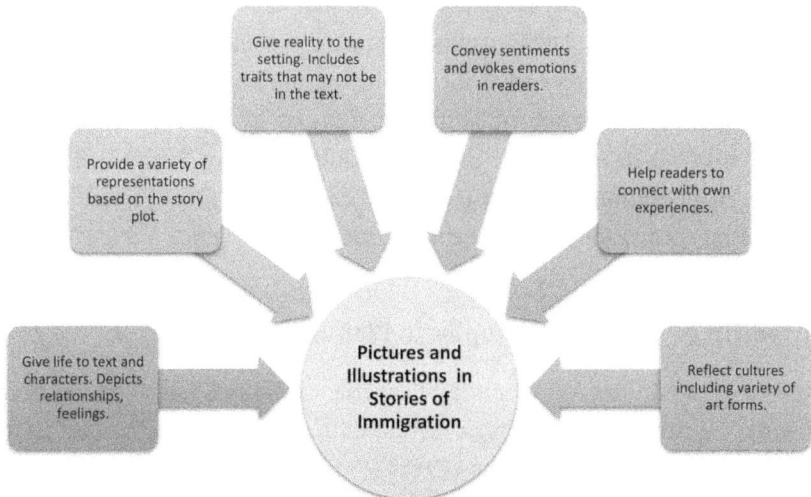

Figure 7.4 Roles of pictures and illustrations in stories of immigration.

Asking yourself what emotions or questions may arise from them is relevant to plan how to address their responses. We suggest to always consider:

- *How would children react or respond to the illustrations?*
- *What prior experiences of children will influence their response to the images?*
- *What will be unusual or unfamiliar in the images for children?*

Some stories of immigration are also wordless books. Before sharing these with children, the need to examine carefully pictures and illustrations is even greater. *Migrants* (Watanabe 2020) and *I walk with Vanessa* (Kerascoët 2018) are two examples of wordless books calling for a careful "reading" of their illustrations before sharing these stories with children. An analysis of what is included and of the representations in the pictures and illustrations would direct you to additional resources that may be needed to bring the story to children. Resources relevant to engage children and to enhance their experience when sharing stories are discussed in the next section.

Don't Rush; Take Time to Choose What Is Appropriate

We also want to share a word of caution about pictures and illustrations, particularly as stories are selected. Together with the story, taking the time to read the pictures, as we stated earlier, is most relevant. Some may not only include unfamiliar items which can be researched and identified, but others may be inappropriate. There may be instances, as well, when images may not be appropriate because of what they represent and how they are represented. Careful attention to respectful representation of immigrants' diversity and culture is critically important. Using your judgment as a teacher will help in deciding with caution not only their age and developmental appropriateness, but also fair representation of diverse ethnic groups.

A Wealth of Themes and Topics to Plan Experiences

Immigration is a broad and multifold experience where a variety of topics and themes are embedded. Children's literature on immigration is a wide avenue where the multiple themes and topics of the immigrant experience are reflected. Organizing and planning learning experiences thematically is another way to integrate stories about immigrations. Consider those that are of interest and age appropriate for the children you teach. Taking the time to review the topics related to themes already in your curriculum also allows you to identify where to integrate stories about the experiences of immigrant children and families. For instance, names are typically a topic of interest to children. An example and suggestions to plan classroom learning experiences is included in Box 7.1.

Box 7.1 Sharing Stories with Children ... Always Meaningful, Stories about Names

Names are always a topic of interest to children. Their interest also offers an opportunity to explore more about the meaning of names, their own and their peers. It is also an opening to learn about the naming traditions and practices of families, especially those of immigrants. Many children may wonder about the long names they have or those of their peers. One of the stories to engage children in exploring and learning about names is *Alma and how she got her name* (Martinez-Neal 2018). Everyone is always interested in finding out about the reasons behind their names and that of their peers. The curious child in the story, who wants to learn why she has such a long name, will help in answering similar questions from children in the classroom. The response from her parent reveals the important meanings of given names. It could lead to an interesting discussion to explore and appreciate given names. They could also explore why some last names may be much longer than others.

> **Expanding on the Topic of Names**
>
> You may want to expand the topic, sharing with children or adding to the classroom library center the story *Marisol MacDonald doesn't match* (Brown 2013). The story addresses the reality of multiracial families denoted in this case through the young girl's name. Combining a Spanish first name with, in this case, a Scottish last name, the story can lead children to an interesting discussion about immigration and names. Children could investigate and trace their names to their places of origin. Another suggested reading is *The name quilt* (Root 2003), which could lead children to further build ideas about the meaningfulness of names. The story and the illustrations reinforce the special role names have as reminders of special people in our lives and of those much-cherished moments with them. As a follow-up activity, children could engage in creating a personal or group quilt of names with those of the group or of their family.

Resources to Support the Sharing of Stories with Children

Getting ready to share stories with children begins as you read the story and reflect on all the possible ways to engage children. Resources including artifacts all help in making the story appeal to and engage children. A key step when planning to share a story is to determine the resources needed to support comprehension. Given the nature of the topics, this is a major step to consider when choosing ways to further their interest and understanding. Learning what resources are available also helps to make topics and characters come alive and connect with children (Giorgis and Glazer 2013). These could include pictures and photos related to the story that can enhance understanding of concepts addressed. Because immigration is a global reality, consider resources including artifacts that would engage children in appreciating cultures and in learning about their meaning, and the places from where they came. These are always helpful in building connections with the narrative and with characters. Some suggested resources are included in Figure 7.5.

Creating an Inviting Setting to Share Stories

Stories of children and immigration address a multitude of experiences and realities. Some are from day-to-day experiences, others are more difficult and emotional. As with any story, but even more, it is critical to prepare a setting that invites children to meet and learn about characters and their experiences,

Photos and Pictures	Photos and pictures related to the setting and to characters of children and families;
Artifacts	Dolls, puppets representing characters, artisan crafts related to the cultures of story characters. Clothing and other artifacts related to stories shared; Music related to cultures of immigrants.
Maps and globes	World globe and maps to locate story settings
Technology	Recorded books; Tablets to encourage reflective writing and to record messages; selected websites to share with children
Art materials	Variety of art materials, paint, markers, paper, and different art media to encourage artistic expression

Figure 7.5 Suggested resources to help connect children with stories.

some that, perhaps, will be just as they are and others unknown and new to them. Sharing stories in a place that is comfortable and that is welcoming sets an inviting tone for read-alouds. Consider resources such as objects related to the cultures explored that may add to the story and that would also draw attention to the theme and actions of characters. Pictures and photos related to the themes and topics that are being addressed will draw attention to a story, providing an invitation for children to explore.

Persona Dolls, a Resource to Address Diversity and Share Stories

Bringing alive a story and engaging children in examining the challenges faced by people is a main goal in our classrooms. Persona dolls is one of the resources that effectively engage children in issues present in their communities and in overall society (Whitney 2002). In essence, they are a tool for building knowledge about needs and realities of people with diverse roots and realities. Basically, they are dolls assigned to represent the diverse traits of a character. The representational character of persona dolls is what imparts value to them, turning them into a didactic resource.

All children benefit from the use of persona dolls, which encourage understanding and empathy as stories about the characters are shared. Persona dolls are also a useful tool when working with immigrant children. Al-Jubeh and Vitsou (2021) reported their effectiveness as a tool working with refugee children, engaging and making them feel confident in their new setting. Because of its representational nature, persona dolls attract children and are effectively used to convey topics from stories addressing key social justice issues such as discrimination and prejudice (Bozalek and Smith 2014; Acar and Cetin 2017). Essentially, a persona doll represents a character from a story. Persona dolls can join the class as guests to "tell" a story and can remain present inviting children into an ongoing exploration about the realities that the doll represents. Having a place designated to house persona dolls invites children to revisit and engage with them as topics continue to be explored in the classroom. A trait of persona dolls is how it facilitates continued interactions as different situations are explored in the classroom. Though generally considered to be effective with younger children, it has been found to be also effective with primary-age children (Al-Jubeh and Vitsou 2021).

Using Story Maps to Promote Reflection and Understanding

Promoting an understanding of what is conveyed in stories is central to embracing their messages. Encouraging what Freire called to "find the hidden voices" (Wallenstein 1987, 35), is what he considered central in uncovering societal issues demanding attention. This is also what we invite you to pursue as you share stories about immigration. Many strategies are aimed at leading readers to focus on issues and realities shared through the events and characters. One that we suggest is building story maps, which essentially, are graphic organizers that bring attention to the key elements in a story (Stagliano and Boon 2009). They can be used while stories are read and help to emphasize important points about the narrative.

Story maps are also a valuable tool to engage all children in constructing what they find to be relevant from a storybook. A variety of graphic organizers can be used to create the story map together with children (Reading Rockets 2022). An example of a story map is shared in Figure 7.6.

Engaging Children in Reflective Conversations: Taking Action for Others

Reading as well as sharing stories of immigration is an opportunity to engage children's agency. Supporting their understanding about the stories shared and leading children to identify the issues at stake is a way to encourage the power of action in children. As stories are shared, reflective conversations with children lead them to more clearly identify the issues and challenges presented in a story. By using reflective questions as prompts to engage a conversation, they can focus attention on a specific issue. Creating an environment that welcomes everyone

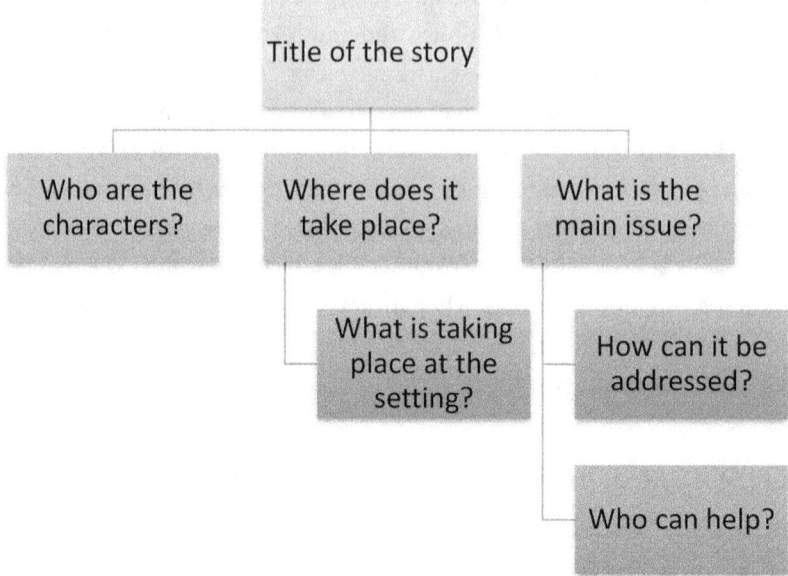

Figure 7.6 Sample template for a story map.

to share comments, allows children to propose and consider actions to engage in as they try to address a challenge. These are also opportunities to further clarify ideas or views. Once they determine what suggested actions to take, these can become a project turning their ideas into concrete actions. This step furthers the sense of agency in children, giving them opportunities to see themselves as agents for change and contributing to enacting in them an emerging sense of civic responsibility. Greater attention needs to be placed in recognizing the potential children have to understand needs and realities demanding actions. Such focus is what is also embedded in the core of anti-bias and social justice efforts (Derman-Sparks and Edwards 2010; Robles-Melendez and Beck 2019). With consideration to what is developmentally appropriate, we can engage children to learn about challenges and invite their thoughtful reflection. This is how we begin to empower children and their promising sense of agency.

A Time for Stories

The time to share and read a story is any time and always. Whether you use them as a motivator to begin exploring a topic or read for a continuing discussion about a theme, stories play a meaningful role in bringing experiences and events to life. This is what makes stories of immigration such a valuable resource to build not only knowledge but to engage children in learning about the living realities in society. We all build a stronger sense of connection when we know and meet those who are experiencing realities in many ways unfamiliar or reflecting our own experience. Even if they are story characters, their realities with their successes and challenges become real as one delves into their experiences. We know that ideas take shape when the first step is taken as you share a story in the classroom, and inviting children to learn about themselves and their peers. In this way, you are leading them to build a sense about respectful living in a society of increasing diversity. The times are now to consider and realize that … "*we can work against racial, cultural, linguistic, and socioeconomic inequalities by creating humane classrooms where students and teachers learn to use language and literacy in critical and empowering ways*" (National Council for Teachers of English 2005, n.p., italics added).

Building your own repertoire of story titles that you plan to share and explore with children, will generate an additional teaching and learning resource. Perhaps, what is more important is that you will have the power of stories that convey and engage learners to critically consider the many circumstances that immigrant children and families experience. A time for sharing a story is always an empowering event as we uncover the many dimensions of life experiences from the pages of a storybook.

A Word before We End … There Is Hope!

After the storm, the calm will come—that is also what we have repeatedly heard over the years. This is also what we have experienced just like the bird that appeared on a tree after a hurricane had battered the community where we live. In the midst of trying to understand, the cardinal that flew in was a welcome message of hope telling us that all would be well again. So is the message that we read in every child, a message of a promising future.

Many have been the experiences, trying moments, some difficult to remember, and others of success overcoming challenges that, define immigration. Many more are also the beginnings across communities and classrooms, wherever immigrant children and their families now live. We hope that in the future, immigrants, especially children, do not have to be concerned about discrimination, feeling like outsiders, or dealing with injustice, but will be welcomed with open arms as in the story *The Refuge* (le Guen 2020), where the refugees were greeted with "smiles and warmth" or in *Stepping Stones* (Ruurs 2016), where "the family has a new home with new sounds and smells, with smiles and people who help." We also hope that immigrants will be given the opportunity to become productive citizens, sharing their many talents because, after all, that is why they came and hope for, as in *Azzi in Between* (Garland 2016), where Father proudly announced, "Now that I can work, we can live here," and in *A Piece of Home* (Levitin 1996), where Papa proudly announced, "work is waiting for me." In the end, that is what immigrants wish for—an opportunity to share their talents and to feel "safe and begin our story again" (Sanna 2016). That is, too, what children aspire to as well, finding an opportunity to showcase who they are, feeling that they belong in the places where they now live.

Reflecting and Beyond

1. Consider the sources where you can locate children's books and other resources to share stories of immigration with children. Decide on what issues or topics about immigration you would like to address with children. Create your own list of resources about the topic or issue that you chose.
2. Choose one of the stories about immigration that were mentioned in this chapter or any other of your preference. Create a web of possibilities and consider the main message that you would like to convey for children of an age group of your preference.
3. Select a trio of stories about immigration with a related theme. Create your own resource box with artifacts and other materials useful to share the stories that you selected.

References

Acar, Hebrun and Hilal Cetin. 2017. "Improving preschool teachers' attitude towards the persona doll approach and determining the effectiveness of persona doll training procedure." *International Journal of Progressive Education* 13(1): 96–118.

Al-Jubeh, Dania and Magdalini Visou. 2021. "Empowering refugee children with the use of persona doll." *International Journal of Progressive Education* 17(2): 210–27. 10.29329/ijpe.2020.332.13.

Bersh, Luz. 2013. "The curricular value of teaching about immigration through picture book thematic text sets." *The Social Studies* 104(2): 47–56. doi: 10.1080/00377996.2012.720307.

Botelho, Maria and Marsha K. Rudman. 2009. *Critical Multicultural Analysis of Children's Literature: Mirrors, Windows, and Doors*. NY: Routledge.

Bozalek, Vivienne and Carol Smith. 2014. "Using persona dolls as an anti-oppressive technique in the South African social work curriculum." *Social Work/Maatskaplike Werk* 46(10): 283–98.

Cai, Mingshui and Rudine Sims Bishop. 1994. "Multicultural children's literature: Towards a clarification of the concept." In C. Genishi and A. Dyson (eds.). *The need for story: Cultural diversity in classroom and community* (pp. 57–71). National Council for Teachers of English.

Comber, Barbara. 2015. "Critical literacy and social justice." *Journal of Adolescent & Adult Literacy* 58(5): 362–7.

Cummins, Amy. 2016. "Refugees and immigrants in children's fiction. New books to build understanding across borders." *English in Texas* 46(2): 24–9.

Derman-Sparks, Louise and Julie Edwards. 2010. *Anti-bias education for young children and ourselves*. Washington, DC: National Association for the Education of Young Children.

Dolan, Anne. 2014. "Intercultural education, picture books and refugee: Approaches for language teachers." *CLELE Journal* 2(1): 92–108.

Epstein, B. J. 2017. "Why children's books that teach diversity are more important than ever." *The Conversation*, February 6. https://theconversation.com/why-childrens-books-that-teach-diversity-are-more-important-than-ever-72146.

Ezell, Helen and Laura Justice. 2005. *Shared storybook reading. Building children's language and emergent literacy skills*. Maryland, MD: Paul Brookes.

Gainer, Jesse. 2012. "Critical thinking: Foundational for digital literacies and democracy." *Journal of Adolescent and Adult Literacy* 56(1): 14–17.

Giorgis, Cyndi and Joan Glazer. 2013. *Literature for young children. Supporting emergent literacy, ages 0-8*. MA: Pearson.

Hilary Janks. (2013). Critical literacy in teaching and research, *Education Inquiry*, 4:2, 225–242.

Hope, J. 2008. "One day we had to run: The development of the refugee identity in children's and its function in education." *Children's Literature in Education* 39: 295–304.

Ikia, Yuko. 2015. "Using multicultural children's literature to teach diverse perspectives." *Kappa Delta Pi Record* 41(2): 81–6.

Janks, Hilary. 2013. Critical literacy in teaching and research.education inquiry, 4(2): 225–242.

Kiefer, Barbara. 1994. *The potential of picturebooks. From visual literacy to aesthetic understanding.* NJ: Merrill.

Lowe, Danielle. 2009. "Helping children cope through literature." *Forum of Public Policy.* https://files.eric.ed.gov/fulltext/EJ864819.pdf.

MacPhee, Deborah and Emily J. Whitecotton. 2011. "Bringing the 'Social' Back to Social Studies: Literacy Strategies as Tools for Understanding History." *The Social Studies* 102(6): 263–7, doi: 10.1080/00377996.2011.571300.

National Council of Teachers of English. 2005. *Position statement. Supporting linguistically and culturally diverse learners in english education.* Illinois: Author.

Nath, L., and Grote-Garcia. 2017. Reading refugee stories: Five common themes among picture books with refugee characters. *Texas Journal of Literacy Education* 5(2): 130–40.

National Association for the Education of Young Children. 2022. *Developmentally appropriate practice in early childhood programs serving children from birth through age 8* (4th edition). Washington, DC: Author.

Norton, Donna. 2013. *Multicultural literature: Through the eyes of many children* (4th edition). MA: Pearson.

O'Neil, Kathleen. 2010. "Once upon today: Teaching for social justice with postmodern picturebooks." *Children's Literature in Education* 41: 40–51.

Orgad, Shani, Dafna Lemish, Miriam Rahali, and Diana Floegel. 2021. "Representations of migration in U.K. and U.S. children's picture books in the Trump and Brexit era." *Journal of Children and Media* 15(4): 549–67. doi: 10.1080/17482798.2021.1882517.

Platts, T. K. and K. Hoosier. 2020. "Reducing Stereotype threat in the classroom." *Inquiry: The Journal of the Virginia Community Colleges* 23(1). Retrieved from https://commons.vccs.edu/inquiry/vol23/iss1/6.

Potter, Cathy. 2019. "Windows and mirrors and sliding glass doors: ensuring students see themselves and others in literature." Guest Blogger, January 25. *Humane Education.* https://humaneeducation.org/windows-and-mirrors-and-sliding-glass-doors-ensuring-students-see-themselves-and-others-in-literature.

Reading Rockets. 2022. *Story maps.* https://www.readingrockets.org/strategies/story_maps.

Reed, Judith, Karen Saunders, and Susan Pfadenhauer-Simonds. 2015. "Problem-posing in a primary grade. Utilizing Freire's methods to break the culture of silence." *Multicultural Education* 23(1): 56–8.

Roberts and Patricia Crawford. 2008. "Real life calls for real books. Literature to Help Children Cope with Family Stressors." *Young Children on the Web*, September: 12–17.

Robles-Melendez, Wilma and Vesna Beck. 2000. *Teaching social studies in early education.* NY: Delmar.

Shor, Ira (ed.) 1987. *Freire for the classroom. A sourcebook for liberatory teaching*. Portsmouth, NH: Boyton/Cook Publishers Heinemann.

Short, Kathy. 2009. "Critically reading the word and the world: Building intercultural understanding through literature." *Bookbird: A Journal of International Children's Literature* 47(2): 1–10.

Smidt, Sandra. 2009. *Introducing Vygostky. A guide for practitioners and students in early years education*. London: Routledge.

Stagliano, Christina and Richard Boon. 2009. "The effects of a story-mapping procedure to improve the comprehension skills of expository text passages for elementary students with learning disabilities." *Learning Disabilities: A Contemporary Journal* 7(2): 35–58. https://files.eric.ed.gov/fulltext/EJ874132.pdf.

St. Amour, Melissa. 2003. "Connecting children's Stories to children's literature: Meeting diversity needs." *Early Childhood Education Journal* 31: 47–51. https://doi.org/10.1023/A:1025136802668.

Temple, Charles, Donna Ogle, Alan Crawford, Penny Freppon, and Codruta Temple. 2018. *All children read: Teaching literacy in today's diverse classrooms* (5th edition). MA: Pearson.

Vazquez, Vivian. 2010. *Gettign beyond the "I like the book." Creating space for critical literacy in the K-6 classroom* (2nd edition). MD: International Reading Association.

Wallestein, Nina. 1987. "Problem-posing education: Freire's method for transformation." In I. Shor (ed.). *Freire for the classroom: A sourcebook for liberatory teaching*. NH: Heinemann. (pp. 33–44).

Whitney, Trisha. 2002. *Kids like us. Using persona dolls in the classroom*. MN: Redleaf Press.

Wolk, Steven. 2003. "Teaching for critical literacy in social studies." *The Social Studies* 94(3): 101–6, doi: 10.1080/00377990309600190.

Children's Books Cited

Davies, Nicola. 2018. *The day war came*. MA: Candlewick.
de Arias, Patricia. 2018. *Marwan's journey*. NY: mineditionsUS.
Deitz Shea, Pegi. 1995. *The whispering cloth*. PA: Boyds Mills press.
Garland, Sarah. 2016. *Azzi in between*. London: Frances Lincoln Press.
Kerascoët. 2018. *I walk with Vanessa*. Canada: Schwartz and Wade.
Khan, Naaz. 2021. *Room for everyone*. NY: Simon & Schuster.
LeGuen, S. 2020. *The refuge*. Seattle: Amazon Crossing Kids.
Mills, Deborah and Alfredo Silva. 2018. *La frontera. El viaje con papá/My journey with Papa*. MA: Barefoot books.
Milway, Katie. *The banana leaf ball*. 2017. Toronto: Citizen Kid.
Naylor-Ballesteros. 2020. *The suitcase*. NY: Clarion Books.
Sanna, Francesca. 2016. *The journey*. London-New York. Flying Eye Books.
Watanabe. 2020. *Migrants*. Mexico: Gecko Press.

Appendix

Topical List of Children's Books on Immigration Experiences

Children and Experiences about Moving

Aliki. 1998. *Marianthe's story: Painted words/spoken words*. NY: Greenwillow Books.
De Regil, Tania. 2019. *A new home*. NY: Candlewick.
Harper, Jessica. 2004. *I like where I am*. NY: Putnam.
Inserro, Julia. 2018. *Nonni's moon*. Jamaica Press, MA: Three Beans Press.
Kim, Patricia. 2015. *Here I am*. North Mankato, MN: Picture Window.
Levitin, Sonia. 1996. *A piece of home*. NY: Dial Books for Children.
Park, Frances and Ginger Park. 2001. *Goodbye, 382 Shin Dang Dong*. Washington, DC: National Geographic Society.
Pérez, Amada. 2002. *My diary from here/Mi diario de aquí y acá*. San Francisco, CA: Children's Book Press.
Umrigar, Thrity. 2020. *Sugar in milk*. Philadelphia, PA: Running Press Kids.
Watts, Jeri. 2016. *A piece of home*. NY: Candlewick.
Wagner, Anke and Eva Eriksson. 2012. *Tim's big move*. NY: NorthSouth.
Winter, Jeannette. 2007. *Angelina's island*. NY: Frances Foster Books.

Experiences at School

Ada, Alma Flor. 1995. *My name is Maria Isabel*. NY: Atheneum.
Aliki. 1998. *Marianthe's story: Painted words/spoken words*. NY: Greenwillow Books.
Ashley, Bernard. 1995. *Cleversticks*. Decorah, Iowa: Dragonfly Books.
Bunting, Eve. 1992. *One green apple*. NY: Clarion Books.
Choi, Yangsook. 2003. *The name jar*. Decorah, Iowa: Dragonfly Books.
Colato Laínez, René. 2009. *René has two last names/René tiene dos apellidos*. Houston, Texas: Piñata Books.
Diaz, Junot. 2018. *Islandborn*. NY: Dial Books.
Gómez Redondo, Susana. 2020. *The day Saida arrived*. San Francisco, CA: Blue Dot Kids Press.

Jiménez, A. 1998. *La mariposa*. Darby, PA: Diane Publishing Company.
Kerascoët. 2018. *I walk with Vanessa. A story about a simple act of kindness*. NY: Wade books.
Khalil, Aya. 2020. *The Arabic quilt. An immigrant story*. Thomaston, ME: Tilbury.
Kheiriyeh, Rashin. 2021. *The shape of home*. Madrid, Spain: Levine Querido.
leGuen, Sandra. 2020. *The refuge*. Seattle, WA: Amazon Crossing Kids.
Levine, Ellen. 1989. *I hate English*. NY: Scholastic.
Medina, Jane. 1999. *My name is Jorge on both sides of the river*. PA: Wordsong.
Mora, Pat. 2003. *The rainbow tulip*. NY: Puffin Books.
Recorvitz, Helen. 2003. *My name is Yoon*. NY: Farrar, Strauss and Giroux.
Sibley O'Brien, Anne. 2015. *I'm new here*. Waterstown, MA: Charlesbridge.
Williams, Kate and Kadra Mohammed. 2009. *My name is Sangoel*. Grand Rapids, MI: Eerdmans Books for Young Children.

Refugees and Asylees

Argüeta, Jorge. 2016. *Somos como las nubes/We are like the clouds*. Toronto, CA: Groundwood Books.
Buitrago, Jairo. 2015. *Two white rabbits*. Toronto, Canada: Groundwood Books.
Bunting, Eve. 1988. *How many days to America*. NY: Clarion Books.
de Arias, Patricia. 2018. *Marwan's journey*. NY: Astra Publishing House.
Davies, Nicola. 2018. *The day war came*. NY: Candlewick.
Deitz Shea, Pegi. 1995. *The whispering cloth*. Honesdale, PA: Boyds Mills Press.
Fakher, Bassel and Deborah Blumenthal. 2020. *Saving Stella: A dog's dramatic escape from war*. UK: Bloomsbury.
Garay, Luis. 1997. *The long road*. NY: Tundra Books.
Garland, Sarah. 2016. *Azzi in between*. Beverly, Massachusetts: Lincoln Press.
Hinojosa, Victor and Coert Voorhees. 2020. *A journey of hope*. Houston, Texas: Six Foot Press.
Kobald, Irena. 2014. *My two blankets*. NY: Clarion Books.
Kumar, Tyshya. 2019. *I am a refugee*. Bristol, UK: SilverWoods Books.
Kunz, Doug and Amy Schrodes. 2017. *Lost and found cat. The true story of Kunkush's incredible journey*. NY: Crown Books.
leGuen, Sandra. 2020. *The refuge*. Seattle, WA: Amazon Crossing Kids.
Maclear, Kyo. 2020. *Storyboat*. Canada: Tundra.
McCartney, Rosemary. 2017. *Where will I live?* Toronto, Canada: Second Story Press.
Meddour, Wendy. 2019. *Lubna and pebble*. NY: Dial Books.
Mills, Deborah and Francisco Alva. 2018. *La frontera. My journey with papá/El viaje con papá*. Cambridge, MA: Barefoot Books.
Milner, Kate. 2017. *My name is not refugee*. UK: The Bucket List.
Milway, Katie. 2017. *The banana leaf ball*. Toronto, Canada: Kids Can Press.

Nuño, Fran. 2017. *El mapa de los buenos momentos*. Madrid: Cuentos de Luz.
Parker, Rubio, Sarah. 2019. *Far from home. A story of loss, refuge, and hope*. IL: Tyndale House Publishers.
Parrilla, Enrique. 2019. *La pequeña emigrante*. Madrid, Spain: Mr.Momo.
Ruurs, Margriet. 2016. *Stepping stones*. Victoria, British Columbia: Orca Book Publishers.
Sanna, Francesca. 2016. *The journey*. London, UK: Flying Eye Books. An imprint of Nobrow.
Van, Muon Thi. 2021. *Wishes*. NY: Orchard Books.
Vescio, Robert. 2019. *The voyage*. Australia: EK Books.
Watanabe. 2020. *Migrants*. New Zealand: Gecko Press.
Williams, Mary. 2005. *Brothers in hope. The story of the lost boys of Sudan*. NY: Lee and Low Books.
Williams, Karen and Kadra Mohammed. 2007. *Four feet and two sandals*. Grand Rapids, MI: Eerdmans Books for Young Children.

Friendship and Kindness

Beckwith, Kathy. 2005. *Playing war. A story about changing the game*. ME: Tilbury House.
Gómez Redondo, Susana. 2020. *The day Saida arrived*. San Francisco, CA: Blue Dot Kids Press.
Kobald, Irena. 2014. *My two blankets*. NY: Clarion Books.
leGuen, Sandra. 2020. *The refuge*. Seattle, Washington, DC: Amazon Crossing Kids.
Meddour, Wendy. 2019. *Lubna and pebble*. NY: Dial Books.
Medina, Meg. 2020. *Evelyn del Rey is moving away*. NY: Candlewick.
Naylor-Ballesteros, Chris. 2020. *The suitcase*. NY: Clarion Books.
Williams, Karen and Kadra Mohammed. 2007. *Four feet and two sandals*. Grand Rapids, Michigan: Eerdmans Books for Young Readers.

Immigration Status

Bunting, Eve. 1994. *A day's work*. NY: Clarion Books.
Danticat, Edwidge. 2015. *Mama's nightingale. A story of immigration and separation*. NY: Dial Books.
de Anda, Diana. 2019. *Mango moon*. NY: Albert Whitman Books.
de la Peña, Matt. 2018. *Carmela full of wishes*. NY: Penguin Books.
Morales, Areli. 2021. *Areli is a dreamer*. NY: Random House.
Williams, Karen. 2021. *Facing fear. An immigration story*. Grand Rapids, Michigan: Eerdmann Books for Young Readers.
Yang, Belle. 2007. *Hannah is my name*. NY: Candlewick.

Family Separation

Colato Laínez, René.2010. *From north to south/Del norte al sur*. NY: Lee & Low Books.
Danticat, Edwidge. 2015. *Mama's nightingale: A story of immigration and separation*. NY: Dial Books.
de Anda, Diana. 2019. *Mango moon*. NY: Albert Whitman Books.
de la Peña, Matt. 2018. *Carmela full of wishes*. NY: Penguin Books.
Juarez, Estela. 2022. *Until someone listens: A story about borders, family, and one girl's mission*. NY: Roaring Brook Press.

Families and Experiences of Immigration

Danticat, Edwidge. 2015. *Mama's nightingale. A story of immigration and separation*. NY: Dial Books.
Fleischman, Paul. 2016. *The matchbox diary*. NY: Candlewick.
Goode, Diane. 1985. *Watch the stars come out*. NY: Puffin Books.
Phi, B. 2017. *A different pond*. Mankato, MN: Picture Window Books.
Polacco, Patricia. 2014. *Fiona's lace*. NY: Simon & Schuster.
Morales, Yuyi. 2018. *Dreamers*. NY: Neal Porter Books.
Say, Allen. 1993. *Grandfather's journey*. NY: Houghton and Mifflin.
Velázquez, Eric. 2004. *Grandma's records*. NY: Bloomsbury USA Children.
Yaccarino, Dan. 2011. *All the way to America. The story of a big Italian family and a little shovel*. NY: Alfred Knopf.

Index

acculturation 48, 129–31, 139–40, 208–9
active zones of war and conflicts 12, 127, 164–71, 181, 223
Ada, Alma Flor
   I love Saturdays and domingos 109, 113
   My name is Maria Isabel 40, 132, 207
Adewumi, Tanitoluwa, *Tani's new home* 137
Afghanistan 164
Africa 9, 175, 183
Aliki, *Marianthe's story: Painted words/spoken words* 110, 148, 200–2, 212
Al-Jubeh, Dania 240
Alva, Alfredo, *La frontera. El viaje con papá/My journey con papá* 77, 112, 170, 235
anti-bias education 21, 233. *See also* education/educational rights
Argüeta, Jorge 70
   Somos como las nubes/We are like the clouds 79, 92, 169
   Xochitl and the flowers 137
Ashley, Bernard, *Cleversticks* 120, 134, 204
Asia 18, 65, 77, 138, 164, 175
asylees/asylum seekers 10, 13, 54, 78–85, 92, 145, 161–2, 164, 168–9, 176–7, 182, 184–5. *See also* refugee(s)
   children's literature about 171–4, 184
The Atlantic 20

Bates, Amy, *The big umbrella* 22
Beckwith, Kathy, *Playing war. A story about changing the game* 215
biculturalism 109, 112–14
Blackburne, Livia, *I dream of Popo* 67
Black Lives Matter movement 119
Bosnian-Serb conflict 181
Botelho, Maria 47–8, 54
Brimmer, Larry, *Without Separation: Prejudice, Segregation, and the Case of Roberto Alvarez* 196

Brown, Monica, *Marisol Macdonald doesn't match* 239
Bruner, Jerome 93
Buitrago, Jairo, *Two white rabbits* 18, 78–9, 169
Bulgaria 122
Bunting, Eve
   A day's work 40, 113
   Gleam and glow 177, 181
   How many days to America 72
   One green apple 199, 213–14

Callanan, Maureen 93
Caribbean 20, 70
Central American migrant caravans 7, 12, 18, 70, 79–80, 92, 145, 164, 169–70
child migrants/immigrants 6–7, 12–14, 23, 37, 40, 47–9, 53–4, 70, 78–81, 89–90, 94, 102–7, 122, 141–4, 161, 163, 172, 178
   building consciousness about 91–3
   challenges of immigration status 143–4
   children's books by authors arrived as 115
   defining moments for 76–94
   experiences of 7, 13, 19–20, 22–3, 31, 32–4, 37, 40–1, 45, 47–56, 63–5, 73–5, 78, 103–4, 116–17, 123–4, 128, 140–2, 149, 164, 170, 208 (*see also* experiences of immigrants/immigration; relocation/moving)
   facing adversity 114, 184–5
   factors influencing to move to new places 140–1
   feelings and sentiments experienced by 126
   hope for 3, 12, 14, 16–19, 76–7, 118, 166
   identity 121, 129, 193, 200, 205–8
   name change (*see* names (identity))
   and pets 68, 76, 83, 142, 180–2

realities of 103, 105, 122–3 (*see also* learnings from realities of immigrant children)
relationship with grandparents 40, 44, 53, 63, 66–8, 70, 85, 101–2, 113, 117, 131, 136, 175–6
rights of 49–55, 78, 105–6, 108, 115, 118–20, 145, 163–4, 194–5, 207–8
social justice for (*see* social justice)
Ukrainian 18, 127, 164, 170–1, 180, 187
value of children 105
children living in war/armed conflict areas 164–70
children's literature 19–20, 32–5, 37–8, 40, 47–8, 78, 93–4, 103, 108, 117, 123, 161, 168, 176, 178, 194, 202, 226–7, 230, 234
choosing/selecting stories 54–5
educational rights in 195
experience of forced migration 161
on immigrant children at school 196–8
immigration status in 144, 146
multicultural 32, 34, 38–40, 47, 54, 107, 230
multidimensionality of 32, 47, 51, 63–4, 125, 131, 226–8
natural disasters in 179–90
pets in 180–1
on refugees and asylum seekers 171–4, 184
roles in children's development 33, 227
and stories (*see* stories)
thematic strands in 173
Children's rights 49–55, 78, 105–6, 108, 115, 118–21, 145, 163–4, 194–5, 207–8
Choi, Yangsook, *The name jar* 40, 130, 194, 208
Civil Rights Movement 39
classrooms 4, 12–13, 21, 31, 34, 40, 44, 48, 52, 54, 56, 66, 73, 76, 89, 105, 114, 122, 124, 138, 173, 185, 244
building conscious awareness on diversity 224–44
building friendships in 214–16
challenge of language 113, 210–11
cultural encounters in 204–5, 209
diversity in 197–9, 201–2, 214

experiences of child immigrants in 107–8, 132–3, 142–3, 192–6, 208–9
immigration status in 216–17
milestone in child's life 193–4
pronunciation of names (*see* names (identity))
responsive experiences in 201, 212–13
social/cultural development for children 217
and stories 194, 196–8
welcoming experiences in 198–205
climate change 179. *See also* natural disasters
Coffel, Cynthia Miller 94
Colato Laínez, René
René has two last names 204, 209–10
Waiting for papá/ Esperando a papá 124, 147
consciousness, building 29, 35, 49, 51–2, 55, 105, 118–19, 123–4, 217
about child immigrants 91–3
analyzing topics and themes 235–6
Freirean approach 233–4
intentionality 119–21
planning 234–5
on social justice issues 231–2
Convention on the Rights of the Child (CRC), Articles of 52, 78, 90, 115, 118–19, 121–2, 145, 163, 171, 194, 207
Cornelles, Jerónimo, *Mariama, different but just the same* 197
Covid pandemic 4, 7, 9, 12, 18, 47, 67, 78, 121, 167
critical literacy 35–6, 232
crossing borders 6, 12, 14, 54, 61, 66, 71–5, 81, 90, 144, 149
with hope 76–7, 144–5
kinds of borders 72
culture(s) 11, 18, 32, 34, 39–41, 49, 51, 54, 62–3, 71, 102–3, 109, 117–18, 120, 128, 135, 138–9, 141, 198, 201, 204–5, 207, 209, 212, 224–5
biculturalism and children's agency 112–14
challenge of language diversity 110–13
cultural characters 45, 71
cultural diversity 17, 204–5, 209
cultural heritage 33, 41, 44, 210

cultural knowledge 43–5
cultural realities 47, 103, 125
host 113, 129–30, 204, 207
learning different language 109–11, 211–13
resiliency 112, 114 (*see also* resilience/resiliency)
and stories 43 (*see also* stories)

Dahl, Audum 93
Danticat, Edwidge
  Eight days 179
  Mama's nightingale. A story of immigration and separation 108, 149
Davies, Nicola
  The day war came 92, 161–2, 164, 174, 235
  Every child a song 118
de Arias, Patricia 78
  Marwan's journey 12, 44, 85, 145, 223–4
Deferred Action for Childhood Arrivals (DACA) 150 n.1
de la Peña, Matt, *Carmela full of wishes* 50, 149
Delpit, Lisa 23
deportation 146, 148–9, 216
De Regil, Tania, *A new home* 82
Diaz, Junot, *Islandborn* 197, 203, 212
discrimination 16, 18, 35, 47, 51–2, 89, 123, 164, 195–6, 205, 241, 244
diversity 4, 10–11, 15, 17, 21–2, 32, 34, 37–40, 47–8, 51–4, 86, 105–7, 120, 124–5, 128, 133, 192, 196, 199, 212
  building conscious awareness on 224–43
  in classroom 197–9, 201–2, 204, 214
  cultural 17, 204–5, 209
  ethnic 11, 22, 32, 198, 238
  through story characters 198
dreamers 119, 150 n.1
Dyson, Ann 31

early childhood 36, 38, 43, 54, 65, 70, 83, 109, 112, 132, 205, 231
  early childhood educators 44, 48, 52, 203–4, 211, 214–15
  education 120
  social justice and 107
  transitions 83–4, 131–2, 143
education/educational rights 10, 13, 16, 36, 50, 52, 93, 194–5, 226
  anti-bias 21, 233
  in children's literature 195
  early childhood 120
educators 3, 13, 19, 34, 38, 44, 48, 51–3, 56, 107–8, 113, 115, 117–18, 131, 142, 161–2, 185, 201, 203–4, 207, 211–13, 228, 230
emotions/emotional 15, 30–1, 36, 38, 41–4, 55, 63, 65, 67–8, 71, 80–3, 85, 90–1, 108, 113, 125–7, 144, 161–2, 175–7, 211, 233, 237
  bonds of children and pets 68, 76, 83, 142, 180–2
  emotional experiences for children 44, 68–71, 83–4, 87–8, 126–50, 172, 175–8, 181
  emotional impact 69, 83, 91–2, 110, 134, 136
  emotional support from friends 214
  and feelings 134–5, 139, 176
  first impressions in classroom 132–3, 193–4, 199–205
  learning different language 109–11, 211–13
  memories (*see* memories)
  names (*see* names (identity))
  need to belong 138–9, 207
  nostalgia and longing for places 135–6, 142–3
  rejection/unwelcoming of immigrants 133, 141–2
  sense of belonging (home/place) 136–8
  sentiments toward immigrants 133–4
  transitions 83–4, 131–2
empathy 21, 37, 124, 138, 144, 181, 183–4, 202, 212, 215, 216, 231–2, 234, 240
enculturation 43
environments 52, 65–6, 70, 83, 86, 88–9, 109, 132, 134–5, 137–8, 141–3, 164, 167, 192, 198–9, 201–2, 228, 232–3, 241
equality 18, 39, 50, 120–1. *See also* inequalities
equity 4, 15, 17–20, 36, 37, 50, 51–2, 116, 121, 134, 232. *See also* inequities

Eriksson, Eva, *Tim's big move* 64
Eulate, Ana, *The sky of Afghanistan* 166–7, 176
Europe/European 5, 7–8, 12–13, 40, 77–8, 122, 164, 166, 180, 208
experiences of immigrants/immigration 4–8, 11–14, 19–23, 34, 37, 39–40, 46–56, 63–5, 73–5, 87–91, 103–4, 117–19, 123–4, 128, 140–1, 150, 161, 170
    change (challenging experience) 66–7, 138
    child immigrants in classroom (*see* classrooms)
    children's diversity in stories 124–5
    emotional experiences 42, 65, 67–8, 70–1, 83–4, 87–91, 109–11, 126–50, 172, 178, 200
    intentional consciousness 119–20
    lived experiences 14, 23, 37, 39, 48, 56, 78, 93, 103–4, 114, 116, 127, 132, 137, 144, 147, 172–3, 192, 203, 226, 231
    living experiences 13, 31, 128, 205–17, 224
    multidimensional experience 63–4, 125
    responsive experiences 200, 212–13
    saying goodbye 126–8, 138, 160–3, 174, 186
    for support and attention 117

fairness in opportunities 3, 10, 15, 17, 19, 33–4, 36–9, 50–1, 108, 119, 172. *See also* social justice
Fakher, Bassel, *Saving Stella: A dog's dramatic escape from war* 181
families, immigrant 3, 5–7, 10, 13–14, 16–20, 23, 31, 37, 39–42, 44–7, 50, 53–4, 65, 67, 69–72, 74, 76, 78, 85, 87, 102, 106, 113, 121–3, 127–8, 140, 145–6, 169–73, 176, 178–82, 184, 187, 198, 201, 216–17, 238, 243–4
family separation 50, 146–9, 170
Faruqi, Reem, *Laila's lunchbox* 204
forced migration 5, 10–11, 78, 82, 84–5, 87, 92, 94, 121, 127, 148, 160–4, 167–73, 175–6, 178, 187. *See also* planned migration
    finding safe place 182–3
    force of nature 179–80 (*see also* natural disasters)
    typology of people impacted by 177
Fox, Mem, *Whoever you are* 23
Freire, Paulo 37, 118, 123, 232
    Freirean approach in building consciousness 233–4
    Pedagogy of the oppressed 36
Freya Blackwood, *My two blankets* 84
friendship, role of 214–17

Gallup World Poll 8
Garay, Luis, *The long road* 78, 89, 92, 137, 169–70
Garland, Sarah, *Azzi in between* 244
Genishi, Celia 31
Gibbons, Gail, *Hurricanes!* 180
Gilliland, Judith, *Sami and the time of the troubles* 165
Gómez Redondo, Susana, *The day Saida arrived* 214–15
Greece 122
green card 77, 95 n.1, 106, 117, 216

Hale, Christy, *Todos Iguales/All Equal: Un Corrido De Lemon Grove/A Ballad of Lemon Grove* 196
Harper, Jessica, *I like where I am* 80
Heide, Florence, *Sami and the time of the troubles* 165
heritage 13, 23, 33, 40–2, 44, 105, 110–11, 120, 124, 128, 130, 139–40, 192, 196, 199, 204, 206–8, 210–11
Hinojosa, Victor, *A journey of hope* 18
Hoffman, Mary, *The color of home* 124
humanity 14, 23, 31, 32, 41, 144, 163, 171, 175, 179, 225

immigration 2–4, 9, 19, 32, 34–5, 39–41, 46–50, 62, 70, 74–5, 82, 94, 102
    and controversies 3–4, 7–8, 15, 20–1, 37–9, 46, 108, 117, 143–4, 226, 230
    forces motivating people to migrate 5, 10–11
    global 6, 8, 225
    growth of international migrants 8
    key reasons for 87
    rise of interest in 3
inequalities 18, 37, 51, 230, 232, 243. *See also* equality

inequities 36–8, 47, 50–1, 119, 124. *See also* equity
Inserro, Julia, *Nonni's moon* 101, 117, 130–1, 136, 138

Jiménez, Francisco
  The circuit: Stories from the life of a migrant child 127, 144
  La mariposa 40, 114, 128, 144
Johnston, Geoffrey 188

Kerascoët, *I walk with Vanessa. A story about a simple act of kindness* 250–1, 231, 237
Khalil, Aya, *The Arabic quilt. An immigrant story* 44, 198–9, 202
Khan, Naaz, *Room for everyone* 225
Kharkiv, Ukraine 165
Kiefer, Barbara 245
Kim, Patricia, *Here I am* 89
Kobald, Irena, *My two blankets* 44, 84, 110–1, 140, 184, 215
Krull, Kathleen, *Maria Molina and the Days of the Dead* 48
Kumar, Tyshya, *I am a refugee* 168, 183
Kunz, Doug, *Lost and found cat. The true story of Kunkush's incredible journey* 99, 180

language(s) 10, 13, 43, 54, 63, 76, 128, 130, 138, 140–1, 200–1, 206, 212–3, 224
  acquisition 109–11, 140, 211
  challenge of language diversity 111–13, 210–12
  heritage 110–1, 140, 199, 210
  learning different language 109–11, 211–13
  linguistic form 43, 110–11, 129, 232, 243
Larsen, Denise 142
Lawlor, Veronica, *I was dreaming to come to America* 112
learnings from realities of immigrant children 105–8
  conscious reading of stories 106
  experiences in classroom 107–8, 132–3, 142, 192–8
  intentional reading of stories 108
Le Guen, Sandra, *The refuge* 108, 180, 205, 214, 244

Lemon Grove schools 195–6
Levine, Ellen, *I hate English* 89, 111, 212
Levinson, Riki, *Watch the stars come out* 53
Levitin, Sonia, *A piece of home* 81, 244
literature. *See* children's literature
London, Jonathan, *Hurricane!* 179
Lukens, Rebecca 97

Maclear, Kyo, *Story boat* 163, 185
Malala Yousufzai, *Malala and her magic pencil* 166
Malta 122
Mandela, Nelson 119
McCartney, Rosemary, *Where will I live?* 88, 185
Meddour, Wendy, *Lubna and pebble* 88, 121, 183
Medina, Jane, *My name is Jorge on both sides of the river* 129, 207–8
Mediterranean 7, 20, 145, 180
memories 3, 30, 63, 66–7, 69–70, 76, 80–1, 113, 115, 126–7, 143, 159–60, 176, 182, 194, 208, 211, 213, 228
  from first days at school 200
  of place of birth 135
  of special relationships 130–1
The Middle East 18, 77, 142, 165, 170, 175, 215
Mills, Deborah, *La frontera. El viaje con papá/My journey con papá* 77, 112, 170, 235
Milway, Katie, *The banana leaf ball* 168, 183, 235
Mohammed, Kadra
  Four feet, two sandals 183
  My name is Sangoel 192–3, 202, 204, 208–9
Morales, Areli
  Areli is a dreamer 217
  Dreamers 76, 146
Mora, Pat, *The rainbow tulip* 111
multicultural children's literature 32, 34, 38–40, 47, 54, 107, 230. *See also* children's literature

names (identity) 130, 206
  change of 128–30, 132, 194, 205–9
  learning naming traditions and practices 238–9

in stories 74, 114, 112, 150, 132, 194, 204, 206–10, 238
narratives of immigration 4, 14–16, 19–20, 23, 31, 35, 37–8, 41–2, 44–6, 49, 53, 57, 74, 81, 84, 92, 102, 106, 130, 135, 144, 148, 168, 172, 175, 177, 183, 185, 198, 205, 209, 215, 232, 234, 239
National Institutes for Health (NIH) 180
natural disasters 78, 89, 162–3, 169, 175, 197–8
Naylor-Ballesteros, Chris, *The suitcase* 231
North America 40, 77, 89, 137
Nuño, Fran, *The map of good memories* 69, 92, 127, 160

O'Brien, Sibley, *I'm new here* 124, 138, 200–1, 203
others/otherness 22–3

Parker Rubio, Sarah, *Far from home. A story of loss, refuge, and hope* 81, 85–6, 187
Park, Frances, *Goodbye, 382 Shin Dang Dong* 63, 66, 131–2, 136, 145
Park, Ginger, *Goodbye, 382 Shin Dang Dong* 63, 65, 131–2, 136, 145
peace, hope for 70, 121, 144, 163–7, 177–8
Penfold, Alexandra, *All are welcome* 133, 191–2, 197
Pérez, Amada, *My diary from here/Mi diario de aquí y acá* 81
pets, children and 65, 74, 85, 142, 178–80
Pfadenhauer-Simonds, Susan 233
Phi, Bao, *A different pond* 53, 66
planned migration 72, 81, 82, 141. *See also* forced migration
population growth, immigrant 6, 8, 11–12
poverty 18, 78, 165
prejudice 3–4, 7, 16, 35, 37, 39, 50, 105, 107, 114, 123, 196, 204–5, 241
Pressley, Soto 207

reader response theory 36
realities of immigration 2–10, 13–15, 18–23, 30–39, 41–42, 46–51, 53, 55–6, 63, 67, 70, 72–3, 77–80, 83, 90, 92–4, 120, 121–2, 131, 134, 142, 146–7, 149, 161, 170, 216, 239
about children's resiliency 114–15
building conscious awareness on diversity 224–44
realities of immigrant children 103, 105 (*see also* learnings from realities of immigrant children)
witnessing 186–7
Recorvits, Helen, *My name is Yoon* 50, 130, 208
Reed, Judith 246
refugee(s) 10, 12–13, 18, 44, 53–4, 78–80, 87, 89, 124, 134, 140, 161–4, 167–8, 170–1, 182–5. *See also* asylees/asylum seekers
agenda for children's protection, UNICEF's 185–6
children's literature about 171–8, 195
refugee camp 167, 182–3
relocation/moving 63–5, 80, 125
change (challenging experience) 66–7, 138
crossing borders (*see* crossing borders)
emotional connections 69–72
emotional experiences 67–8, 70–1, 83–4
emotional impact of 91
leaving special relationships 69–70, 125, 130–1, 136, 147–8
multidimensional experience of 64
objects/items 80–1
special places and connections 66
and well-being of children 89–91
resilience/resiliency 112, 114, 135, 166, 179
realities about children's 114–15
Rogoff, Barbara 97
Rohingya 85, 164, 168
Root, Phyllis, *The name quilt* 239
Rosenblatt, Louise, reader response theory 36
Rudman, Marsha K. 48, 54
Ruurs, Margriet, *Stepping stones: A refugee family' story* 78, 144–5, 178, 244

Sanna, Francesca, *The Journey* 15, 37, 78–80, 168
Saunders, Karen 233
Say, Allen, *Grandfather's journey* 10, 12, 15, 40, 135
Schrodes, Amy, *Lost and found cat. The true story of Kunkush's incredible journey* 99

sense of control, children's 66, 85
Serres, Alain, *I have the right to be a child* 119, 163
Shaefer Bernardo, Susan, *Sun kisses, moon hugs* 136
Shrodes, *Lost and found cat. The true story of Kunkush's incredible journey* 180
Silva, Quintana, *Kalak's journey* 86
Simon, Seymour, *Hurricanes* 180
Sims Bishop, Rudine 34, 37, 39, 41, 48, 73, 106, 227
Smith, Bridges 41
Smith, Jacquelin 94
social justice 3, 15–19, 32, 34, 37–9, 46, 54–5, 93–4, 107, 118–21, 149, 150, 161, 205, 217, 229, 241
  awareness for children from stories 227
  building consciousness on issues of 231–2
  for immigrant children and their families 17–18, 20–1, 37–8, 50–2
  learnings from children's books 229–30
socially mediated learning 227
Spain, migrants from Africa 9
specter of war conflict 170
Stanek, Muriel, *I speak English for my mom* 113
stories 7, 11–12, 14–16, 19–23, 29–31, 33, 39–42, 73, 75, 78–9, 86–7, 105–6, 117–18, 148–50, 161, 176, 212
  challenges of immigration status 145–7
  children's diversity of experiences 124–5, 197–5
    through story characters 198
  and children's literature (*see* children's literature)
  children's stories 35–6, 53–4, 75, 93, 104–6, 122–4
    by authors arrived as child immigrants 115
    choosing/selecting children's books 54–5
    and immigration experience 47–9, 63–5
    responsive experiences in classrooms 203, 212–13
  connecting children to 228–30
  conscious/intentional reading of 106, 108, 119

and cultural knowledge 43–4
on forced migration 173–5
Freirean approach to engage children in 233–4
on immigrant children at school 194, 196–8, 205
influential characters in 231
life at refugee camps 182
memories (*see* memories)
and names (*see* names (identity))
narratives (*see* narratives of immigration)
persona dolls 240–1
pictures and illustrations in 235–8
realities of conflict for children 174–84
reflective conversations with children 241–2
resources of 239–41
responding to 36
sentiments 31, 36, 66, 69, 89, 91, 93, 94, 117, 126–7, 128, 131, 133–4, 136, 138, 145, 172, 176, 180–1, 232
sharing 45–9, 194, 232, 237, 239–43
story maps 241–2
topics and themes (analyzing/planning) 235–6, 238
values and roles of 42–3, 226–8
storybooks 4, 20, 33–4, 36, 102, 105–6, 183, 194, 229, 236, 241, 243
storytelling 41

Takanishi, Ruby 47, 120
technology 175
Thompkins-Bigelow, Jamilah, *Your name is a song* 130
Thompson, Lauren 142
Tonatiuth, Duncan
  Pancho Rabbit and Coyote: A migrant tale 169
  Separate is not equal: Sylvia Mendez and her family's fight for desegregation 195
transitions 70, 73, 80–1, 83–5, 88, 125, 131–2, 135, 138, 141, 143, 194, 213
transnational families 147
trauma/traumatic 81, 128, 141, 148, 163, 166, 174, 178, 181, 183, 185

Tutu, Desmond 120
Twiss, Jill, *The someone new* 132–3

Ukraine, 2022 war crisis in 127, 165, 167, 170–1, 180, 187, 224
Umrigar, Thrity, *Sugar in milk* 131–2, 136, 142
uncertainty 63, 65, 79, 85, 92, 115, 146, 161, 164, 166, 182
undocumented/unofficial immigration 144–6, 148–9, 150 n.1, 216
UNESCO 41
unfairness, social 16, 21, 125, 161, 170, 226, 232–3
UNICEF 78, 92, 122, 163–5, 167–8, 171, 185
    agenda for children's protection 185–6
    For every child 168
The United Nations 94, 115, 119, 121, 167. *See also* Convention on the Rights of the Child (CRC), Articles of
United Nations Refugee Agency 167
The United States 2, 5–6, 8, 9–13, 20, 77, 134, 143, 145, 149, 150 n.1
    child migrants in 6–7, 13, 67, 76, 90–1, 113–14, 120, 122
        educational rights for 195
        language in classrooms 211
        name change 207, 210
        school enrollment 197
    family separation 148
    green card 77, 94 n.1, 106, 117, 216
    population growth in 8, 11

value of children 105
Van, Muo Thin, *Wishes* 114–15, 117, 168
Velázquez, Eric, *Grandma's records* 44, 63, 66, 70, 176
Ventura, Marne, *Kunkush: The true story of a refugee cat* 180

violence 10, 15, 18, 79, 86, 92, 120, 144, 162–4, 166–8, 172
Vitsou, Magdalini 230
Voorhees, Coert, *A journey of hope* 18
Vygostky, Lev 227

Wagner, Anke, *Tim's big move* 63
Wallenstein, Nina, hidden voices 36, 235, 241
Wall, John 118
Watanabe, Issa, *Migrants* 108, 169, 178, 237
Watts, Jeri, *A piece of home* 68, 90
Weiner, Sandra, *Small hands, big hands* 39
well-being of children 10, 52, 68–9, 74, 89–92, 108, 114–16, 118, 122, 140, 142–3, 149–50, 163–5, 167–8, 171, 179, 195, 206–7, 211, 214
Williams, Karen
    Facing fear. An immigration story 146, 216
    Four feet, two sandals 183
Williams, Kate, *My name is Sangoel* 192–3, 202, 204, 208–9
Williams, Mary, *Brothers in hope. The story of the lost boys of Sudan* 168, 183
Winter, Jeannette, *Angelina's island* 65, 70, 89, 136, 138, 141–2
Woodson, Jacqueline, *The day you begin* 193

Yaccarino, Dan, *All the way to America. The story of a big Italian family and a little shovel* 86
Yang, Belle, *Hannah is my name* 12, 65, 77, 106, 117, 216
Yashima, Taro, *Crowboy* 37
Yohani, Sophie 142
young children. *See* child migrants/immigrants

www.ingramcontent.com/pod-product-compliance
Lightning Source LLC
Chambersburg PA
CBHW071814300426
44116CB00009B/1305